REVENGE, POLITICS AND BLASPHEMY IN PAKISTAN

ADEEL HUSSAIN

Revenge, Politics and Blasphemy in Pakistan

OXFORD
UNIVERSITY PRESS

OXFORD
UNIVERSITY PRESS

Oxford University Press is a department of the
University of Oxford. It furthers the University's objective
of excellence in research, scholarship, and education
by publishing worldwide.

Oxford New York

Auckland   Cape Town   Dar es Salaam   Hong Kong   Karachi
Kuala Lumpur   Madrid   Melbourne   Mexico City   Nairobi
New Delhi   Shanghai   Taipei   Toronto

With offices in

Argentina   Austria   Brazil   Chile   Czech Republic   France   Greece
Guatemala   Hungary   Italy   Japan   Poland   Portugal   Singapore
South Korea   Switzerland   Thailand   Turkey   Ukraine   Vietnam

Oxford is a registered trade mark of Oxford University Press
in the UK and certain other countries.

Published in the United States of America by
Oxford University Press
198 Madison Avenue, New York, NY 10016

Library of Congress Cataloging-in-Publication Data is available

ISBN: 9780197659687

Printed in Great Britain by Bell and Bain Ltd, Glasgow

CONTENTS

ACKNOWLEDGEMENTS

I would first like to thank Shruti Kapila. Shruti's deep scholarly insights into the history of South Asia were critical in my intellectual development. Anshul Avijit has been an intellectual companion for my entire journey into the subcontinent and has contributed to the development of the arguments in more ways than I can acknowledge. Siraj Khan's invaluable comments on early drafts have significantly shaped this book, and I thank him for his continued friendship and intellectual generosity. Tripurdaman Singh has offered important input throughout the writing process. Faisal Devji has been a constant source of inspiration and support over the last decade. His writings on Muslim thought and the nationalist moment remain foundational for this book and my broader thinking on South Asia. As always, Tahir Kamran has provided crucial insights on an early manuscript draft and has offered support throughout my academic career. Armin von Bogdandy provided a hospitable academic home at the Max Planck Institute for Comparative Public Law and International Law, where this book took root. Alastair McClure has offered insights into the legal structure of colonial India and helped mould the argument of the first part of the book. The late Sir Christopher A. Bayly provided helpful guidance and encouragement in my early scholarly engagements with South Asia, and he remains a model for intellectual integrity. I would also like to thank Simon Wolf, Adam Lebovitz, Samuel Zeitlin, Saumya Saxena, Tilmann Röder, Jonah Schulhofer-

Wohl, Jojo Nem Singh, Daniel Thomas, Letizia Lo Giacco, and Thomas Clausen for their friendship and support.

Michael Dwyer has been a publisher extraordinaire. I thank him for believing in the potential of this book and for bringing it into existence. The anonymous peer-reviewers have greatly enhanced the scope of this book, and to work with the editorial team at Hurst has been any author's dream. To complete this book, I have benefitted from institutional support at the University of Cambridge, the Max Planck Institute for Comparative Public Law and International Law, and Leiden University. I would also like to thank the archivists at the libraries I consulted for this research.

My parents and sisters have encouraged and fostered my intellectual curiosity, for which I remain forever grateful. My wife, Mariam Chauhan, who is also my most critical reader, has helped me finalise this project and offered important advice at all stages of writing the book. I dedicate this book to her. Unless they formed a crucial part of a legal case, blasphemous assertions against the Prophet Muhammad (peace be upon him) have not been repeated. As per scholarly convention in academic works, the Islamic honorifics for the Prophet Muhammad have been omitted.

Leiden, March 2022   ADEEL HUSSAIN

INTRODUCTION

Sometime in 2015, Tahir Naseem, a taxi driver in his early fifties from Illinois, began receiving dreams he believed were from God. Naseem had come from Pakistan to the United States more than thirty years previously to escape the persecution of the religious sect to which he belonged, the Ahmadiyya. This sect put an enormous emphasis on dreams. In most of their yearly gatherings, the spiritual head of the Ahmadiyya, the caliph, who is usually a descendent of their nineteenth-century founder Mirza Ghulam Ahmad, would read out dreams of his followers at great length as proof for the group's divine connection. A large number of these dreams were merely personal journeys of converts. Others related to more earthly matters like health, career, family, and education. Yet, there was a line in the narration of these dreams that was not to be crossed: dreams in which God disclosed theological insights were reserved for the caliph alone. Naseem's spiritual visions, however, were of this nature. They increasingly mirrored those of the sect's founder. Naseem began to publicly claim that he was a spiritual reformer, a *mujaddid*, and soon after upped the stakes and asserted that he was the Messiah and a prophet, too.[1]

Naseem's claims were no longer compatible with Ahmadiyya teachings, and he soon left the group to accept a following of his own. He amplified his spiritual message through social media and plugged himself into a circuit of spirited fellow travellers. This group consisted of other self-proclaimed prophets, zealous conspiracy

1

theorists, diligent hobby theologians, and members of other cults who were now holding their spiritual leaders to task by radically challenging the very premises of their former beliefs. Many of them had South Asian roots and they would meet online to debate the latest visions they had allegedly received from God or share insight on scriptural references they felt confirmed their exalted status.

Many of their conversations ended up on YouTube. In one such debate, from May 2018, Naseem discussed his mission with Zahid Khan, another aspirant to prophethood. After assessing their relative status as prophets and generously conceding that there could be more than one prophet on earth at the same time, Khan, who had grown up in Lahore, urged Naseem to cancel his upcoming missionary trip to Pakistan. 'They will do worse things to you in Pakistan than the Jews did to Jesus', Khan pleaded from his living room in Frankfurt, perhaps hoping that the reference to earlier prophets would dampen Naseem's drive to carry his message to the motherland.[2] 'Allah has given you a brain ... use it!'[3]

Despite these explicit warnings, Naseem flew to Peshawar, an ancient city bordering Afghanistan along the eastern edge of the Khyber Pass. As expected, Naseem failed to convince anyone of his prophetic status. Instead, he quickly ran into problems with the law. After preaching to a teenager at a Peshawar mall, he was put in jail on charges of blasphemy. The boy, a madrassa student, testified that Naseem had first contacted him via Facebook and claimed to be a prophet. Later, Naseem had repeated this statement at the mall, where they had met for ice cream. In Pakistan, a country with strict blasphemy laws, any claim to prophethood is punishable under criminal law. It violates section 295 of Pakistan's penal code, where a series of anti-blasphemy laws enshrine offences against religion and seek to punish any blasphemous expressions against the Prophet Muhammad with a mandatory death sentence.

In July 2020, after more than two years of solitary confinement, Naseem appeared before the Peshawar High Court. Around the same time, his videos began to receive renewed attention, and his view counts on YouTube soared. A swarm of members from the *Tahreek-e-Labaik Pakistan*, a political party with the primary purpose of hounding blasphemers and avenging insults against the Prophet

Muhammad, was fuming in the comments section. Naseem's claim to prophethood, they alleged, had violated the theological principle that the Prophet Muhammad is God's last Prophet, a principle enshrined in the sacred Quranic doctrine of *khatam-e-nabuwwat* [finality of Prophethood].

Under a since-removed YouTube video, many commenters encouraged Naseem to schedule an appointment with a psychiatrist. More zealous ones, who easily made up the majority, demanded blood. 'My life's only wish is to kill this cursed dog, even if it means that I will be martyred as a result. I will not hesitate for a second to sacrifice my life to uphold and protect the finality of Prophethood,' a commenter wrote without even a cursory attempt to obscure his name or profile picture. Hundreds of commenters followed in the same vein. The gist of their expressions of rage was that Naseem had lost the right to live and that it had become mandatory for Muslims to kill him. In the more technical language of Islamic polemicists, Naseem had become *wajib-ul-qatl*, worthy of killing.

Naseem did not live to stand trial and receive a court ruling regarding his blasphemy charges. Faisal Khalid Khan, a lanky fifteen-year-old Pashtun, gunned him down inside Peshawar High Court, killing him on the spot. As opposed to fleeing from the scene, Khalid calmly sat down on a bench in the waiting area, leaned back, crossed his legs, and began speaking into mobile phone cameras that the court's security guards pointed at him. 'This cursed man was not just an enemy of Islam but also an enemy of humanity and Pakistan. I have killed him because of his false claim to prophethood'.[4]

It took only hours for Pakistan's religious right to turn Khalid into a hero. Hundreds of photoshopped images with rose petals showering down on his picture popped up on Twitter, backed with passionate hymns playing in the background which hailed Khalid as a holy worrier, a *ghazi*. Some even added the picture of a lion behind Khalid to accentuate his masculinity and bravery. In solidarity with the shooter, two Sindh Assembly members changed their Facebook profile photos to pictures of Khalid. A Member of the National Assembly immediately lobbied for a presidential pardon in parliament.[5] Lawyers began bowing in front of the teenager and several kissed his feet when he appeared in court.[6] The Peshawar police squadron tasked with transporting him from his jail cell to court posed with Khalid in smiley, thumbs-up selfies.[7] Despite a raging COVID-19 pandemic, tens of thousands of protesters took to the streets to voice their support for Khalid killing a *gustakh-e-Rasul*, a person who had insulted the Prophet Muhammad.[8]

Attention around blasphemy laws and vigilante killings of blasphemers has surged in recent decades. According to the United States Commission on International Religious Freedom, a bipartisan commission tasked by Congress and the US President to monitor freedom of belief, Pakistan spearheaded this trend in both state-backed persecution and extra-judicial violence. From 2014–18, almost a third of the 674 globally reported arrests and convictions for religious insults took place in Pakistan.[9] In extra-judicial violence, Pakistan even accumulated half the reported incidents, ranging from beating blasphemers with sticks to public lynchings.[10]

How has Pakistan come to dominate the global field on blasphemy? Accusations of blasphemy against the Prophet Muhammad, in something close to their modern South Asian form, first appeared as a concept in the early nineteenth century. Traditionalist Muslim scholars invented blasphemy to stem the rising tide of Enlightenment rationality, which threatened to tear apart their theological cosmology. These traditionalist scholars, or ulema, identified two sources of danger. Internally, they levelled blasphemy charges against the Shias and Sunni reformers like Shah Ismail Dehlvi, a Sunni reformer who sought to purify Islam from what he considered polluting Hindu customs and, given the similarity in his doctrinal approach towards religion, is often mislabelled as a 'Wahabi'.[11] Shah Ismail had set out a program for puritanical rejection of all deviations prevalent in South Asian Islam. Externally, traditionalists flagged the British East India Company as the main threat. The Company had begun their India operations as a mercantile firm in the seventeenth century but quickly metastasised into a company-state that was rapidly hollowing out the Mughal crown.[12]

To resolve the internal dispute, Sunni traditionalists adopted the habit of calling all reformers *gustakh-e-Rasul*, blasphemers against the Prophet. After consulting medieval Islamic jurisprudence works, traditionalists went further and began to argue that these rationalist reformers should be killed for their blasphemous transgressions. A particularly outspoken proponent of this view was Fazl-e-Haq Khairabadi, who had spent much of his life rampaging against anyone he suspected of demeaning the Prophet Muhammad.[13] Such acts were grave crimes, Khairabadi contended.[14] Even a diverging scholarly opinion on theological issues, often dense and theoretical and mostly without any immediate practical significance, could, in Khairabadi's eyes, qualify as blasphemy and trigger a sentence of death. In his most prominent academic debate with Shah Ismail Dehlvi, Khairabadi quickly declared Shah Ismail a *kafir* (infidel) and therefore *wajib-ul-qatl*.[15]

In their preceding discussion that led to this stern fatwa, Shah Ismail had argued that Allah's power was absolute. It was thus well within his powers to create another prophet.[16] Though Shah Ismail agreed with Khairabadi that Allah would not do so, as he had promised it in the Quran, Khairabadi chastised him for opening the theoretical possibility that Allah may dispatch other prophets in the future. Khairabadi held that such hypothetical statements, albeit purely academic, undermined the status of the Prophet Muhammad as humanity's last guiding light. Anyone who thought that the creation of another prophet was not beyond God's power, just as the creation of another God was beyond His power, Khairabadi insisted, was committing blasphemy by violating the doctrine of the finality of Prophethood.[17]

To suppress Shah Ismail's rationalist advances, Khairabadi commissioned Mirza Ghalib, India's foremost poet, to compose a *masnavi* to highlight Shah Ismail's blasphemy.[18] Apart from rebuking Shah Ismail, Ghalib's involvement would have increased public attention to this otherwise niche scholarly debate.[19] But Ghalib was not excited about this prospect. For one, he feared being dragged into a tiresome academic discussion of the kind he had avoided throughout much of his life. Ghalib also never had a particularly doctrinal approach to religion. Born into a Sunni family, he had embraced much of Shia thought towards the end of his life. In defiance of the obligations prescribed by both denominations, he never fasted in the month of Ramadan and actively neglected his five daily prayers. As he repeatedly reminded his readers, his best poetry was written while sipping wine. Yet this removal of Islam's dogmatic shell seems to have brought Ghalib closer to the Prophet's veneration and he eventually agreed to Khairabadi's request and penned a short tract that chastised the 'Wahabi' desecration of the finality of Prophethood doctrine.[20]

With the internal dispute ostensibly won through poetry, Khairabadi sought to overcome the external threat to his traditionalist doctrine by signing the fateful fatwa of 1857, which declared jihad to rid India of the British. In this military effort, many otherwise rivalling ulemas joined him. This surprisingly diverse group consisted of the Ahl-e-Hadith movement, another proto-rationalist offshoot that had begun to take roots in India, as well as Shah Ismail's followers, who had already gained some practical jihad-experience in the 1830s battling the Sikhs in Punjab. Yet their jihadi striving during the Indian Rebellion of 1857 proved unsuccessful. After the crushing defeat against the British in 1858 and the humiliating dethroning of Bahadur Shah Zafar, the last Mughal king, Muslims had to renegotiate their place in India.[21] In the process of reasserting themselves as political actors, Indian Muslims splintered into different factions, which ranged from past-minded isolationists to future-centric modernists. During much of the latter part of the nineteenth century, vigilante killings of blasphemers remained scarce, if not altogether absent, while at the same time rivalling sects continued, like Khairabadi had done, to call each other kafir and *wajib-ul-qatl*. The name-calling had little impact on Muslims' overall conduct with each other, which remained largely cordial. For instance, students continued to freely drop in and out of courses and lectures of rivalling madrasas without feeling any obligation to implement the strongly worded fatwas of their school's founders unambiguously declaring death sentences upon the other denomination.

Therefore, much of this former inner-Islamic scholarly posturing remained markedly distinct from our current age's preoccupation with insults against the Prophet Muhammad and the real repercussions that flow from them.[22] Today, such cases mainly involve non-Muslim insulters and passionate Muslim displays of love for the Prophet Muhammad which cultivate a seemingly binding ethical obligation on individual Muslim believers to avenge these insults in blood.

Historians and anthropologists of South Asia have tracked the story of how we got here from various points, whether from the circulation of Enlightenment principles, where a form of epistemological violence pressed colonial subjects into venting their suppressed emotions, as in Pankaj Mishra's *Age of Anger*;[23] or from colonial policies and laws, for instance the implementation of India's first anti-blasphemy legislation in 1927, which pushed Muslims to perform their outrage to receive legal recognition, as in Asad Ahmed's *Adjudicating Muslims*;[24] or from the nationalist movement in the 1940s that rallied for an Islamic state on Indian soil, as in Venkat Dhulipala's *Creating a New Medina*;[25] or from Zia-ul-Haq's Islamisation program in the 1980s, which sharpened the state's legal toolkit to hunt blasphemers, as in Ayesha Jalal's *The Struggle for Pakistan*;[26] or from individual state organs like the judiciary, which despite its colonial roots nudged Pakistan towards shariatic principles, as in Martin Lau's *The Role of Islam in the Legal System of Pakistan*.[27] Whichever way, for whatever reason, blasphemy has continued to dominate Pakistan's citizenship-state relationship, with the result that to run for public office, or even to vote, Pakistani Muslims have to solemnly swear that they are 'not the follower of anyone who claims to be a prophet [...] after Muhammad (Peace be Upon Him).'[28]

There is another way of telling the story of blasphemy, however. In this telling, blasphemy did not emerge from high-brow debates between rival Muslim sects in the late eighteenth and nineteenth centuries, nor did it materialise through colonial policies or later political forms. Rather, this view frames blasphemy and the need for individual believers to defend the Prophet's honour as developing in tandem with Hindu revivalist and nationalist thought.

The following chapters will show that Pakistan's blasphemy fixation started as a debate between two North Indian revivalist movements to pursue spiritual supremacy. These movements are the Arya Samaj and the Ahmadiyya. I argue that these sects remained central reference points in Muslim conversations about blasphemy in colonial India and Pakistan. Both movements also had a disproportionate impact on the development of Hindu nationalist thought. Yet, for all their political and theological importance, scholarship has failed to credit them for their impact. Research endeavours on the Ahmadiyya, for instance, have largely bracketed them within a medieval eschatological Islamic discourse, labelling them as a more enterprising and modernist Sufi order.[29] Studies on the Arya Samaj, on the other hand, have framed them as a feeble attempt to produce a religion tailored to the sentiments of a growing middle-class salariat in North Indian urban centres.[30] Scholars have also largely explored these two movements as distinct from each other as opposed to inextricably intertwined.[31] This book, in contrast, positions these two movements as foundational for Indian politics and fundamentally geared towards each other.

The history of Muslims and their political activism in modern South Asian history and public memory has drawn substantive interest in recent years.[32] With the rise of new political leaderships in India and Pakistan, the central question of what a republic means has again become fiercely contested.[33] Some historians have argued that research on the constituent assembly can settle these debates, as the assembly forms the backbone or foundational moment of any republic.[34] The knowledge gained in this way, they hold, could be made politically useful for the ongoing scuffle with increasingly muscular executives. Scholarship on popular movements has disagreed with this approach. They note that such approaches focus too squarely on institutional machinations and ignore the everyday lives of citizens. They also point out that such approaches marginalise the broader lived experiences and fail to explain how political concepts acquire meaning on the ground.[35] Several studies from this scholarly field have assessed religion's role in political mobilisation and touched upon the role that insults against the Prophet Muhammad played in drawing Muslims together as a political force.[36] However, to date, little work has been done to address the central question of the *emergence* of blasphemy against the Prophet as a trope to rally around.[37] As a result, scholarship endorses a narrative that characterises blasphemy mainly as one of the many responses to colonial modernity, both in British India and in Pakistan.

This book provides a more differentiated historical genealogy and roots the legal and political emergence of blasphemy against the Prophet on the Indian subcontinent in a forgotten debate between Mirza Ghulam Ahmad and Pandit Lekh Ram, two provincial clerics far from the traditional centres of religious learning or worldly power.[38] Through a close examination of earlier untapped speeches, private diaries, letters, newspapers, pamphlets, court records, and police reports, I show how Indian Muslims, and later Pakistanis, moulded blasphemy into a central ethical, legal, and political idea. As a first conceptual move, I relocate blasphemy in Pakistan from its present place in historical and legal scholarship to a more appropriate location in the longer historical narratives of South Asian history.

I broadly structure the attitude of Indian Muslims towards blasphemy into three stages, or Weberian ideal types, that signify the inherent conceptual shifts. In the first stage, Indian Muslims viewed insults against the Prophet as a sin that Allah would punish in the hereafter. In the second stage, roughly from the 1880s onwards, they regarded it as a sin that Allah would penalise in this world, and not just in the hereafter. In the third stage, beginning in the early twentieth century, South Asian Muslims started to view the avenging of insults against the Prophet, especially when these insults came from non-Muslims, as an individual ethical duty and a barometer of their faith. At its most interventionist, this book argues that Mirza Ghulam Ahmad, the founder of a small nineteenth-century Muslim reform movement called the Ahmadiyya, helped popularise today's pervasive emotional response towards blasphemy. On the flip side, this book holds that, although almost entirely written out of history books today, Pandit Lekh Ram had an outsized impact on Hindu nationalist thought by way of preconfiguring its relationship with Indian Muslims.

In the first part of the book, I track Mirza and Lekh Ram's polemic encounters and their broad impact on Indian politics. In the last three chapters, I show how the religious and political groups in Pakistan utilised an augmented version of Mirza's sensitivities towards blasphemy. In the conclusion, I briefly sketch out how the Arya Samaj–Ahmadiyya conversation set the conceptual paradigm for Hindu nationalist thought.

This book thus offers a fresh angle to the conventional scholarly accounts on the development of legal and constitutional sensitivities of South Asian Muslims, the rise of Hindu–Muslim conflict, and the effect of religious revivalist movements on politics. It also attempts to fill the gap in scholarship on the role of blasphemy in Pakistan's legal and political history. This history is older than Pakistan's creation and arguably stretches well into the colonial period.[39] In this book, I link the emergence of many of the tropes that inform blasphemy and constitute the bedrock of Pakistan's agitational politics and constitutional structure to religious revivalist sects in the late nineteenth century.[40] By emphasising how they cultivated religious sentiments, the idea of a separate Muslim nation drew many of its conceptual cues from debates that were wrestled over for at least half a century before.[41]

Like all works of history, this book cannot cover the entirety of the complex and often intersecting issues that relate to blasphemy in Pakistan, especially issues between Muslim sects. Anti-Shia extremism, for instance, which followed as a direct consequence of the Iranian Revolution of 1979, and was mobilised by militant Deobandi sectarian outlets, continues to haunt Pakistan's Shia minority for their alleged revilement of the Prophet's family and companions.[42] Pakistan's penal law also reflects this sentiment with an explicit prohibition on hurling insults at the family or the companions of the Holy Prophet in 298-A Pakistan Penal Code.[43]

At various times, and with different intensities, disputes over the role of the Prophet Muhammad have also flared up in intra-Islamic constellations between different Sunni *maslaks* (sub-sects). Significantly, the Deobandi and Barelvi dispute has in recent decades metastasised into hardened fronts with periodic spouts of violence between these sects.[44] For many Barelvis, who constitute the overwhelming majority in Pakistan, failing to display emotionally forceful responses to religious transgression—as in their eyes the more rationally minded Deobandis fail to do—points towards a corrupted religious sensibility and may even compromise one's Muslimness and political belonging.[45]

However, unlike the Ahmadis and other non-Muslim minorities, Shias and Deobandis have not experienced constitutional and political exclusion based on their religious beliefs. Instead, they are attacked (and in turn attack other groups) based on their ritualistic performance. While rendering Muslims as non-Muslims through fatwas, a process known as *takfir*, has spiked in recent decades, none of these Islamic legal rulings has placed other Muslim groups unconditionally outside of the pale of Islam. Such a total exclusion has only been awarded in the case of the Ahmadiyya, which makes their entanglement with blasphemy qualitatively different from other occurrences in the context of intra-Islamic sectarian violence in Pakistan.[46]

The irony of persecuting Ahmadis for blasphemy when this movement had historically positioned itself at the forefront to silence non-Muslim blasphemous voices is best understood in the context of religious revivalist movements more broadly. In the late nineteenth century, movements like the Ahmadiyya and the Arya Samaj had, despite their heterodox beliefs, gained some acceptance of their respective faiths from the orthodox mainstream for their ability to convert new followers into their religious fold and for fighting back conversion efforts from other religious groups.[47] With Hindus and Christians largely purged from Pakistan after 1947, and even more so after the loss of East Pakistan, where more than ninety per cent of non-Muslim Pakistanis lived, in 1971, the threat, imaginary or real, of Muslims converting to other religions had evaporated.[48] Ahmadis were few, but their higher education level had allowed them to flourish under the colonial administration. When Pakistan was born, they still occupied a prominent position in public life; However, without the looming fear of Hinduism advancing, Ahmadis quickly became the subject of conspiracy theories which, stoked by state actors and political calculations, spiralled into outright constitutional exclusion.[49]

1

REBIRTH

I

It began with a prophecy. In February 1893, three years after his contentious claim of being the rebirth of Jesus and the final incarnation of Krishna and Vishnu, Mirza Ghulam Ahmad stood before an expectant crowd of turbaned men in the remote village of Qadian, Punjab.[1] Mirza, a fifty-year-old former law clerk who had devoted much of his worldly life looking after his shrinking family estate, had spent the last months in strict isolation. During this period of withdrawal, he had prayed intensely to Allah for a heavenly sign that would prove his messianic status and boost membership of his nascent reformist movement, the *Ahmadiyya*.[2] Facing the crowd, Mirza bent forward and announced that Lekh Ram, an ex-police constable turned celebrity Arya Samaj [Hindu] preacher from Peshawar,[3] would soon be 'cut into pieces like a lifeless calf'.[4]

Wrapped in thick woollen shawls to fend off Punjab's creeping cold, the audience likely looked unfazed, as Mirza had made such prophecies about Lekh Ram before. In an earlier pamphlet that was widely circulated at the time, Mirza had announced that 'Allah will punish him for using foul and degrading language against the Prophet Muhammad peace be upon him'.[5] But it was not some common

13

illness that would bring Lekh Ram down. Quizzed by some of his followers, Mirza elaborated quite meticulously on how Lekh Ram's punishment would play out: '[i]n my vision, I have seen a frightening figure of enormous height and blood dripping from his eyes, who looked at me and groaned: "Where is Lekh Ram?"'[6] After pondering over this vision at some length, Mirza concluded that 'Allah has now designated an angel specifically for the task of punishing Lekh Ram.'[7] Despite the involvement of a heavenly messenger, Mirza remained somewhat vague when asked to provide a clear time frame in which his prophecy would materialise. He only commented that 'it will happen in the next six years and happen in such a way that the world will be able to witness the truth of Islam.'[8]

Five years later, in 1897, just within the time frame Mirza had laid out, a man fatally stabbed Lekh Ram at his home. Lekh Ram had spent the day milling around the Arya Samaj mandir down the road from his rented flat in Wachowali *galli*, a characteristically narrow lane that lent Lahore's Walled City an aura of majestic decay.[9] He had returned home early to avoid the soundscapes that accompany Eid-ul-Fitr, the Islamic festival that concludes the fasting month of Ramadan, as he felt Lahore's Muslims cheered extra loudly when they passed the Arya Samaj temple. While not enthused over the end-of-Ramadan feast, Lekh Ram, a lifelong vegetarian, vastly preferred it to the other Islamic holy day, Eid-ul-Adha, where Muslims slaughter goats, calves, and cows in a ritualistic sacrifice, flooding the alleys in the Walled City with animal blood.[10]

Once home, Lekh Ram asked his wife and his mother not to disturb him and busied himself in chanting hymns. Ever since his only son had died as an infant a few years previously, Lekh Ram had adopted a strict routine of chanting religious mantras in seclusion. But on that day, he was not humming alone. Accompanying him was a slightly built young man, a former Muslim who now wanted to convert to Hinduism through *shuddhi*, a recently invented 'purification' ceremony that was a speciality of the Arya Samaj.[11] After shadowing Lekh Ram for about three weeks and worming himself into his confidence, the conversion candidate declared that he was now ready for the *shuddhi* ceremony. Lekh Ram had brought him home for this very reason. The man looked sickly: his cheeks sunken from lousy nutrition, his face freckled with birthmarks, and two jutted teeth sticking out whenever he spoke. Concerned about his general health, Lekh Ram had even called upon a nearby doctor to examine the man, and he had immediately proscribed vitamins upon seeing him.[12]

Just at the moment when Lekh Ram was getting ready to unspool the complicated steps involved in the *shuddhi* procedure, his guest pulled out a razor-sharp dagger and sliced into Lekh Ram's stomach, taking his time to rotate the knife. As Lekh Ram's intestines quilled out, he could still wrestle the assassin to the floor. Alarmed by the screams, Lekh Ram's wife and mother sprinted up the stairs, both armed with *chapati* rollers. They stormed into the room where Lekh Ram had pinned down the assassin.[13] 'This wretch came to receive *shuddhi* but has stabbed me instead!'[14] Lekh Ram squeaked before his mother dealt the assailant several strong blows to the head with her *chapati* roller. The man swirled around with his knife, cutting Lekh Ram's wife in the process, but knowing that there was no other escape, as now both Lekh Ram and his wife were clutching onto his weapon, shawl and shoes, he peeled out of them, whisked down the stairs and fled, with his blood-soaked *kameez*, into Lahore's teeming bazaar.[15]

Alerted by the screams, Lekh Ram's neighbours ran into his house and rushed him to Mayo Hospital, Lahore's premier clinic, on a *tanga*. Around the turn of the century, knife crimes were commonplace in Lahore. Social frictions had swelled in the city after an influx of migrants over the preceding three decades. Another factor that had turned Lahore into a hub of petty crime was the relative degradation of the city's population and its rapidly disintegrating social structures.[16] Knife attacks and *lathi* blows were a regular occurrence in the motions of city life. Just a few weeks before Lekh Ram's stabbing, during a courteous meeting between two rival wings of the Arya Samaj, an argument over the consumption of meat had enraged the sentiments of vegetarians and left a carnivorous student, who had suggested a dietary change in the school's canteen, dead with a fractured skull.[17] Yet Lekh Ram's case stood out, both for the severity of the wound and for the public attention it received. An intern at the Mayo clinic recalled Lekh Ram's condition in the following way:

The house surgeon called me over. He told me to take a close look at a 'serious case'. And there he was. A six-foot-tall man with his stomach slashed open squirming on a stretcher. His eight-inch cut was glaring at me. Most of his intestines were coiling out and, on the doctor's orders, I stabilised them with a hot water sponge.[18]

This intern also remembered the dying words of the pandit. 'Look at my *kismet*, not even a real doctor is here to attend to my wounds', Lekh Ram groaned, likely confusing the Indian house surgeon for just another studious intern. When Lekh died the following day, the local Arya Samaj community took him to the cremation grounds, where over twenty thousand Hindus had assembled, making it one of the most attended funerals in Lahore that year. In their eulogies, Lekh Ram's Arya Samaj companions declared him the 'first martyr of his faith'.[19] They were also quick to note that this looked like the work of a Muslim fanatic who had punished Lekh Ram for his 'scholarly' allegations against the Prophet Muhammad and Islam.[20]

Mirza was an obvious suspect. Immediately upon hearing of Lekh Ram's murder, Mirza had rapidly curated dozens of posters and plastered them in the village squares around Qadian. For him, Lekh Ram's death warranted a celebration, as his prophecy had come true. Mirza's announcements did not go unnoticed, and soon major newspapers, from the gossipy *Akhbar-e-Aam* to the reticent *Tribune,* collectively pointed the finger at him. These accusations perturbed Mirza and soon he pushed back against charges that he had ordered the murder. To him, the indictment was baseless, as no spiritual leader could order an obedient disciple to commit a killing:[21]

> It's an entirely ridiculous idea that I ordered one of my disciples to kill Lekh Ram. The relationship between a disciple and his spiritual master is a very fickle one. Even the smallest imbalance can destroy it. Some of the members of my movement have begun sowing doubts about my claims for trivial reasons. [...] Once, I was forced to drink tea with my left hand because my right arm was broken and weak. I later came to know that some of my disciples had started circulating this story, accusing me of having violated the traditions and practices of the Prophet

Muhammad [it is *sunnah* for Muslims to eat/drink with the right hand].[22]

For anyone questioning Mirza's innocence, he had a 'complete solution'. In an open letter, he challenged doubters to take a vow in front of him that they considered him guilty. Any such person, Mirza foretold, would suffer the wrath of Allah within a year, just like Lekh Ram had. If for some reason no heavenly sign materialised, Mirza announced in characteristically dramatic fashion that 'you should punish me like a murderer'.[23]

Then Mirza's defence took a personal turn. He began to indulge in speculations surrounding the motive of the assassin. 'I read in the *Paisa Akhbar* that Lekh Ram had an illicit relationship with a local woman. Lekh Ram's killer may well have been this woman's father or husband, who had some honour left in him. I am quite surprised that nobody is digging deeper into this matter.'[24] Even after Lekh Ram's death, Mirza still seemed infuriated by the vile insults the Arya Samaj pandit had levelled on Islam and its founder, the Prophet Muhammad. Maybe it was for this reason that Mirza wrote a biting message to the mourning Hindus commiserating with them on Lekh Ram's martyrdom, mocking that Lekh Ram was not a martyr once but twice over. His first martyrdom? Getting 'knifed by the beauty of a woman'.[25]

II

The story of Mirza's family and upbringing reflects the peculiarity of two centuries of Punjabi politics. In the latter part of the eighteenth century, the Mughal Empire rapidly fragmented at the fringes.[26] Maharaja Ranjit Singh, a Sikh, managed to unite the bickering warlords who had risen up as a direct consequence of waning Mughal sovereignty. Their unity ensured Ranjit Singh's swift succession to the throne of what was then one of India's most prosperous provinces. To quell potential rebellions, Ranjit Singh disowned and banished all Muslim landowners who had in any way resisted his march to power.[27] Atta Muhammad, Mirza's grandfather, had sided with the Mughal Empire and, as a punishment, had to leave Qadian. But whereas other Muslims found themselves entirely without protection, the Raja of Kapurthala invited Atta Muhammad to take up a salaried position in his army and offered him residence in a village just twenty kilometres from Qadian.[28] Atta Muhammad died in exile soon after.[29]

In 1818, Ranjit Singh launched several military campaigns in Peshawar and Kashmir. He did this partly to quash Muslim rebellions in those areas as well as to extend his empire to the East and North-West.[30] On the lookout for fresh recruits, Ranjit Singh offered Mirza's father, Ghulam Murtaza a position in his troops. In exchange, Mirza's family was permitted to return to Qadian.[31] They were also granted the deed to some scrubby patches of land around their former ancestral seat. Ghulam Murtaza was a good fighter. His efforts helped to consolidate Sikh rule over much of India's North-West as well as Kashmir. By the time Mirza was born in 1841, he had received a sizable amount of land in reward for his military feats.[32]

But the glory of a Sikh Raj waned soon after that. Already in Ghulam Murtaza's lifetime, the East India Company started making inroads into the closed market economy of the Punjab, which was rich in agricultural produce, particularly sugar, rice, indigo, wheat, and cotton.[33] After a series of wars in the 1840s, the Company annexed Punjab and incorporated it into British India in 1849. For the most significant part, the British upheld the existing power distribution. The Company praised Mirza's family for having 'remained faithful and steady subjects' after the annexation and would, therefore, 'never forget your family's rights and services'.[34]

Having fought loyally for the Sikhs, Ghulam Murtaza recognised the window of opportunity that the Indian Mutiny of 1857–58 opened. Together with his eldest son and many members of his extended family, he swapped allegiance to enlist with the East India Company. John Nicholson enlisted them for his regiment. Mirza Ghulam Ahmad, who was sixteen at the time, did not participate in the fighting. This had less to do with his age and was more due to his bookish nature that did not lend itself to horseback warfare.[35]

Ghulam Murtaza had faced Nicholson as an opponent during the two Anglo–Sikh Wars in the 1840s. In previous military campaigns, Nicholson had developed a reputation for impulsiveness and brutality. He fully lived up to this notoriety on his march to Delhi. In the few months that it took him to reach the epicentre of the Mutiny, Nicholson had indulged in the following activities: he had blown prisoners of war from the muzzles of guns, shot and hanged them without trial, and suggested that in cases where murder or rape involved European women a 'new kind of death' of the perpetrators would be appropriate, one that should include 'flaying alive, impalement, or burning'.[36]

After quelling the Sepoy Mutiny, Nicholson wrote a recommendation for Ghulam Murtaza that would be crucial for the family's fate after the British Crown absorbed the East India Company in 1858. Services in battle now transformed into sources of income, and the British Government endowed Ghulam Murtaza with a pension of 700 rupees and an additional *khilat* of 200 rupees.[37] Ghulam Murtaza could cover the majority of his running costs from this pension alone. But his desire to bring their formerly owned landholdings back into the family estate soon plunged him into a series of litigations that massively drained his resources. According to Mirza, his father had spent around eight thousand rupees on lawyers and court fees alone.[38]

Apart from being born in the Sikh *Raj*, and witnessing the catastrophic events surrounding the Mutiny from close range, Mirza Ghulam Ahmad's early life was mostly uneventful. Those who knew him reported that he was a recluse and preferred to spend his time at the mosque or studying religious books. What helped him to decipher the technical debates around tricky questions of Islamic jurisprudence, Hindu mythology, and Christian eschatology was a thorough training in Farsi, Arabic, and Urdu that he had received in his youth. For his non-scholarly family, however, Mirza's detachment from worldly affairs was a concern. When a guest of the family asked Ghulam Murtaza where Mirza was, he responded that the guest might want to 'search him in the nooks of the mosque; and if you still do not find him there, then check to see the person who stowed away the prayer carpets did not inadvertently roll him up and leave him stashed away in it.'[39]

It was thus very much in character for Ahmad to write a sentimental letter to his father lamenting the worldliness he saw around him, which pressed him to yearn for 'seclusion away from the company of people'. He penned that only radical detachment would allow him to spend all his time 'in the remembrance of the Eternal Being'.[40] What was out of character, however, was that Ahmad, aged twenty-four, when sent to pick up his father's pension from the government offices in Lahore, ran off with his cousin Imam-ud-Din and squandered the entire sum. When Imam-ud-Din tried to make good on their steep financial loss by robbing a tea-caravan on their way home, he was caught instead and put on trial for theft. Fortunately for the pair, the charges against Imam-ud-Din were soon dropped, but Mirza was so deeply ashamed about his impulsive behaviour that he did not return home to Qadian, where his wife and two sons were waiting.[41] Instead, Mirza picked up meagre employment at the district court in Sialkot, a lively cultural hub near Lahore, and began working as a law clerk.[42]

Mirza's Sialkot years, from 1864–68, were the most impactful for shaping his future messianic mission. Here, he met people from all parts of India and engaged with them about the differences in their respective faiths. He was particularly fascinated by Christian missionaries and befriended John Taylor, an Urdu-speaking Scottish Presbyterian minister.[43] Taylor had arrived in Punjab as a missionary shortly after the Mutiny with big plans for proselytising and converting Punjab's Hindu, Sikh, and Muslim population entirely to Christianity. For this purpose, he felt that the approach towards preaching that missionaries had conventionally adopted had to change radically. It was no longer sufficient to announce the word from the pulpit. Instead, the word had to be brought directly to the people living in villages. 'The people see so little of us', Taylor wrote to his church's board while asking for more funds, '[and are therefore] so little impressed with our services.'[44] Taylor was also amongst the first to recognise the value of native preachers and staffed his mission stations with them, an approach he found more successful than importing culturally illiterate missionaries from Britain. According to Taylor, with just 'a few well-trained native preachers', the church was guaranteed to expand quickly in the coming decades.[45]

Syed Mir Hassan, a follower of Syed Ahmed Khan of Aligarh fame and a devout rationalist, who would later become a distinguished scholar of Arabic, was another close acquaintance of Mirza. They shared a fondness for Arabic and discussions on religious matters. These discussions ranged from medicine and sexuality to jurisprudence and theology. Most of these conversations occurred at night when the discussants had finished their day's work at government offices. They would convene at a corner store opposite Mirza's residence and continue their discussions well into the night. The following excerpt provides a glimpse of how such discussions unfolded:

> Conversation once turned to dress. A group argued that pants that were loose at the ankle, as were commonly worn in India, were preferable to pants that were tight at the ankle (like harem pants). Others held the opposite viewpoint. Mirza sahib stated, 'For the purpose of hiding nakedness, pants that are tight at the ankles are preferable because such pants conceal more completely, and the tight fit at the ankles hides the nakedness even from the earth.' All those present liked his reply.[46]

Like much of the colonial world in the late nineteenth century, Punjab was adopting rapidly to modernity.[47] In Lahore, the British Government set up a liberal arts college to train future civil servants. They were also recruiting a professor of Arabic. Mir Hassan suggested that Mirza apply to this position as he thought him qualified enough and because it would pay in two months what he was earning in a year as a law clerk.[48] Mirza refused. As he later professed to Mir Hassan, he feared that such a high-ranking position might change him. Mirza thought that 'most people [in positions of power] misuse their knowledge and make it into an instrument of mischief and illegal acts.'[49]

The other reason that likely held Mirza back from applying to the professorship was his feudal upbringing and the relative independence of his time management that came with it. Such attitudes did not lend themselves well to salaried employment. Mirza wrote the qualifying examination to become an attorney to break free from his mundane existence as a clerk.[50] When he took the exam in 1868 and failed, Ghulam Murtaza asked him to return to Qadian and look after his mother, in her declining health, and the

21

estate. To Mirza's great sorrow, his mother died before he was able to reach the village.[51]

But the Sialkot years endowed Mirza with a specific subjectivity that emerges from the experience of having one's core beliefs challenged. On top of this, he saw from close range what it meant to work as a tiny cog in the enormous imperial legal bureaucracy that was, at least in its self-professed claim, running impartially and without any nepotism. More than his father's loyalty towards the British during the Mutiny and the decades that followed, it was Mirza's direct experience of working in the colonial bureaucracy that endowed him with lifelong enthusiastic support for British rule over India. What he took from Taylor was the notion that locality mattered tremendously for global religions and that the missionary efforts of a few men can attract large swathes of converts. From Syed Mir Hassan, he took the scholarly confidence to write and participate in public debate. From the discussions in the corner store, he picked up the importance of engaging in religious discourses with rationality and reason, regardless of how much it was spiced with irrational hypotheticals.

Back in Qadian, Mirza quickly fell back into his old routine of praying and studying. For as long as his father was alive—until 1876—he was able to do this without much financial pressure, even though this meant that he occasionally had to attend court hearings on their family's land disputes. After his father's death, his financial worries spiked. Now it was his elder brother, Ghulam Qadir, who managed the estate and provided Mirza with a stipend. It was during this time that Mirza set out to accomplish by far his most ambitious project: a fifty-volume book project, titled *Barahin-e-Ahmadiyya*, which would contain, as he wrote in the blurb, '300 inconvertible rational arguments' to cement the superiority of Islam over all other religions.[52]

Barahin-e-Ahmadiyya was, Mirza promised, to be unlike any other book on Islamic apologetics. Other books that attempted to defend Islam, Mirza outlined in the first volume 'have been written in the context of a particular faith'. They were, therefore, 'confined to refuting the specific beliefs of that faith.'[53] In the past, Mirza argued, doctrinal threats to Islam had mainly arisen from the viewpoint of Christianity. Therefore, Muslims had only churned apologetic literature to meet Christian critics. In India, however, Christianity was not the most significant threat. Islam was facing a much more substantive danger from the dual attacks of atheism and modernity. Mirza worried that these forces would soon bring about a society in which, 'instead of the traditional salutation [*Assalamu 'alaikum wa rahmatullahe wa barakatuhu*], one would hear "goodbye" and "good morning".'[54]

Mirza did not follow rationality in any strict sense. In successive steps towards the fourth volume, the *Barahin-e-Ahmadiyya* becomes infused with revelations that he received. Receiving revelation was a significant break, both from the debating style of Christian missionaries and the Arya Samaj. But there was enough rational pondering in his books that gave some credibility to his claim that the *Barahin-e-Ahmadiyya* had demonstrated Islam's divine origin strictly through logical argument. Either as a clever marketing ploy or out of sincere conviction in the strength of his ideas, Mirza also announced a monetary reward for anyone who could refute his arguments 'from his own scripture', which is to say, anyone who was able to prove a denser rational logic that was holding his religious world-view together.[55] Where Mirza broke the conventional script and remained somewhat unintelligible to objective observers was in his insistence that divine revelations constituted the bedrock of his book. This fact made it challenging to deconstruct any single argument, as Mirza could always claim that it had been revealed to him directly from God. What looked rational could be classified as revealed, putting it outside the scope of being challenged by reason.

In what would become his signature style of engagement, Mirza announced a reward of 10,000 rupees to anyone who could disprove any argument in his book. The prize was roughly equivalent to the value of his entire inheritance. There was a small but important caveat to his challenge, however. Before paying out an award, three mutually agreed-upon judges would have to assess the challenger's submission in a 'reasonable' way.[56] If the judges did not arrive at their decision in a way Mirza considered reasonable, their award would not be binding upon him. It was thus of little surprise that nobody came forward to claim the prize money, despite Mirza's generous offer that any challenger would only have to provide 'one-fifth' of his arguments.[57] Still, the publicity feat worked. Mirza started appearing in the obscure and nativist sections of magazines and newspapers across India. Sometimes his fame even crossed borders and continents. A letter that Mirza mailed to the Bishop of Lahore, ruminating over his life's mission as similar in spirit to that of Jesus, led directly to a page-long profile in a German magazine for Christian missionaries. Had Mirza translated it into Urdu, he would not have been pleased that the magazine cited at length the Bishop's harsh assessment of Mirza as 'not fanatical but daydreaming'.[58]

Given his heightened sense of mission, it may be somewhat surprising that Mirza had a single person in mind to whom he devoted his book, a man who was neither an atheist nor a Christian. As he writes in *Barahin-e-Ahmadiyya*, his 'primary addressee' was Dayanand Saraswati,[59] a Gujrat-born *rishi* and the founder of the Arya Samaj movement.[60] Dayanand had attracted a sizable following amongst the emerging professional classes of the Punjab during this time. One reason for his success was his message to uplift Hindu political consciousness, which resonated well with upper-caste Punjabi Hindus, especially those who had received an English education but remained deeply rooted in their native culture. In short, Dayanand wanted to make Hinduism fit for the modern world, cleanse it of all corrupting influences and bring about some form of *swaraj* (self/home-rule). His nationalist leanings spoke directly to the concerns of Punjab's upper-caste Hindus, especially the urban intelligentsia. They were tired of being denied self-rule. Dayanand's message, predictably, did not bode well with supporters of the colonial regime. The Oxford don Max Müller, who trained colonial administrators for a living, called Dayanand the 'most perverse interpreter of the Vedas', not least to downplay his political importance to the palpable independence movement.[61] In his magnum opus *Satyarth Prakash* [The Light and Meaning of the Truth], written in 1875, Dayanand Saraswati laid out the contours of how such a new political entity may look like, with a marked emphasis on ridding a people of foreign subjugation.[62] Educated Hindus flocked to Dayanand's teachings in droves.

Several factors fuelled Mirza's phobic attachment to Dayanand. For one, Mirza was impressed by the audacity of Dayanand's message. In the early stages, Mirza still taunted Dayanand for being outside the fold of orthodox Hinduism.[63] Later, Mirza mirrored Dayanand's position by spinning toward the margins of Islamic orthodoxy himself. The second point that Mirza admired about Dayanand was his unrelenting drive for transforming social and religious structures through public debates. Mirza, too, adopted a similar approach to propagate his renewal of Islamic teachings. But mostly Mirza was impressed by the following that Dayanand had attracted: young urban degree holders, mainly working in lower to mid-level government services. Throughout his life, Mirza never tired of reminding his readers that there were BA and MA degrees holders as well as government servants amongst his followers. Partly Dayanand's success amongst the literate classes stemmed from his outreach efforts to university campuses. Government College, Lahore was one such place. The Arya Samaj impact was so strong that a student from the class of 1878 recalled: '[m]ost of the college students enlisted themselves as Samajists'—though he truthfully added that many 'deserted the new sect shortly after [graduation].'[64]

Even before presenting any argument in his book, Mirza punched hard against Dayanand. He promised that once he had written all fifty books of the series, he would be interested to know whether Dayanand 'still want[ed] to live or will contemplate suicide'.[65] Dayanand did not respond to any of these provocations and ignored the countless letters, pamphlets, and books Mirza addressed to him. Mirza was also ignored by Syed Ahmed Khan, arguably the most impactful socio-religious reformer in nineteenth-century India.[66] Instead, Mirza found himself debating with a brooding bunch of amateur theologians: there was one middle-school teacher from Chiniot, an art teacher from a nearby government college, and some novice writers who never picked up the pen again after their brief spat with Mirza.[67] Only after Dayanand passed away did one of his most enthusiastic disciples, a man in his early twenties who had recently given up government service to devote himself to full-time preaching, begin to respond to Mirza's challenges. Lekh Ram lacked the social standing that Mirza would have preferred as a debating partner. He did not fit the profile of a learned scholar respected by his peers. Even if defeated in argument, Lekh Ram would not give any immediate scholarly credibility to Mirza. Lekh Ram was more akin to the hobby theologians from which Mirza sought to move away. At the time, Lekh Ram was also hardly known outside narrow North Indian Arya Samaj circles.

In 1885, after publishing the fourth volume of the *Barahin-e-Ahmadiyya*, Mirza decided to issue an open call to invite people to Qadian. Anyone who would live with him for a year, he promised, would be able to witness 'heavenly signs'. In case the visitor was not satisfied, Mirza promised to pay 2,400 rupees as a fine. Lekh Ram was eager to come to Qadian and see Mirza perform miracles up close and hoped that such an arrangement would allow him to promote the Arya Samaj. Mirza was not keen to host him in Qadian. One reason for this was Lekh Ram's relatively low status in the religious hierarchy of the Arya Samaj at the time. But Lekh Ram's nagging insistence made it difficult for Mirza to deny him a ticket to Qadian. What also may have swayed Mirza to invite Lekh Ram to Qadian was the fact that nobody else wanted to take up his challenge. Before coming to Qadian, however, Mirza insisted that Lekh Ram acquire the signatures of several senior Arya Samaj leaders. These leaders should also verify, Mirza insisted, that Lekh Ram would take up the challenge on their behalf. When Lekh Ram failed to secure the necessary letters, Imam-ud-Din, with whom Mirza had once squandered his father's allowance, and with whom he had a bad relationship since, stepped in to host Lekh Ram. After a year of haggling, Lekh Ram finally arrived in Qadian on 18 November 1885. Together with the ten or so local Arya Samaj members and equipped with the religious interpretations of Dayanand Saraswati, Lekh Ram began to plan a large public debate against Mirza, where they would conclusively settle the Islam versus Hinduism debate.[68]

III

If one were to ask Dayanand Saraswati what drove him to discard the traditional path that Brahmin boys from India's conservative belt regarded as their birth right, his answer would perhaps involve a Shiva statue and a mouse.[69] As a child, Dayanand liked to recall, when his devout parents had assembled food offerings in front of a Shiva statue, he witnessed how a mouse silently crept up from behind and started nibbling on the food reserved for the Gods. This incident gravely shook Dayanand. Was this the omnipotent God that had the power to destroy nations? How was this God then not able to 'protect itself even from the impertinence of a mouse'?[70]

A rebellious mind from a young age, Dayanand's life was markedly distinct from the more pliant one Mirza had led in his early years. Dayanand spent it on the run. His first flight was from his own wedding. At the age of twenty-one, in 1845, when Dayanand's family had fixed his marriage, Dayanand took off the night before his big day—leaving behind a grieving would-be wife, a mourning mother, and a manic father who immediately hired men and horses to chase him down. He was soon captured, returned, but managed to escape again. From then on, Dayanand made sure to keep a proper distance from his ancestral home and, whenever asked, refused to share any details about his parents. 'If my relations knew of me, they would call me back, and then, once more face to face with them, I should have to remain with them, attend to their wants, and touch money.'[71] Dayananda feared that dipping back into household duties would prevent him from completing his destined mission to perform 'the holy work of [Hindu] reform.'[72]

It was during one of his lengthy wanderings through the Indian hills and plains where he met his master, Swami Virjanand, a reclusive Vedic scholar with rather unorthodox views. Dayanand was mighty impressed, for instance, when the Swami threw a *murti* into the street and declared that this was not God but merely a moulded piece of rock. Swami Virjanand also pondered a lot about the correct interpretation of the Vedas and came to see them as a book of revealed knowledge from a monotheistic God. Dayananda carefully studied and eventually adopted Virjanand's views. He abandoned the preaching in Sanskrit, a language that only the learned few had access to, and began writing in the vernacular so that he could reach ordinary people.[73] Observing the mushrooming of Christian mission schools all over North India, Dayanand realised the need to establish parallel institutions to teach Vedic knowledge alongside modern sciences.[74] He set up a number of such schools and quickly built a

27

solid reputation as a Hindu reformer and, as the *Pioneer* of Allahabad aptly captured, 'the hater of idolatry'.[75]

Dayanand was keen on showcasing his knowledge at public debates, where he emerged as a staunch iconoclast. An early poster put up in Banaras advertising Dayanand's arrival promised that he would refute, next to the worship of images,

> the incarnation of God, the son of God and his power of mediation in behoof of his votaries and of procuring them salvation, the commission of prophets to preach religion, the uplifting of mountains, the raising of the dead, the splitting of the moon, the belief in the creation of the world without cause, the unbelief of God or atheism, the self-assumed title of Brahma, the identity of soul and God, the telling of a rosary, the sandal badge on the forehead, the wearing of the chaplets of the berries of the *elaeocarpus* round the neck, Shivism, Vishnuism, Ganeshism, and the similar forms of heathenism, which are all contrary to the nature of God [...][76]

This outright iconoclasm won Dayanand mixed reactions. People sympathetic to his calling grouped together as the Arya Samaj and clustered together in centres around India. His relentless refutation of 'idolatry, caste, polygamy, infant marriage' had glimpses of Raja Ram Mohan Roy, another Indian socio-religious reformer, but there was something novel in Dayanand's message.[77] Unlike Roy, Dayanand was highly critical of both Islam and Christianity.[78] Lecturing on this topic in Ajmer, a city of saintly significance to Indian Muslims as it contains the shrine of the Sufi Moinuddin Chishti, Dayanand devoted an entire session to go through 'a long list of errors' he perceived in the Quran.[79] Amid the audience was a man who felt elated by Dayanand's words and who would soon devote his entire life exclusively to the Arya Samaj movement and become their go-to theologian for matters concerning Islamic theology: Lekh Ram.[80]

Born into a Brahmin family during the tumultuous years of the Mutiny, in Saidpur a village just a stone's throw away from Jhang, Lekh Ram grew into maturity in Peshawar, where he stayed with his uncle, a deputy inspector with the police force. One of the reasons his parents gave for sending him away at a young age was that he could learn 'everything involved in being a police officer'.[81] Both Jhang and Peshawar had significant Muslim populations, and Lekh Ram, who excelled at the local government schools, learned Persian and Arabic.[82]

It was in Peshawar that Lekh Ram began identifying more closely as a Hindu. Partly this was due to the influence of his uncle's secretary, an old Sikh. He studied the Bhagavad Gita with him in Gurmukhi, the script of the Punjabi language, and trained Lekh Ram in the practice of *samadhi* [meditative absorption].[83] Lekh Ram immediately took to the spiritual side of theology. It was during this phase that his uncle once returned from work and found Lekh Ram sitting on his bed in a state of deep meditation. Upon calling him, Lekh Ram turned around but entranced as he was, wobbled for a bit, and then fell flat on his face on the ground.[84]

With his uncle's recommendation, Lekh Ram joined the Peshawar police corps in 1876 but continued to devote himself to the teachings of the Gita. Within the police, he became known as the person who chanted *shlokas* and praised Krishna wherever he was stationed and for sustaining himself on a single self-cooked meal a day. Most of his fellow servicemen were Muslim, and Lekh Ram repeatedly clashed with them in debates over religious doctrine.[85] This desire to debate Muslims made him stand out in the more liberal-minded Anglicised lot that had adopted the Arya Samaj creed. Unlike these mostly urban city-dwellers, who came to Dayanand for his message of self-empowerment against the British, Lekh Ram was primarily interested in Indian Muslims.

Three issues marked Lekh Ram's tenure at the Arya Samaj. Firstly, as a rebellion against the languages he was taught at school, Lekh Ram promoted Hindi as the sole medium of instruction in all government schools across the Punjab. Secondly, Lekh Ram was passionate about protecting cows from getting slaughtered. And lastly, and most importantly, he was vehemently opposed to Islam. After sharpening his debating skills under the tutelage of Dayanand Saraswati, whom he viewed as his *guru*, Lekh Ram eventually left the police force in 1884 to devote himself wholly to the propagation of the Arya faith. Like in the case of Mirza and Dayanand, Lekh Ram's family was not happy about his religious devotion. Questioning his ability to provide for his betrothed, they broke off the engagement and married her to Lekh Ram's younger brother instead.[86]

On the lookout for debating partners and possible spheres of activity, Lekh Ram quickly stumbled over the writings and 'challenges', which Mirza had published in local Urdu papers across the Punjab. Maybe it was even Mirza's 1885 declaration, where he stated that Allah had appointed him as the *mujaddid*, the Islamic reformer of this age. In this declaration, Mirza invited all seekers to come to Qadian and see him perform 'true revelations, miracles, prophecies, explanations of earthly mysteries, true visions, and acceptance of prayer.' A significant proof of his elevated status in the eyes of Allah was, Mirza attested, 'the *Barahin-e-Ahmadiyya*, which will consist, upon completion, of about 300 sections [arguments], 37 of which have already been printed.'[87] A debate with such high stakes and such a low bar to enter was precisely what Lekh Ram had been looking for, and he began writing letters to Mirza Ghulam Ahmad to explore the possibility of a potential debate in Qadian.

IV

In their frequent exchange of letters, Lekh Ram interrogated Mirza Ghulam Ahmad along two broad lines. The first was personal. He challenged Mirza to expose and publish the names of the 'Arya Samaj members of Qadian' who had, as Mirza's books claimed, witnessed many miracles proving Mirza's divinely inspired status. All Arya Samaj members who Lekh Ram had asked to confirm Mirza's account, he scoffed, had not corroborated a single one of Mirza's claimed events. 'The Aryas of Qadian have exposed the veneer of your spirituality,' Lekh Ram taunted Mirza in his first letter.[88] In the *Barahin-e-Ahmadiyya*, mainly in parts three and four, Mirza had indeed pointed to several incidents that seekers could verify by confirming the events with the Hindu inhabitants of Qadian. There was an ominous case of tuberculosis, for instance, where Mirza claimed to have healed a 'Hindu Aryah boy, who lived in Qadian and still does' through his prayers alone. According to Mirza, the story could be verified from '[s]ome Hindus who were with me at the time and who still live here.'[89] Mirza did not mention the name of these witnesses in his book. If a person wanted to confirm his account and check with the witnesses, there was no other way but to ask Mirza himself.

When Lekh Ram arrived in Qadian in November 1885, he set about finding these people independently and, when he could not locate them, insisted that Mirza had lied in his book. Mirza merely mirrored this accusation back at Lekh Ram and claimed the Arya witnesses were readily available. After a fierce exchange of heated letters, the two began preparations for Lekh Ram to debate Mirza's son, Sultan Ahmad, who had stepped in after his father rejected a direct encounter with Lekh Ram. Both camps drummed up support from their respective quarters. As sentiments were running high, the local administration eventually stepped in and cancelled the event for safety reasons. Mirza then scheduled a second debate with Lekh Ram, but that too fell through. Each side blamed the other for withdrawing out of fear of losing the contest, and Lekh Ram left Qadian for Lahore, where he took over the prestigious editorship of the *Arya Gazette*, the Urdu-mouthpiece of the Arya Samaj.[90]

Even though a verbal debate between the two never materialised, Lekh Ram and Mirza would remain intimately connected through their hostility for more than a decade. Their primary quarrels were over religion. Lekh Ram believed Hinduism to be superior to Islam, which he considered a primitive form of spiritual engagement, a weak structure for a societal organisation, and opposed to reason. He also suspected that Islam's theological core fed off human lust. These convictions are visible from the list of things that Lekh Ram repeatedly associates Islam with: cow slaughter, meat consumption, miracles that contradict physics, treatment of women, *jihad*, revelations, and the concepts of heaven and hell, as well as its origins in Arabia.[91] His exhaustive catalogue of writings, later collected as the *Kulyaat-e-Ariya-Musafir*, reveals occasional traces of creativity, especially when he is not stooping to the level of insults. But for the most part, Lekh Ram followed the well-trodden path of Christian polemicists, which positioned the Prophet Muhammad, and with him the entire Islamic faith, as infused with the desire to maximise sensual experiences in this world.[92]

Mirza clashed with Lekh Ram over the social and moral relevance of Islam and the doctrines of Hinduism. Here their topics were composed of Mirza's criticism, which ranged from the transmigration of souls to the concept of *moksha*. Mirza collected his attacks on Hinduism in a booklet *Chashma-e-Ariya*, which he published in 1886.[93] Like Lekh Ram, Mirza acknowledged his indebtedness to Christian missionaries, who had levelled most arguments against Hinduism before him. Karl Gottlieb Pfander, an early polemicist and missionary, loomed large as a source of inspiration in Mirza's writings.[94]

Around the same time, Lekh Ram accelerated his critique of Islam with two publications, the *Takzeeb-e-Barahin-e-Ahmadiyya* and a lengthy exploration of the use of violence under Islamic empires called *Risala-e-Jehad*.[95] Regardless of the significance of their differences in theological outlook, the fact that the two men were able to cause hurt to each other suggests that they were operating from a similar moral horizon. Insults regarding moral transgression only work if both parties draw their restrictions from a comparable moral code. For Lekh Ram and Mirza, this moral code was not so much a product of religion as it was a product of the region they inhabited. In their case, this was the Punjab.[96]

Their shared Punjabi identity would also explain why both men spent much of their time writing and thinking about themes of little practical importance to their co-religionists. Most Muslim men did not consider marrying a young girl in old age, as Lekh Ram repeatedly insinuated was the Muslim way of life. And most Hindus had other things to worry about than *niyoga*, an ancient practice whereby a woman would be sent to a Brahmin to beget a child if her husband was impotent, as Mirza vehemently maintained constituted an everyday Hindu practice.[97] Only in the moral languages of the Punjab did both of these cases constitute instances of transgression. Perhaps for this reason, both Lekh Ram and Mirza focused intently on such stray cases. Aside from the joint moral plateau of the Punjab, the most potent stimulus to their antagonism was that they recognised each other as legitimate representatives of their respective faiths. Lekh Ram held Mirza to be the authorised representative of the Muslims, and Mirza, after early reluctance, accepted Lekh Ram to represent Hinduism. The more Lekh Ram and Mirza spiralled away from the theological orthodoxy of their respective faiths, the more they relied on one another for recognition.

V

On 21 June 1908, more than five thousand people huddled together in Lahore's University Hall to listen to Mirza's last written words. Mirza had died from a prolonged illness some weeks before. His final text, titled *Paigham-e-Sulh* [Message of Peace] addressed the graduating class at Punjab University and, given the title, most attendees thought it would revolve around issues of reconciliation and peace. There was a bitter need for such a message. Violent encounters between Hindus and Muslims were on the rise. Punjabi Muslims began flirting with the idea of abandoning the All India Congress Party, India's primary nationalist organ. Many even thought of joining the All-India Muslim League, an exclusively Muslim political movement founded in Bombay.[98]

Mirza's speech was read out in measured word by one of his most trusted disciples, Khawaja Kamal-ud-Din. It began promisingly: 'In this country, Hindus and Muslims are intertwined with each other. If one of them suffers, the other group will also suffer. If either one group insult the other, to boost their ego or out of vanity, it will not escape disgrace itself.'[99] But then his speech took a characteristic turn. Mirza ruminated over Guru Baba Nanak, a sixteenth-century holy man and founder of the Sikh religion. He suggested that Nanak had converted to Islam, performed the Hajj and attempted to bring about religious reconciliation by advising Hindus to convert to Islam.[100] Sikh and Hindu members in the audience were incensed when they heard these words from Kamal-ud-Din. Mirza lost more goodwill when he turned to history. Stating that religious conflict in India was primarily the fault of Hindus, as they had rebuffed Baba Nanak's invitation to Islam, Mirza moved on to his proposal for religious harmony. He suggested that Hindus and Muslims should sign a legal pledge. Hindus should first contractually agree to abstain from abusing the Prophet Muhammad. Then Mirza and his community would refrain from making disparaging comments about the Vedas. But Mirza would accept their contractual pledge only if ten thousand Hindus of high standing would sign the following:

We believe in the divine message and Prophethood of Hadrat Muhammad Mustafa Rasulullah [the Messenger of Allah] may peace and blessings of Allah be upon him. We deem him to be a true Prophet and Messenger. From now on, we will remember him with reverence and respect as is the duty of any believer. If we fail to adhere to this outlined principle, then we will transfer a large fine, of not less than three hundred thousand rupees, to the leader of the Ahmadiyyah Jama'at.[101]

This pledge was reflective of Mirza's debating style: the fascination for legal contracts, a seductive lure of prize money, the desire to be recognised as the sole spokesman for Indian Muslims, and the conviction that the Prophet Muhammad was under attack and in dire need of protection. The last point was particularly dear to Mirza. He pointed out that Indian Muslims were very sensitive when it came to insults against the Prophet Muhammad. Such remarks were equal to accusing 'someone's mother of unchaste conduct'.[102] According to Mirza, Hindus had to sign his legal pledge first because until they had promised to stop levelling insults against the Prophet Muhammad, Muslims were more likely to 'make peace with the serpents fed on brackish soil and the wolves of the wilderness,' than with people 'who attack our dear Prophet, whom we love more than our life, more than our mother, and more than our father.'[103]

Three hundred thousand rupees was the highest prize money in any of Mirza's challenges. But before Khawaja Kamal-ud-Din could read out Mirza's entire message, the chairperson of the conference called the meeting off. Another group required the University Hall for their scheduled function.[104] The attendees began to disperse gradually, but there was a small but noticeable contingent who refused to leave. They stipulated that Mirza's message deserved to be delivered in full, even if that meant cancelling all scheduled functions for the day. Leading this faction calling for Mirza's last words to be shared in full was Rambhaj Dutt Chowdhary, a leading member of Lahore's Arya Samaj.

2

BETRAYAL

I

On a chilly afternoon in December 1926, Abdul Rashid, a fifty-something calligrapher with a stubbly beard, trudged down Burn Bastion Road, a wide lane connecting Delhi's railway station with its brimming bazaars north of the city wall.[1] Under his creased brown blanket, Rashid had carefully nestled a slightly chipped Belgian handgun—an FN M1910, a model that acquired notoriety after Gavrilo Princip used it to shoot Archduke Franz Ferdinand in the neck.[2] It was easy to find such weapons in Delhi after the First World War, as Indian soldiers had brought back thousands from their military campaigns on European battlefields.[3] Rashid leaned against a wall and inhaled several big puffs of *charas*, a gritty cannabinoid extracted by gently patting the buds of a marijuana plant, through a small clay pipe that he then quickly stowed away in his pocket.[4]

He calmly exhaled a cloud into the frosty air. Then he set foot into a *haveli*, where a servant ordered him to leave. Rashid insisted, however, that he was here to see Swami Shraddhanand, an Arya Samaj preacher in his early 70s and a close confidant and biographer of Pandit Lekh Ram.[5] When the servant snubbed his request by telling him that the Swami was recovering from pneumonia and could not receive guests, Rashid became noisy. Overhearing the kerfuffle unfolding in the corridor, Shraddhanand promptly called Rashid into his room on the condition that he remain silent. 'My friend, you can talk with me to your heart's content after I get well', the Swami feebly murmured, 'But now I am bed-ridden.'[6] Once in the Swami's chamber, Rashid asked the servant to fetch him some water. The very moment the housekeeper walked out of the room, Rashid pulled out his pistol and fired twice at the Swami, killing him on the spot.[7]

Rushing back into the room, the servant leapt on Rashid and wrestled him to the floor. Alarmed by the gunshots, the other inhabitants of the building stormed into Shraddhanand's chamber and kept Rashid pinned to the ground.[8] By the time the police arrived, a dozen people were swirling around Shraddhanand's bed. They had stripped Rashid of his gun and turned him over to the police.[9] Once in police custody, things moved quickly for Rashid. With overwhelming evidence against him, the Sessions Court sentenced Rashid through a speedy trial within a few weeks. Even his formulaic appeal against the death sentence meted out by the Sessions Court was rejected only four months after the murder.[10]

Rashid was not a particularly religious man, but he was not a non-religious man either. His legal defence team clustered around Zafarullah Khan, a devout follower of Mirza Ghulam Ahmad, who would later represent Indian Muslims at the Round Table Conference in London and become one of the early constitutional architects of Pakistan. Zafarullah advised Rashid to deny the murder charge and instead proposed a counter-narrative, a set-up of sorts, in which someone had called Rashid into Shraddhanand's house by shouting, 'Sir, come in.'[11] Upon entering, this ominous person had 'knocked and gagged' Rashid, who had then only regained full consciousness when police constables jolted him into their car.

After the Court poked holes in Zafarullah's narrative—far too many witnesses had seen Rashid posing with the pistol before the murder—he swapped positions and began to portray Rashid as mentally unstable.[12] From Zafarullah's eclectic defence, we learn what constituted mentally unstable in his eyes: Rashid used two waterpots to clean himself after using the toilet; repeatedly forgot to pull up his pants after urination; on at least two occasions casually danced naked at his workplace; told people that he was the king of Delhi; showered several customers with ink when they pointed out mistakes in the books they had given him to copy; broke several flower-pots; and, midway during communal prayer at Delhi's biggest mosque, turned around and pretended to be the *imam*. When all these stray incidents failed to move the judges, Zafarullah called upon a critical witness who testified at some length that he once observed Rashid in the mosque's washroom kicking empty waterpots for pleasure.

Zafarullah Khan also claimed that Rashid suffered from bouts of depression. To prove this, Khan invited Rashid's childhood friends from Bulandshahr, a sleepy town halfway between Delhi and Aligarh. Falling somewhat short of what Zafarullah had hoped for, their testimonies only established that as a young boy, Rashid had often worn old and torn clothes.[13] None of their statements rendered Rashid incapable of knowing that murder was wrong.

According to Justices Broadway and Skemp, the two British judges attending to this matter, it rather seemed that the opposite was true. They held that plenty of signs spoke for Rashid's sanity. For instance, he was known to beat his former wife severely. And whenever he pondered over the physical and mental damage he had inflicted upon his wife, Rashid 'stopped and began to weep.'[14] For Skemp and Broadway, such flashes of moral clarity proved that Rashid had a decent understanding of right and wrong. They also trusted the medical opinions that had come in from Lahore's mental hospital, where the authorities had Rashid locked up for a month before the trial. All attending doctors at the hospital cleared Rashid from even 'temporary fits of insanity.'[15]

II

Swami Shraddhanand was born Munshi Ram Vij in Talwan, a small village in the rural hinterland of Ludhiana, Punjab.[16] His was an agricultural family, yet they had adapted to the bureaucratic apparatus of the colonial regime relatively fast. Munshi Ram's father, a man he loathed and respected in equal measure due to his violent outbursts and strict demands for obedience, had joined the police force early in his life. So had Munshi Ram's uncle and most other male members of his family. His father's employment forced the family to resettle frequently, and Munshi Ram grew up in a handful of second-tier cities across the United Provinces. After successive promotions, however, his father became the chief police officer in Banaras, an influential post in the colonial administration, which allowed the family to lead a cushioned existence.

Munshi Ram's origin story begins in Banaras, when, at the age of seventeen, he was stopped from entering a temple by two police officers. They told him that the Maharani of Rewah, a small princely state with a surprisingly high revenue stream, was praying at the temple and had ordered them to seal the gate.[17] Munshi Ram, not used to low-level police officers speaking back to him, felt humiliated and began to question the very rationale of entering the temple in the first place: to conduct idol worship. As a direct consequence of this encounter, Munshi Ram decided to convert to Christianity. Mustering all his courage, he walked up to a nearby Catholic Church, opened the priest's door, only to find a sparsely clad holy man exchanging hot kisses with a nun.[18] Disgusted, Munshi Ram turned away and never went back to a church again. After this encounter, temples, shrines, and mosques exuded no particular attraction to him as the premise of institutionalised religions seemed flawed. Much later in his life, when a follower asked him about his religious inclinations at this stage of his life, Munshi Ram reminisced that he thought of himself a 'thorough atheist'.[19]

His sense of spirituality did not return with his mother's sudden death. For much of his twenties, Munshi Ram indulged in all things gluttonous: nautch parties with prostitutes, binge drinking with college friends, and excessive gambling. His only genuine interest, as he was never shy to point out, was in wrestling matches.[20] Then he had a fateful encounter with Swami Dayanand Saraswati. Munshi Ram's father, now a senior police officer, was tasked to keep order during one of Dayanand's meetings in Banaras. He brought Munshi Ram along in the hope that listening to Dayanand may help him find a path back to religion, though not in his wildest imagination could he have foreseen the profound transformative impact that Dayanand was going to exude on Munshi Ram. In the autobiography that he wrote shortly before his death, Munshi Ram had this to say about Dayanand:

> I came to maturity in an India that forced Hindu youths to mock their religious ideals. [...] The British said that Indian culture was barbarous and uncouth; they said that Indians had no history. Indians could only achieve something if they followed the template of European civilisation. [...] But Rishi Dayanand changed this perception and showed the Indian youth that they could be proud of their mighty past. He also exposed the hollowness of Western pretension to constituting a civilisation.[21]

After a rocky start in government service as a *tahsildar*, Munshi Ram secured a place to study law in Lahore. He did this by making use of his father's extensive network. Now a married man with a child on the way, Munshi Ram attempted to earn more money and toyed with different business ideas. Eventually, he settled on opening a provision store in Lahore's Anarkali bazaar, a bustling hub for textiles, garments, and traditional foods. Munshi Ram had to shut the store after only fifteen days upon discovering that one of his partners had run off with the meagre two-week profits. Munshi Ram was not the best reader of people, and just like business, the study of academics did not come easy to him. When studying law books for his degree, he would get distracted easily. Instead of studying, Munshi Ram preferred to spend his time hanging out with friends and drinking wine, or any other liquor for that matter. When his finals came closer, in 1882, Mushi Ram changed his life dramatically and stopped socialising altogether. All his time was spent in exhaustive study, and he confidently faced the final law paper. After writing the law exams, he moved back to his birth village and awaited his results. A letter from the examination board soon arrived with the message that Munshi Ram had failed.

Approaching his mid-twenties and having been in gainful employment for roughly two weeks of his life, when one counts his stint as a shop owner in Lahore's oldest bazaar, Munshi Ram was justified to feel 'a little anxious' about his future. But as he made clear in his autobiography, it was not so much any financial pressure that persuaded him to look for proper employment but rather his desire to kick the habit of excessive drinking. 'I became an unrestricted drunkard. It caused me not only intoxication but also a little unconsciousness.' The more he had drunk, the less of an effect alcohol had on him, a sure sign that the habit had gotten out of hand. 'Even after a full bottle [of brandy] my head would not reel, and I would be speaking temperately.'[22]

After the failed exam, it was his wife who pulled him back to the books and sobered him up. Munshi Ram intensified his focus on his textbooks and spent his days frequenting solitary study places in central Lahore. His nights were no longer spent drinking, but he was now reading Walter Scott's novels for pleasure. Following this strict disciplined routine, Munshi Ram passed the law examination. Perhaps because he had written off his son as a drunk, his '[f]ather's joy knew no bounds' when he received the news. Around the same time that Dayanand Saraswati died, Munshi Ram started his professional career as a *mukhtar* (lawyer) in Jalandhar. While not fully established in the Arya Samaj yet, Munshi Ram could already pull a few prominent speakers, Pandit Guru Dutt and Lala Hansraj, to hold a condolence meeting for Dayanand in Jalandhar. Then he suffered another setback. Much like his business partner in Lahore, his law clerk disappeared a few months after taking a big loan in Munshi Ram's name and squandering the money on prostitutes and liquor. Despite this setback, Munshi Ram's practice eventually picked up and, while not fully profitable yet, he experienced some moderate success. But even this went to Munshi Ram's head, and he began to drink again. It reached a point where he was finding it difficult to 'read anything for more than half an hour', and slipping further down the drinking hole, he now found it impossible to 'concentrate [for] even a few minutes.'[23]

Things ultimately changed after a night of royal debauchery. A well-established fellow *mukhtar* had invited him to a party, where Munshi Ram was cheerfully gulping up 'eggs, wine, and chicken.'[24] After eating and drinking some more, he walked a drunk friend home and had great difficulty stopping him from running into a whorehouse. Once he had dropped his friend and returned to the party, he carelessly walked into one of the rooms of the house, just in time to prevent his other colleague from forcing himself on a screaming teenage girl. 'Had I been a minute late, she may have been outraged,' is how Munshi Ram recalled the incident in his autobiography. To digest the eventful night, he poured himself a large glass of wine, and after taking a sip, he suddenly had a vision. Dayanand appeared in front of him and asked if Munshi Ram still believed in God. To underline that his answer was a resounding 'yes', Munshi Ram raised his wine glass and smashed it against a nearby wall. Leaving no doubt that he believed in God, Munshi Ram also tossed the half-filled bottle against the same wall.[25]

On the next day, Munshi Ram packed his bags and left for Lahore. He was now aiming higher in his educational aspirations and enrolled to pass the examination to become a *vakil* (a lawyer that can plead in higher courts). It was rare for people without B.A. degrees to clear this examination. Even people with prestigious university degrees routinely failed. But Munshi Ram had a secret weapon. What was to put him in the right mindset for studying was a newly established Arya Samaj student association. Upon arriving, he not only rekindled his ties to Dayanand's followers but ended up moving in with six of them in a Samaj-owned fraternity house. Two of his house-mates were also planning on taking the same *vakil* examination.

Reading and re-reading the *Satyarth Prakash*, Dayanand's pivotal work, Munshi Ram increasingly absorbed its spirit. He first noted the change when he began to be repulsed by meat. It happened gradually and then all at once. During supper at the Arya Samaj dining hall, he was handed a plate with chicken curry. Disgusted by the smell of meat, he cautiously picked up the plate and hurled it against the wall of the dining hall. Then he sat down and calmly told his friends that whenever he smelled cooked meat, a nauseating feeling mounted within him. His friends paused for reflection and perhaps thought that if Munshi Ram was so repulsed by meat, he could have shown it without smashing the plate.[26]

Munshi Ram's symbolic action of tossing food and drink against walls gained him some notoriety and even a growing following. He began touring the Punjab and speaking against the evils of alcoholism and child marriage, a practice that was still prominent amongst North Indian Hindus. The debating skills he gained from lecturing unassuming villagers about their social mores came in handy for his

41

study of law. While *vakil* candidates had no dedicated college that they attended, sitting and former judges informally organised their classes in the rooms of Lahore's Government College. E. W. Parker, a district judge and close friend of Rudyard Kipling, taught jurisprudence.[27] For this, he used a recently published textbook by Thomas Erskine Holland, an early believer in international law and legal positivism.[28] Munshi Ram soaked up the liberal ideas that Parker offered in his lectures. But he did not limit himself to the prescribed curriculum. In his free time, he oscillated between Scott's lively novels and the purposefully dry and scholarly works of Bentham and Austin. At that time of his life, Munshi Ram had tuned his future ambition towards 'one day becoming a Judge of the Chief Court.'[29]

Despite his newly discovered determination and focus, Munshi Ram failed the oral examination. He blamed it on the ignorance of the Indian examiners, appealed the assessment, and eventually passed. What disturbed him was that many weaker candidates had also cleared the exam without any trouble. Rather than studying, as he did, they had transferred a bribe to Mr Larpantan, the Registrar of Punjab University. For passing the *vakil* examination, the going rate was an eye-watering 500 rupees. As degree names were not as common and standardised as they are today, some of the early bribe-paying *vakils* thought that the LLB they had received stood for Lawyers who had paid Larpantan, a Bribe.[30] Eventually, in 1888, a commission headed by Parker dismantled Larpantan's elaborate bribery scheme. This incident drew immense public attention and came to be known as 'The Great Punjab Bribery Case'.[31]

When Munshi Ram finally set up his legal practice in Lahore in 1885, the expectations he had for his staff were low. He wanted to hire a Muslim clerk as he had heard that Muslims were not 'inclined towards drinking' and because he sincerely hoped that his clerk would also not squander his money in 'a public woman's house' as his last clerk had done.[32] This enterprise was moderately profitable, and Munshi Ram felt the need to celebrate his success again. On one occasion, he came dangerously close to the bottle. However, when some of his colleagues grabbed him at a party, forced his mouth open and poured wine into it, Munshi Ram became so disgusted by alcohol that he swore never to touch it again.[33]

After his father died, Munshi moved to Jalandhar, where his wife's family lived, and opened up a new chapter of the Arya Samaj. His other motivation for moving was that the competition between *vakils* in Lahore had become cut-throat. Most of his time in the years from 1886 onwards was spent as a defence attorney in criminal cases or service to the Arya Samaj. But not all of his clients appreciated his new clean way of living. As Munshi Ram recalled, especially the 'local jats were under the impression that only those who were given to worldly pleasures would make good criminal lawyers.'[34] By joining forces with other Arya Samaj lawyers, however, Munshi Ram successively built a solid network and a reputation for his law firm that stretched well beyond state lines.

In 1888, after careful deliberation, Munshi Ram laid the foundation for the Jalandhar chapter of the All India National Congress, a political party that had been created three years earlier in Bombay to amplify the voices of elite Indians within the colonial system. At the time when Munshi Ram joined the movement, even most English-educated people did not know what the Congress was or what it stood for. If you asked them, he quipped, they would not be able to tell whether the Congress party 'was a man, an animal or a fetish.'[35] It was the Congress's liberal bent that may have attracted Munshi Ram, who was himself trained in the latest methods of positivist jurisprudence. Through his efforts, three hundred of 'the leading men of Jullundhur' came together to jumpstart the Congress party. In their first resolution, they elected Munshi Ram as the local President of the party's executive committee. What Munshi Ram himself found noteworthy about the early days of the Jalandhar Congress, as he revealed in an article written for the *Tribune*, was his ability to convince a large group of Muslims to enter the Congress as well.[36] In much of the rest of India, the Congress remained an overwhelmingly Hindu affair. In Jalandhar, however, Munshi Ram claimed, only those Muslims had remained opposed to the Congress, who had adopted the 'bitterness and unprincipled character of' Sir Syed Ahmed Khan.[37] Sir Syed, a Delhi-born liberal reformer in his own right, had advised Indian Muslims to stay aloof of the Congress, as he considered it primarily a Hindu body. Even worse, in his view, Sir Syed thought it was overwhelmingly Bengali.[38] Munshi Ram found that 'more intelligent, enlightened and liberal section[s] of our Mahomedan countrymen' had understood that the Congress was not a Hindu project but that it represented the only viable path that India could take to acquire meaningful political participation.[39] This opinion did not make Munshi Ram a strict secularist by any stretch. His views resembled those that Mahatma Gandhi would articulate decades later, for instance, when Munshi Ram proclaimed that for the Congress's survival, 'religious inspiration would be essential if [it] was to become popular.'[40] Even after he laid down his position as the President of Jalandhar's Congress committee, to focus more fully on his work for the Arya Samaj, Munshi Ram remained closely tied to the developments in the nascent political party.

Like most Congress members, Munshi Ram cycled through many disillusionments and re-enchantments with the party. His first disillusionment with the Congress took place in 1892 at Jalandhar railway station. As one of forty-one elected delegates, Munshi Ram had come to the station to board the train to Lahore for the ninth Congress Session. To his surprise, none of his fellow delegates had turned up. Instead, Munshi Ram witnessed how the secretary of the party desperately tried to recruit ordinary travellers to become delegates at the platform itself.[41] And even though he had little success, the secretary continued his futile attempts to convince random travellers at every stop until they reached the venue in Lahore. With great disappointment, Munshi Ram found that it was not just the local secretary of the Jalandhar branch attempting to swell the numbers through such tactics. A high-pitched version of this hypocritical behaviour was prevalent at the session as well. To break Sir Syed Ahmed's curse that Muslims should stay away from a Bengali-dominated Hindu party, the Congress had resorted to radical measures: all Muslims could attend the session 'free of charge'.[42] They were also permitted to eat and stay for free. Munshi Ram was against such open pandering because he feared that such actions would cultivate a feeling of distinctiveness amongst Muslim members and could easily lead to resentment from non-Muslim members. With its overly zealous hospitality towards Muslims, the Congress was also leaving itself open to attracting Muslim delegates who were not particularly interested in emancipatory politics:

These [Muslim] delegates stopped in the Pandal [temporary shed] only a few minutes in the beginning and were to be found enjoying creature comforts [...] outside of the Pandal for the rest of the sitting. This aspect of politics again disgusted me with the Congress propaganda work.[43]

During this period, Munshi Ram began thinking about large-scale programs for social uplift. As his first act in this direction, he founded a school for girls. Munshi Ram developed the idea after an encounter with his young daughter, who was attending the local mission school, and one day declared that 'Christ was the Prophet. No price is required to mention his name. Christ is my anchor.'[44] Munshi Ram also donated a large part of his inherited property to set up a *gurukul*, a school modelled after the ancient Vedic system of education, where students would live and study close to their teachers.[45] Additionally, Munshi Ram also set up a newspaper, an Urdu weekly called *Saddharma Pracharak*, through which he propagated the message of Dayanand and, taking inspiration from Lekh Ram, levelled arguments for the superiority of the Hindu faith against Christian missionaries and various Muslim sects.

At the 1891 Kumbh Mela in Hardwar, a significant Hindu pilgrimage along the banks of the Ganges that recurs roughly every twelve years, Munshi Ram joined forces with Lekh Ram. The conditions at the Kumbh that year were dire. As there was no system of sanitation, thousands of pilgrims had simply defecated behind any structure that would offer them a minimal degree of privacy. Cholera was rampant. According to conservative estimates, two hundred thousand pilgrims died as a direct result of attending the Kumbh. With this bacteriological catastrophe unfurling around them, Munshi Ram and Lekh Ram continued their efforts to invite people into the Arya Dharm. In many ways, they were ideological twins. Both men belonged to the *mahatma*-wing of the Samaj, which distinguished itself from the so-called 'college wing' in that they promoted a militant version of vegetarianism. Lahore's Arya Samaj was evenly split between these two groups and over the issue of vegetarianism. In Jalandhar, however, Munshi Ram's influence had kept meat-eaters at bay.[46] After a few days of rampant infection rates, and people dying at the pilgrimage site, many pilgrims reluctantly decided to leave early.[47] Munshi Ram and Lekh Ram parted ways as well. When Munshi Ram arrived home from this arduous journey, he received news that shook him to the core: his wife had died while giving birth to a stillborn baby.[48]

The trauma of losing his father, his wife, and his child in a short time drew Munshi Ram even closer to the Arya Samaj doctrine. He also became more aware of family responsibilities and friendships. When he heard about Lekh Ram's stabbing in 1897, Munshi Ram was on the first train to Lahore. Munshi Ram was by Lekh Ram's bedside when he passed away as a result of the stabbing. Hearing that Lekh Ram's death was in part caused by his relentless efforts for *shuddhi* (conversion to Hinduism), Munshi Ram swore to carry on Lekh Ram's missionary legacy and bring Muslims into the fold of Hinduism. While Munshi Ram had shown little interest in *shuddhi* before, it would, later in his life, become one of his greatest fields of activity. But first he continued with opening more schools for children from the lower castes. In 1902, in a fit of piercing insight into India's spiritual and educational needs and with a dash of courage, Munshi Ram began planning and building a school in the middle of a jungle. What seemed like an outlandish idea quickly grew into one of the most innovative school systems in colonial India. The curriculum was progressive and included both Western sciences and the study of sacred Hindu texts. Though punctuation and grammar were also part of his new curriculum, Munshi Ram squeezed his educational philosophy into a single long-winded sentence:

> The Gurukul is an educational institution, founded with the avowed aim of reviving the ancient institutions of Brahmacharya, of rejuvenating and resuscitating ancient Indian philosophy and literature, conducting researches into the antiquities of India, of building up a Hindu Literature, incorporating into itself all that is best and assimilable in Occidental thought, of producing preachers of the Vedic Religion, and good citizens possessed of a culture, compounded of the loftiest elements of the two civilisations, which made their home in this ancient land of sages and seers, and of retaining, in a permanent form, for the use

of humanity, the perennial features of the virile and vitalising civilisations of the ancient Aryans, by moulding and shaping its institutions to suit the altered environments of the times.[49]

To further spread this message of vitalism amongst the Indian elite and to attract much-needed donations for his school project, Munshi Ram attended the Congress session in Lucknow. His first impression was very encouraging. A lot more Muslim delegates were in attendance than what he scornfully remembered from Lahore, and it seemed that they were attending to advance India's now palpable freedom struggle.[50] But, upon closer inspection, Munshi Ram became suspicious. What triggered him were several Muslims strolling around in gold-plated garb. He found out through a colleague that wealthy Hindu merchants had sponsored Muslim delegates and offered them clothing and food in return for attending the session.[51] Just like in Lahore, Munshi Ram lamented, the Congress had drawn men from the surrounding 'opium dens' to boost the number of Muslim delegates.[52] Munshi Ram distanced himself from what he considered a poorly staged and scripted spectacle. While he was in disagreement with the Congress leadership over the way they incorporated Muslim members in their ranks, Munshi Ram's fundraising tour was overwhelmingly successful, and he secured enough funds to finance his *gurukul*.

Already in the first decade of its existence, Munshi Ram's *gurukul* rose to national fame. Its basic anthropological premise was simple, as it saw intellectual parity between Indians and Europeans: '[t]he Indian brain is no way inferior to the European brain.' Munshi Ram's sojourn into education sparked the interest of British and Indian leaders alike.[53] On separate occasions, Sir James Meston, the Lieutenant Governor of the United Provinces, Viceroy Chelmsford of India, and Gandhi visited the school to learn if Munshi Ram's teaching methods could be implemented in other schools.[54] In 1917, perhaps in anticipation of his next phase in life, Munshi Ram took the *sannyasa*, a religious vow taken in the later years of one's life to signal the renunciation of material desires and prejudices. Devoting himself entirely to Arya Samaj service and social reform, Munshi Ram changed his name to Swami Shraddhanand Saraswati.

After fifteen years of working in relative quiet on the educational uplift of India's poor, the step towards taking the *sannyasa* was but a natural progression.

III

From 1919 onwards, Shraddhanand began to dabble in national politics. Like most Indians, he was disappointed with the British, who had increased intrusive policing measures despite Indian soldiers contributing significantly to Britain's victory in the First World War. Many political overseers had predicted swift constitutional reforms and that Indians would acquire a more substantial say in domestic governance. However, even after the war had ended, there was little movement on that front. With the Rowlatt Act (The Anarchical and Revolutionary Crimes Act of 1919), the government continued to guard jealously and, in some spheres, even extend their already broad executive powers.[55] Shraddhanand disappointedly remarked that instead of any 'delicious dishes' which Indians were deservedly expecting, the colonial state had served them 'stones'.[56]

Representatives of the Crown, so the common understanding went, now had the legal right to clamp down even harder on the press; to sentence anyone suspected of terrorism; to arrest people without a warrant; and to adjudicate political trials without a jury.[57] Amongst the politically minded subsect of the Indian population, these planned provisions were known in shorthand as '*na vakil, na dalil, na appeal*' (no lawyer, no argument, no appeal).[58] In a quest to unite the extremist and moderate wings of the Congress party behind him, Gandhi took to the streets in Bombay and invited Shraddhanand to lead a *satyagraha* (passive resistance) in Delhi. Shraddhanand agreed to Gandhi's request and, in his first message to the gathered crowds, cautioned them to refrain from violating the holy trinity of 'life, person and property.' If protestors would embrace *ahimsa* (non-violence) in full measure, Shraddhanand promised, in Gandhian terms, they would not only 'save the Indian nation' but 'would again make this ancient land the spiritual teacher of the World.'[59]

On 30 March 1919, after a tiring day of giving public speeches against the Rowlatt Act at the Congress pandal, Shraddhanand led a massive procession of forty thousand people towards Delhi Town Hall, a location in the centre of Chandni Chowk.[60] The crowds were shouting *hartal* (a form of general strike) slogans.[61] Given the sheer number of protesters, the government was on high alert, with hundreds of soldiers patrolling the streets. A majority of these soldiers had no local ties. They were Gurkhas from Manipur, who were deployed in Delhi precisely for the reasons for the relative unfamiliarity of the place—a policy that the British had adopted to avoid a native rebellion in their troops. When the protesters came closer to Delhi Town Hall, they found a contingent of twenty-five Gurkhas positioned in double-file blocking the road. Their rifles were loaded, unlocked, and pulled out.[62]

On seeing far more protesters than they had expected, the Gurkhas vacated the roadblock and moved towards the footpath. Assuming that the soldiers would no longer hinder them on their march to Delhi Town Hall, Shraddhanand proceeded forward only for a Gurkha to fire a warning shot. Clad in the saffron robes of a sanyasi, Shraddhanand continued to march on and only stopped when two Gurkhas pointed their rifles directly at him. 'We will pierce you with our bullets,' the Gurkhas threatened. 'I am standing here, fire your bullets!' Shraddhanand responded, according to witness reports.[63] Ten more rifles were now pointed at him, and for three long minutes, Shraddhanand and the Gurkhas remained in this standoff. Before any serious bodily harm could ensue, a nearby British officer, who had been alerted by the shot, rode towards the men on his horse and ordered the Gurkhas to stand back.[64] The protesters were now able to continue their march and, perhaps due to exaggerated retellings of this event Shraddhanand was turned into a hero of sorts.

Not all *satyagraha* demonstrations in Delhi remained non-violent. Especially younger *satyagrahis* paraded up and down market roads, forced shopkeepers to shut their businesses and participate in the general strike. Such violent acts went against the principles of Gandhi, who had envisioned the *satyagrahis* remaining calm and non-violent, but in many ways, they were predictable.[65] During one such skirmish at Delhi's central station, the station master prevented the forced closure of a food stall selling Indian sweets (jalebis) with the help of nearby Gurkha soldiers. Three *satyagrahis* were subsequently arrested and taken into custody by the railway police. Within an hour of the arrest, hundreds of *satyagrahis* gathered around the railway station and demanded that their friends be immediately released from detention. Yet, instead of deescalating the situation by releasing the three *satyagrahis*, the police opted for full-fledged confrontation. Forcing the gathered *satyagrahis* into the nearby Queen's garden, they started shooting.[66] Dozens of *satyagrahis* were injured, and eight Muslim protesters died, among them a teenage boy.[67] Their corpses, once released from the administration, were taken to the Jama Masjid for burial.[68] Swami Shraddhanand led the funeral procession with a crowd of over fifty thousand people in attendance of their last rites.[69]

At this high-point of Hindu–Muslim unity, Swami Shraddhanand addressed twenty thousand Muslims from the *minbar* (pulpit) of Delhi's Jama Masjid, right after the Friday prayers. His short speech cemented his reputation as the flagbearer of Hindu–Muslim unity and of being the man whose words, according to Gandhi, were nothing short of the 'law in Delhi.'[70] There was pin-drop silence when Shraddhanand calmly uttered the following prayer:

> O God of Hindus and Muhammadans [...] Grant us power that we may not be afraid of worldly strength; that we may regard military force as worthless and may recognise the piety of the martyrs. May we be prepared to sacrifice ourselves for the freedom and progress of our country. Grant powers into us Asiatics. Give to thirty-two crores of Asiatics the strength of sixty-four crores that we may oppose the power of all materialists and bring forth the reign of peace and tranquillity.[71]

Increasingly frustrated with the mounting violence, Gandhi felt that the *satyagraha* no longer lived up to the high moral ideals he had dotted down on board the *S.S. Kildonan Castle* in a short pamphlet with the name *Hind Swaraj* (Indian Home Rule). The other important factor that disheartened Gandhi from continuing with his peaceful protest turned bloody was that he feared losing the goodwill of the more liberal British. For his passive resistance to work, Gandhi needed the colonisers to identify with the pain of those colonised. Colonisers had to disown their system of oppression first before the colonised could shake it off through passive resistance. Well before he called for nationwide *satyagraha*, Gandhi had thought deeply about this point and communicated it openly. For instance, Gandhi shared the following story from his South Africa years, where he had ignited the first *satyagraha* campaign, with J.L. Maffey, the Viceroy's secretary:

> All the time that satyagraha was going on in South Africa, I had the privilege of addressing General Smuts through his Private Secretary, Mr. Lane. As the struggle developed, Mr. Lane became the Angel of Peace between the government as represented by General Smuts and Indians as represented by me. Without his unfailing good nature and courtesy probably the satisfactory result which was arrived at might not have been achieved [...][72]

In early April, the thought process of the colonial government played out on the streets of Delhi in real time. After mowing down the first wave of protesters and limiting the movements of the protest leaders, colonial officials began to understand that they only possessed a limited number of options. Some were ruled out immediately. Delhi's Chief Commissioner, for instance, rejected an attempt at large-scale imprisonment of protesters on the grounds that it would only draw more people into the *satyagraha*.[73] Chelmsford, India's Viceroy, attempted to beat Gandhi at his own game. He arrived at a plan that displayed naivete and genius in equal amounts. The only way to bring Gandhi's passive resistance to an end, he declared in a telegram to his secretary, was for the government to organise a 'counter passive resistance movement.'[74]

To the colonial state's delight, Gandhi called off the *satyagraha*.[75] On 14 April 1919, the day after Reginald Dyer ordered his soldiers to fire indiscriminately into a crowd of unarmed Indian civilians in Amritsar, killing 379 Indians and injuring hundreds more, Gandhi wrote a lengthy letter to the Viceroy's secretary. In his letter, Gandhi repented that he may have 'over-calculated the measure of permeation of Satyagraha amongst the people.'[76] He had also 'underrated the power of hatred and ill will.'[77] Gandhi promised that he would correct his error in the future. 'Until I feel convinced that my co-workers can regulate and restrain crowds and keep them peaceful, I propose to refrain from seeking to enter Delhi or the other parts of the Punjab.'[78]

Gandhi's sudden suspension of passive resistance came as a blow to those who had worked hard to bring people together. Heavily disappointed, Swami Shraddhanand withdrew his commitment to the ideas that underpinned Gandhi's *satyagraha*. He articulated his grievances in a lengthy letter, where he declared that Gandhi's philosophy of protest rested on a logical error. For Shraddhanand, 'the civil breaking of laws, without producing an upheaval among the masses [...] is impossible.'[79] If violence was to occur in the aftermath of civil disobedience, the moral blame had to fall on the state, not carried by peaceful protesters. Especially in cases of 'wilful provocation' by the government, and excessive 'horrors perpetrated in the name of "law and order"', the responsibility of non-violence could not simply be the duty of peaceful protesters.[80]

What alienated Shraddhanand further from Gandhi's way of thinking about violence was the latter's approach to untouchability. Shraddhanand despised the very concept of untouchability and the caste system and saw it as a system of perpetual violence. As he put in an angry letter to Gandhi: the Congress had not taken a single step towards 'the absorption of the depressed classes.'[81] For Shraddhanand, the Congress had for too long focused on Gandhi's pet-project to rid India of foreign cloths as if through such acts they would magically attain self-rule.[82] Shraddhanand also disagreed with Gandhi's symbolic action of burning all foreign fabric in public bonfires. He sent a wire to Gandhi that such clothes were better 'distributed among the starving and naked poor of India.'[83] His concern for the wasting of cloth was not exaggerated. Only months before Gandhi's call to set large amounts of foreign cloth on fire, Shraddhanand had written an urgent letter to the *Leader* pleading 'cloth merchants in Delhi, Calcutta [...] to send cheap cloth for distribution'. The plea continued chillingly that in some parts of India, the situation was so dire 'respectable poor women cannot go out for want of clothes.'[84]

Swami Shraddhanand then reshuffled his political options and aligned himself closer with Pandit Madan Mohan Malviya and Pandit

Motilal Nehru, both lawyers with strong Hindu leanings. Together, they brought the Congress session to Amritsar with the purpose of returning to the place where the colonial government had massacred hundreds of innocent Indians. In December 1919, scores of Congress delegates and visitors stormed into Amritsar to attend the thirty-fourth Congress session, and with Swami Shraddhanand as the president of the reception committee, they were greeted by a sanyasi dressed in saffron robes. During this Congress session, Shraddhanand's public visibility was at its height. Many of the sixteen thousand attendees present on that day saw him on par with the stature of Gandhi. A small but vocal minority with strong Arya Samaj leanings would even give Shraddhanand the clear edge over Gandhi.

In his welcome speech, Shraddhanand touched upon topics ranging from the religious creed of the Arya Samaj, the massacre in Amritsar, the Delhi riots, the Montagu reforms, to Hindu–Muslim unity and social uplift. But his main message was that religion and politics belonged together. Shraddhanand explained that, in times of crises when people are living under oppressive rule, it was vital for religious men 'to join hands with the political leaders.'[85] Speaking about the Amritsar massacre, Shraddhanand defiantly proclaimed that the violence that the colonial state had unleashed on the Punjab had not diminished but 'stimulated its political activity.'[86] A province once regarded as lagging fifty years behind the rest of India, he exclaimed proudly, now stood 'abreast of the other more advanced provinces.'[87]

Shraddhanand saw more positive effects of the recent disturbances and killings. By far, the most important was 'Hindu–Mohammadan unity.' He recalled that what had allowed fifty thousand mourners from all religions to come together in Delhi was the martyrdom of a Muslim boy. Through the sacrifice of his blood, the martyr had 'united the hearts, estranged from ages, at his grave.'[88] Shraddhanand wanted the Congress to embrace religion as a constitutive element of politics, and he saw it as the only path through which colonialism could end: '[T]he Congress had long been doing political work and it was solely political in character but the time has come for it to accept for its motto "Politics is Religion".'[89]

It was in many ways a continuation of Shraddhanand's ideological convictions that led him to reignite Lekh Ram's dormant *shuddhi* campaign. Shraddhanand had laid bare the conceptual architecture of his *shuddhi* activism already in 1911 when he wrote a lengthy tract with the name *The Arya Samaj and Its Detractors: Vindication*. There he explicitly singled out the Mirza Ghulam Ahmad–Lekh Ram encounter and lauded him for his *shuddhi* work:

> The reclaiming of Hindu converts to Muhammadanism became an every-day occurrence. The faith of hundreds of born Muhammadans even began to be shaken. At last a remedy was found. Mirza Gulam Ahmad's prophecy [that Lekh Ram would die an unnatural death] was fulfilled. A Muhammadan fanatic went to the renowned Arya preacher in the garb of a candidate for reclamation and stabbed him in the heart while he was engaged in writing Swami Dayanand's biography. But was the missionary activity of the Arya Samaj slackened? The threat of daggar [sic] and of sword was of no avail. Pandit Lekhrama's posthumous works were printed in thousands and sold extensively.[90]

For Shraddhanand, the Muslim creed was chequered with instances of violence. As he continued writing in his book, 'that Lekh Ram is murdered in broad daylight and Englishmen and even harmless English women are murderously assaulted not only in the hills of the Frontier but in the most crowded street of Anarkali in Lahore! Truly has the Prophet of Arabia said that "Paradise lies under the shadow of swords."'[91] Reducing Islam to violence and attributing disputed sayings to the Prophet Muhammad as Shraddhanand did was offensive to Muslims. But it still took for Shraddhanand to roll out a large-scale *shuddi* campaign of Malkana Rajputs in 1923, for his Muslim followers to dwindle away.

Partly, Shraddhanand's withdrawal from national politics had to do with his total disillusionment with Gandhi. Already during the first *satyagraha*, Shraddhanand had found Gandhi's behaviour erratic and mystifying. He then still normalised it by telling himself that any man trying to conduct a sincere *satyagraha* without training in the study of Hindu scriptures would run into similar problems. Gandhi openly acknowledged his weaknesses regarding scriptural knowledge and often asked Shraddhanand's advice as a 'younger brother,' though he would mostly ignore it when it ran counter to his politics of non-violence.[92] Shraddhanand's disillusionment turned into resentment at the Congress session of 1921 in Ahmedabad. During a speech that Gandhi gave there, he moved a resolution that would make him 'the sole Executive authority of the Congress and invest him with the full powers of the All India Congress Committee.'[93] Shraddhanand worried about the potential downsides of passing a resolution of this nature and the disarray that it could cause to the Congress. His only way to rationalise Gandhi's move was by thinking that the 'illiterate masses consider Gandhiji to be an incarnation of God,' the only way to dispel that 'Avatar theory' was to let him use his method until exhaustion.[94]

Another reason for Shraddhanand to mourn Gandhi's attempt to obtain institutional power was because there was no credible alternative or opposition to him. Most Congress senior leaders had been in prison: from the Allahabad father-and-son duo Motilal and Jawaharlal Nehru to Deshpande C.R. Das, Maulana Azad, and Lala Lajpat Rai, none of the Congress stalwarts were able to challenge Gandhi and steer the party in a more democratic direction. Muhammad Ali Jinnah, who stood between the moderate Gokhale-wing and the more extremist Tilak-section, had already been sidelined by 1920. Gandhi had come to dislike Jinnah for his opposition to the Khilafat movement, which Jinnah had renounced for pandering to Muslim fanaticism, and his opposition to *satyagraha*, which Jinnah thought was just a sophisticated Sanskrit word for anarchy. Shraddhanand's main problem with appointing Gandhi 'as Dictator' was that it would allow him to 'appoint [his] own successor without the sanction of the Working Committee.'[95] Even when one trusted Gandhi not to misuse his extensive power, it was difficult for Shraddhanand to accept that any successor Gandhi thought fit could inherit 'all his aforesaid powers'.[96] A chain of such successorships without any democratic accountability could quickly throw Congress into chaos.

For Shraddhanand, the lack of democratic governance within the Congress party also reflected a more significant problem. It went back to the question of the critical role of violence in politics. Shraddhanand proposed a change in the Congress policy. He argued that the Congress should not rule out violence per se, but seriously consider it as a potential, even desirable, outcome of another passive resistance movement.[97] Until they were ready for this step to embrace violence formally, Shraddhanand held that their best path would be to participate in the Indian Legislature and work with the first glimpses of *swaraj* that the colonial state had opened up through the Montagu-Chelmsford reforms.[98] Gandhi rejected Shraddhanand's suggestion outright. He even ridiculed him and claimed that the proposal would never garner the necessary votes to pass as a resolution. Still, Shraddhanand pressed on that he was just as much entitled to interpret the political situation as he saw it. 'Mahatma! I, too, have a conscience and if by acting according to its dictates I am reduced to a minority of one, I shall only be following you in standing to my guns.'[99]

After a prolonged silence, Gandhi eventually acknowledged that Shraddhanand's amendment to his politics of non-violence would make it impossible to stick to the resolution to extend his powers in an open session. Upon hearing this, Shraddhanand offered to withdraw his amendments on the condition that he would be allowed to resign from 'the active work of the Congress'. On 12 March 1922, Shraddhanand ultimately submitted his resignation to the President of the Delhi Provincial Congress Committee. As a reason for leaving the Congress, Shraddhanand explicitly singled out Gandhi's approach to politics, which for him failed to grasp the Indian political condition: 'I believe the time will never come when a non-violent calm atmosphere, according to the high ideal propounded by Mahatma Gandhi, could be produced among the Indian masses and therefore to agree to the proposition that Civil Disobedience of laws could be started at all in the near future, would, for me, be acting against my conscience.'

IV

A realist conception of politics had weaned Shraddhanand away from Gandhi's idealist non-violent idealism. For the Swami, Gandhi's policies had produced more disillusionment than hope. Witnessing excessive police brutality against peaceful Sikh wood-collectors at a shrine in Amritsar further strengthened Shraddhanand's resolve that violence in response to such state acts should never be ruled out, even when one adhered to the eternal rules of *ahimsa*.[100] According to Shraddhanand, *ahimsa* was one path to achieving truth, but it had to go hand in hand with concrete and sometimes violent measures of protecting limb and property. At his own school, for instance, Shraddhanand always kept a large stock of firearms to fend off roving tigers and bandits just in case they refused to adhere to the *gurukuls* philosophy of non-violence.[101] Gandhi rejected Shraddhanand's path entirely. He renounced any retaliation measures, regardless of the degree of violence first ushered in by the colonial state. In an angry note to protesters, Gandhi categorically declared that '[n]o amount of provocation by the sub-inspector could possibly justify retaliation by the non-co-operators.'[102]

In early 1923, Motilal Nehru invited Shraddhanand to join the Swaraj Party, a political party that grew out of the Congress due to the conflict on the role of violence that Shraddhanand had prophesied. Gandhi had again suspended the non-cooperation movement after protests in Chauri Chaura, a small town in the United Provinces, turned bloody. Riot police had fired into a peaceful march and killed three protesters. In retaliation, the protestors resorted to violence and burned down the police station, killing many more and leading Gandhi to call off his campaign. To accommodate the potential for such incidents better in their anti-colonial struggle, Motilal Nehru, Chittaranjan Das, and Vithalbhai Patel, all established Congress dons who were now in the Swaraj Party, urged Shraddhanand to return to national politics. But Shraddhanand declined their invitation as he wanted to devote his time entirely to the Arya Samaj, where his role in the freedom struggle, perhaps second only to Lala Lajpat Rai, helped push him right to the top of the Arya movement.

Shraddhanand went about his work of 'reclaiming Muslims' through two organisations: the Arya Samaj and the Hindu Mahasabha, both heavily co-dependent outlets that sought to give weight to the place of Hinduism in Indian society.[103] Initially, Shraddhanand's *shuddhi* campaigns did not ignite an immediate backlash from Indian Muslims.[104] For one, Muslims felt confident enough that Hindus could not revert a significant amount of them to make conversions politically relevant.[105] As late as 1923, when Shraddhanand's campaign to convert Muslims to Hinduism was in full swing, the editor of the Muslim-owned *Oudh Akhbar* from Lucknow still felt comfortable to announce that 'much good' had come from the Mahasabha.[106] Indian Muslims had also been distracted. They were pouring much of their energies into the Khilafat cause and had busied themselves with fighting for a transnational pan-Islamic *ummah*.[107] The Khilafat movement, as the street parades of hundreds of thousands came to be known, was centred around the somewhat dubious demand to reinstate the Sultan of Turkey as the rightful custodian of the Khilafat. Yet, the Sultan's throne had precious little to do with the particularities of Indian politics. Most Indian Muslims had not even heard his name, and only ardent cosmopolitans would have been able to identify him in a photograph. Perhaps because of the utterly non-instrumental nature of Indian Muslims fighting for the Sultan of Turkey, Gandhi whole-heartedly supported them for much of the Khilafat campaign, up until it slowly fizzled out in the early 1920s.[108] Gandhi also found supporters in the enterprising Ali Brothers, two former civil servants with a penchant for flashy dress and symbolic performances, who spearheaded the Khilafat campaign.

Predictably, the Khilafat evaporated without any significant permanence after the British refused to petition Mustafa Kemal, the secular leader of the Young Turks, to reconstitute the Sultan's religious titles. Indian Muslims had spent much of their political capital on the Khilafat. Its implosion left them scattered, disoriented, and without any outstanding individual to direct their energies and attention to any domestic political objective. Right into this void of political purpose, Shraddhanand embarked on the biggest *shuddhi* campaign yet.[109] His new campaign targeted Malkana Rajputs in North India, and fighting against this campaign gave Indian Muslims more of a fresh lifeline and political purpose after the collapse of the Khilafat.[110] It also radically redefined how Muslims engaged with Indian politics for the next quarter of a century to come.[111]

For the colonial state, the Malkana Rajputs had always caused considerable headaches when it came to classification. 'In various parts of India groups are found,' laments the Census Report of

1911, 'whom it is difficult to class definitely either as Hindus or Muhammadans.'[112] For the colonial official who penned the report, Malkana Rajputs were the most prominent of these groups. He had classed them as 'Muhammadan' in the census but thought them to be 'far from being genuine Muhammadans.'[113] Many ritualistic practices that the Malkana Rajputs performed made the colonial officer doubt that he had grouped them in the appropriate religious category. 'Their names are Hindu; they mostly worship in Hindu temples; they use the salutation Ram, Ram; they intermarry amongst themselves only.'[114] Yet, he maintained that the Malkanas also had a 'strong Muhammadan flavour': '[t]hey sometimes frequent a mosque, practise circumcision and bury their dead; they will eat with Muhammadans if they are particular friends; they prefer to be addressed as Mian Thakur.'[115] Asking them directly how they identified did not help the census official either. 'They admit that they are neither Hindus nor Muhammadans, but a mixture of both.'[116]

Shraddhanand's *shuddhi* campaign on the Malkana Rajputs was markedly distinct in scale from the *shuddhi* Lekh Ram had run. Lekh Ram had only targeted stray individuals, often at the margins of society, whereas Shraddhanand's efforts were directed at an entire sub-caste of Rajputs, numbering roughly five hundred thousand. Though such numbers would also have a considerable effect on potential election outcomes in a future democratic assembly, Shraddhanand seemed not primarily driven by political considerations for increasing the number of Hindus. Instead, as he wrote in the last tract he published before his murder, it was an encounter with an Indian statistician that led him to throw himself 'heart and soul' into the *shuddhi* campaign.[117] After scanning the numbers of diligently written colonial census reports, Shraddhanand had become convinced that Hindus were decreasing at a rate of five per cent each year.[118] He feared that in a few hundred years, the Darwinian nightmare of extinction would come true and that there would be no Hindus left. Immediate action was required, and Shraddhanand identified *shuddhi* as the only way of fighting for cultural and religious survival.

Shraddhanand also found dubious historical justifications to engage in *shuddhi*. From the eighth century onwards, Shraddhanand historicised, Muslims had seduced illiterate Hindus to join their faith.[119] Many Hindus had accepted their offer. According to the Swami, they were drawn to Islam as it provided them with a path out of the rigid caste structure that Hinduism had wrongly imposed upon them. Muslim preachers promised equality, as in Islam, 'all men are equal in the sight of Allah.'[120] According to Shraddhanand's analysis, the vast majority of the Muslim population of India was, therefore, 'originally Hindu'.[121] Some still carried easily identifiable names like 'Rajputs, Jats, Arain, Gujar, Mochi, Turkhan, and Teli,' which to him signalled that they derived their ancestry from Indian stock.[122] Shraddhanand elaborated that today a large number of Untouchables were on the brink of becoming Muslims. As caste Hindus had abused them for centuries, these Untouchables were no longer willing to put up with their mistreatment. Shraddhanand hoped that by knotting them closer into the Hindu social and religious fold through an increase in their rights and status, he could stop Untouchables from converting to Islam.

For Shraddhanand, conversions constituted a straightforward way through which untouchability could be abolished. To frame Shraddhanand's actions as a sophisticated political ploy to increase the numbers of Hindus within a system of colonial representation falls short of acknowledging his ideological convictions.[123] Predictably, however, it was this period in his life that also transformed Shraddhanand into the most vilified and abused Hindu figure in Muslim political circles. Because he had been one of the highly trusted national leaders for Hindu–Muslim unity during the days of non-cooperation, his fall from grace was steep. The Muslim Nation School of Delhi, for which he had secured enormous funds in the preceding years, even removed his portrait from their dining hall.[124] Muslims increasingly began to define and fear *swaraj* as a democratic clad coup towards Hindu domination. The hometown of Abdul Rashid, Bulandarshah, constituted the backdrop of the sight of Hindu–Muslim agitations. Hindus had thrown a pig into the main mosque to let it bleed out there.[125]

Wherever *shuddhi* campaigns managed to convert a section of the Muslim population, which they often accomplished through attacks on the Prophet Muhammad, riots followed. A series of at least two dozen riots took place, which left more than thirty dead and hundreds severely injured.[126] A large number of these riots could be directly linked to places Shraddhanand had visited. In July 1923, when the Swami had come to Shahjahanpur to promote *shuddhi*, a fistfight broke out between Muslims and Hindus. A Muslim boy was severely injured. Taken for dead, Muslim protesters paraded him around town for an hour, and once they had tired of performing their grief, they found that the poor boy was still breathing. He was rushed to the hospital and survived.[127] The incidents that followed were more serious. Three Muslim men were beaten to death during other protests directly in response to Shraddhanand's *shuddhi* campaign.[128]

To gauge the impact of the *shuddhi* campaign on Indian Muslims, one only needs to look at the names of organisations that mushroomed in its shadow, and that still have a strong presence in Indian Islam today: *Tabligh-i-Jamaat* (Society for Spreading the Faith), *Anjuman Razi-e-Mustafa* (Society for the Protection of the Honour of the Prophet Muhammad), *Anjuman Tahaffuz-e-Islam* (Society for the Conservation of Islam), *Anjuman Hifazat-e-Islam* (Society for the Protection of Islam), and so forth.[129] Amongst the groups most vocal in their opposition to the *shuddhi* campaign were also the followers of Mirza Ghulam Ahmad, though they were now split into the Qadian wing led by his son Mirza Bashir-ud-Din Mahmud, and the more urban and educated Lahore faction, headed by members of Mirza Ghulam Ahmad's former advisory council. Even the more bookish Deobandis participated in fighting the Hindu conversion efforts. It was at this time the majority of Muslim organisations altered their theological outlook toward primarily catering to the principles of *tabligh* (propagation of Islam) and the protection of the honour of the Prophet Muhammad.

On 11 September 1923, with communal tension at a boiling point, the Congress attempted to pacify ill-feelings between Hindus and Muslims by bringing Swami Shraddhanand in conversation with Motilal Nehru, Jawaharlal Nehru, Abul Kalam Azad, Madan Mohan Malviya, Hakim Ajmal Khan, Saifuddin Kitchlew, Vithalbhai Patel, the Ali Brothers, and a few maulanas from Deoband at the old Alliance Bank building in Delhi.[130] They were only to leave this meeting if they had reached an agreement on the *shuddhi* issue. Irritated by the lengthy kowtowing to Gandhi by the other participants, Swami

Shraddhanand began his speech in defence of *shuddhi* by stating that he had severe problems with the Mahatma. 'Gandhi thought of Non-cooperation only three years ago while I began Non-cooperation 30 years ago when I gave up my [legal] practice.'[131] Regarding *shuddhi*, Shraddhanand was initially not willing to cede any ground. Proselytisation was 'the right of every religion.'[132] His was also not a sly conversion of illiterate Muslims through personal attacks on the Prophet Muhammad. Instead, he insisted that he had only 'approached those persons who were Hindus in all their customs and ways'.[133] When the other participants, especially the Muslim representatives, pushed him to abandon his *shuddhi* efforts, Shraddhanand insisted that he would not. Only after a lengthy talk with Madan Mohan Malviya did Shraddhanand soften and curb his *shuddhi* movement, but on the condition that the Muslim would also withhold from practising *tabligh*.[134]

Scholars from the Deoband, whom the Congress had designated to represent the Muslim *tabligh* faction, reluctantly agreed to this consensus.[135] However, the Congress had miscalculated its influence over Indian Muslims. While the Deoband had some heft in the hilly borderland to the North, their power in the Punjab and the United Provinces, the main sites of the *tabligh* and *shuddhi* efforts, was limited at best. Thus, the Deobandi agreement to abandon *tabligh* did not translate to other Muslim organisations to freeze their conversion efforts. In a particularly visible act to ridicule the agreement the Deoband had signed, the Ahmadiyya and others redoubled their efforts to attack their old foes of the Arya Samaj. Resuming the print war of their founder Mirza Ghulam Ahmad, the Qadianis accused Hindu women of bestiality in a pamphlet with the name *Kufr Tor* (Breaking of Unbelief), and in another work, entitled *Unisveen Saddi Ka Maharishi* (The Great Sage of the Nineteenth Century), attacked Dayanand Saraswati for having led a life of filth and sexual transgression.[136]

Such pamphlets from Qadian came as a response to those already written by the Aryas: *Rajput*, *Lal Jhandi* (Red Flag), *Taranai Shuddhi* (The Slogan of *Shuddhi*), and *Malaksh Tor* (Destroy the Beloved). In these pamphlets, the Arya Samaj alleged that the Prophet Muhammad had led a life of sensuality and that these traces could still be found in Indian Muslims today. The most visceral booklets came from the Lekh Ram wing of the Samaj. Pandit M.A. Chamupati, a close ally of Lekh Ram, who also started writing his biography, penned at least two pamphlets that set the lowest standard yet: *Bichitra Jeevan* (A Strange Life) and *Rangila Rasul* (The Colourful Prophet).[137] As the most visible and recognisable face of the *shuddhi* movement, the majority of Muslims began to associate Swami Shraddhanand with these insensitive publications.

V

Abdul Rashid's murder of Shraddhanand in 1926 was just the most visible in a string of killings that followed in the aftermath of the Arya Samaj–Ahmadiyya pamphlet war. Relations between Hindus and Muslims, strained enough in regular times, seemed broken beyond repair. In this atmosphere of communal antagonism, political figures from the Hindu Sabha, the Khilafatists, and the Congress tried to score easy political points. It was only a matter of time before Delhi flared up in riots.[138] Amid this violence, followers of Shraddhanand from all over Punjab as well as other parts of North India rushed into the city throughout late December to participate in his funeral procession.[139] More than two hundred thousand people performed his last rites and silently watched his funeral pyre set ablaze by the banks of the Jamuna river.[140]

Two days after Shraddhanand's murder, at the 41st session of the All India National Congress at Gauhati, a sleepy town nestled behind leafy hills in India's North-East, Mohandas Gandhi offered his condolences for Shraddhanand's death. In Gandhi's first appearance in more than a year, he called Shraddhanand a 'noble patriot,' 'a hero among heroes,' and 'the bravest of the brave'.[141] This part of Gandhi's reaction was in line with the sentiments that other politicians and religious leaders had expressed about Shraddhanand's murder. At a special session of the Hindu Mahasabha, Pandit Madan Mohan Malviya also grieved the murder of the Swami, but unlike Gandhi he connected it to a call to action. Malviya encouraged his co-religionists to continue Shraddhanand's work: 'Swami Shraddhanand was the pioneer of the Suddhi movement. It was he who really felt about the desire of those Hindus who had once forsaken their religion [Muslims] and he inaugurated the Suddhi movement. Up to the last day of his life he fought for Suddhi, and Sangathan.'[142] Unlike Shraddhanand, Malviya regarded the conversion of Muslims not as a religious imperative but a political tool to keep Muslims in check. As he made clear to a large number of what he called 'village and hill-folk' in attendance,[143] '[i]f the Mussalmans stop their Tabliq I would like to see the Hindus also give up their Suddhi.'[144] Malaviya also felt that Hindus should follow Shraddhanand, and the broader Arya Samaj project, as this was the only way to preserve and protect 'the life blood of the Hindus.' As potential pathways to achieve this aim, Malviya suggested the banning of child marriages, allowing widows to remarry, guarding temples, and protecting cows from slaughterhouses.[145]

That the Mahasabha claimed Shraddhanand as one of their own was not surprising. As a movement that encouraged Hindus to think more coherently about their place in colonial India, the Mahasabha had been founded in the Punjab of the 1910s.[146] Much of its leadership ranks came directly from the Arya Samaj's Lekh Ram wing.[147] Early writings on the Mahasabha acknowledged this intellectual lineage very clearly. In the introduction to the first book on the foundations of the Mahasabha, Bhai Parmanand, who Veer Savarkar considered 'the foremost champion of the Hindu cause', credited the Arya for having laid the groundwork to change 'the mental attitude of the Hindu Community.' When Bhai Parmanand looked at the Mahasabha, he saw 'an enlarged and more comprehensive edition of the Arya Samaj.'[148] Arya Samaj and Mahasabha political aims largely overlapped: they wanted to bring about a political awakening amongst Hindus, breathe manliness and solidarity into the Hindu community, and, perhaps most importantly, fight back hard against what they considered Muslim bullying.[149] In its early years, the Mahasabha also put great emphasis on stopping Muslims from seducing Hindu women.[150] Though more imagined than based on facts, the idea of Muslim men chasing after Hindu women went a long way in the recruitment efforts of the Sabha.[151] Most of their annual meetings contained speeches that whipped up emotions in this regard. Swami Shraddhanand had also participated in such rhetoric. 'I wish that my

Hindu brethren be wiped off this earth if they cannot protect their sisters, daughters, and others, and cannot save the honour of our religion,' he proclaimed in one of his early presidential speeches to the Mahasabha.[152]

Not too far from Shraddhanand's Delhi residence, the All India Muslim League held its eighteenth session a few days after the murder in an atmosphere of utter communal distrust. In a spacious and heavily decorated temporary shed in front of Ajmeri Gate, the who's who of Muslim intelligentsia had gathered. Amongst them were Muhammad Iqbal, Muhammad Ali Jinnah, Zafarullah Khan, and Abdur Rahim. Their speeches all had a similar bent. Hindus were secretly plotting to establish a Hindu Raj, in which there was no proper place carved out for Indian Muslims. To fight back against this sinister vision, they asked for constitutional protections, a more significant share in government offices, and more influence in Indian cultural organisations.[153] Sheikh Abdul Qadir, the incoming President of the League, devoted much of his speech to Swami Shraddhanand's killing, which he denounced as a 'dastardly murder.'[154] Then he went on to condemn the act in even stronger terms: 'No man could render a greater disservice to Islam or lend a stronger impetus to the Shuddhi propaganda than he [Rashid] had done by this foul deed'.[155] In a resolution that Muslim League delegates passed the next day, they condemned both the murder of the Swami and the killing of a Muslim teenager that allegedly took place in retaliation.[156]

Gandhi did not stop his speech after lauding Shraddhanand as the bravest of the brave. In characteristically Gandhian fashion, his speech found a way to cause resentment among Hindu and Muslim delegates. A large section of the Mahasabha was already appalled when Gandhi had referred to Abdul Rashid as his 'brother.'[157] But they found it unacceptable when Gandhi lectured them that he did 'not even regard him [Abdul Rashid] as guilty of the Swami's murder.'[158] Instead, Gandhi lashed out against the press. 'Guilty, indeed, are all those who excited feelings of hatred against one another.'[159] Such statements outraged the Muslim leaders of the Khilafat movement as well, who were still closely aligned with the Congress at the time. Their intense efforts in establishing a closely knit network of printing presses and newspapers to spread political awareness were dismissed by Gandhi as altogether harmful. 'I am sure that India would lose nothing if 90 per cent of the papers were to cease today.'[160]

VI

On 27 January 1927, the *Hindu Punch*, a Calcutta-based weekly newspaper close to the Arya Samaj, eulogised Swami Shraddhanand's death as a drama with the name *balidan* (sacrifice).[161] The first scenes depict a *shuddhi* ceremony and a murder. Two Muslim men come to Dayanand Saraswati, founder of the Arya Samaj, and ask to be brought back into the Hindu fold. Saraswati calls upon his most trusted disciple, Lekh Ram, to conduct the conversion. After Lekh Ram performs the rites and the two men leave the scene, another Muslim man appears. He wants Lekh Ram to convert him back to Hinduism. But just as Lekh Ram is getting ready for the next *shuddhi* ceremony, the man stabs him in the stomach instead.[162]

When a telegram with the news of Lekh Ram's murder reaches the house of one Bhoj Dutt, a prominent Arya Samaj publisher, he is shocked but not surprised. Instead, he goes on a lengthy tirade that it was in the 'nature of the Moslem to take revenge on the Hindu by fraud and breach of confidence.'[163] In the last scene, Swami Shraddhanand lies in bed to cure an illness. When a Muslim enters who wishes to convert, he allows him in, only to be shot dead with a revolver. Upon his death, Mother India appears with a list of complaints against Indian Muslims. They had tormented her 'for 1,000 years and tyrannised over the Aryans, killing cows, and practising injustice and excess.'[164] They had forgotten 'whose salt was in their bones' and that they were also descendants of the 'Aryan religion'. If Indian Muslims could no longer live in India peacefully, they 'should go to Arabia'.[165]

The *Hindu Punch* faced a severe backlash against this piece. A charge of promoting enmity between Indian groups, under Section 153A Indian Penal Code, was slapped on Iswari Prasad Sharma and Mukund Lal Burman, the editor and the printer. Both men were active members of the Calcutta branch of the Arya Samaj. The High Court of Calcutta sentenced them to six years and four months imprisonment.[166] Shraddhanand's short-lived dream of Hindu–

Muslim unity soon dissolved, with an increasing number of Muslims abandoning the Congress for the Muslim League. After hearing of Shraddhanand's death, the Qadiani faction of the Ahmadiyya was jubilant. Digging deep in their archives, the son of Mirza Ghulam Ahmad claimed that just like in the case of Lekh Ram, Shraddhanand's murder too had been foretold by his father. He publicised the following note:

> [Shraddhanand's killing] is in accordance with the prophecy of the Promised Messiah [Mirza Ghulam Ahmad]. He made a prophecy about the murder of two people. One was Lekhram, and the Promised Messiah did not recall the name of the other. The interesting fact is that Shardhanand was previously named Munshi Ram and when he was killed his name was Shardhanand. That is the reason that the Promised Messiah could not recall his name [...] Many of the events relating to his murder resemble Lekhram's murder. Lekhram was murdered on Saturday, the day after 'Id. Shardhanand was killed on Thursday, which also adjoined the Friday. In both cases the murderer had wrapped himself in a blanket. In both cases an attempt was made to stop the entry of the murderer, but he was permitted to enter afterwards.[167]

At a speech in Banaras, Gandhi found some soothing words for those grieving the Swami. 'Swami Shraddhanand is not dead,' the Mahatma concluded while addressing a gathering of lower-caste women, 'he lives in our hearts. He was brave; he had a noble soul. [...] May God impart to us some of his qualities so that we can carry on his work.'[168] Gandhi also advised Muslims to continue condemning the murder. 'Let there not be a single Mussalman who approves this killing of Shraddhanandji even privately.'[169] However, Gandhi's words fell on deaf ears. After the execution of Abdul Rashid in November 1927, fifty thousand Muslims broke through the police barrier, snapped up Rashid's dead body, and paraded him through Delhi as a martyr.[170] When the police finally regained possession of the coffin, two Hindu shopkeepers had been killed, hundreds more injured, and dozens of stores looted.[171] Riots caused counter-riots, and the spiral of Hindu–Muslim violence escalated to the national stage.

3

SIN

I

After returning in December 1928 from Kohat, a town built on rocky land in the arid North-Western Frontier Province, Ilm Din gleefully took to urban life in Lahore.[1] In Kohat, Ilm Din had scraped, sawed, and carved wood into shape on a nine-month carpentry stint with his father. Kohat was ablaze with riots. Ilm Din witnessed how Muslim tribes ejected Hindus from their homes in retaliation for an Arya Samaj publication that mocked the Prophet Muhammad's private life called *Rangila Rasul*.[2] This slim twenty-four-page pamphlet brought public life in the province to a screeching halt. Written in 1924 by Pandit Champuti, who worked as a teacher at Swami Shraddhanand's *gurukul*, the pamphlet was first released through Rajpal Malhotra, a Lahore-based publisher and an avid follower of Pandit Lekh Ram's *mahatma*-wing of the Arya Samaj.[3] It never had much of a circulation. After the Ahmadiyya cried foul for the distasteful depiction of the Prophet, the colonial administration banned the book and seized all copies. But in 1927, Mirza Mahmud, the son of Mirza Ghulam Ahmad, who was now heading the Qadian wing of the Ahmadiyya as caliph, sought to reignite his father's feud with the Arya Samaj. Plastering town squares in Lahore and Amritsar with posters that carried the most offensive bits of the *Rangila Rasul* pamphlet, Mirza Mahmud sought to rekindle the decade-old enmity with the Arya Samaj.[4]

One of those posters ended up in the hands of the wandering Deobandi Mullah of Chaknawar, a staunch combatant with a talent for exciting crowds. In 1919, during the Third Anglo-Sikh War, Chaknawar had ordered his followers to join the *jihad* against the British or go home to their wives and swap clothes with them.[5] Triggered by the poster, Chaknawar ripped it off the wall and took it with him to Kohat. Once there, he began to read out the excerpt at tribal gatherings. Predictably, this had the desired effect of whipping up emotions. To express their grief, Chaknawar advised the tribesmen to rid the entire border region of Hindus.[6] Some of the tribesmen were indebted to Hindu moneylenders and saw this as a welcome opportunity to eliminate their debt as well. Yet others were genuinely driven by hurt feelings after hearing the curated version of the most suggestive lines in the pamphlet.

While these riots were going on, Ilm Din and his father had continued working on their building project. Once back in Lahore, Ilm Din picked up a part-time job at his uncle's convenience store and spent the rest of his time loitering around with his childhood friend Muhammad Hussain, or Fatta as he affectionately called him. They liked spending time at Din Muhammad's paan (betel leaf) stall in Lahore's Sirianwala *mohalla*, a township with a sizeable Sikh community.[7] Apart from Fatta and Din Muhammad, Ilm Din was on good terms with many street kids who frequented the small bazaar and were always on the lookout for a hot meal or a few *anas*. Amongst them, Ilm Din particularly liked Sadiq Qasib, Haji for short.[8] But one day, when Fatta and Ilm Din were at Din Muhammad's paan stall, Haji refused to acknowledge Ilm Din.[9] Their friendship further deteriorated when Haji shunned Ilm Din's invitation to accompany him to the *Mela Chiraghan* (festival of lamps).[10] This annual festival was held in remembrance of Madhu Laal Hussain, a heterodox Sufi saint of the sixteenth century, and the royal Shalimar Gardens turned into a spectacle of dizzying drums and whirling dances. Ilm Din was still pondering why Haji was ignoring him when he bumped into Ghulam Nabi, another boy from the neighbourhood, who told him that he had recently 'committed sodomy on Haji'.[11]

Shocked by this revelation, Ilm Din rushed back to Haji and confronted him with Nabi's statement. Haji denied and proposed to stomp the rumour by forcing Ghulam Nabi to repeat it in his presence. On the next day, Ilm Din found Ghulam Nabi goofing around with friends at Din Muhammad's pan stall. Ilm Din called Haji over, and together, they walked up to Ghulam Nabi to confront him about the incident. Ghulam Nabi quickly backpaddled. He claimed that he had never said anything in this regard and that Ilm Din had invented the story. Angered by what he considered was a blatant lie, Ilm Din slapped Nabi across the face. Fatta and Din Muhammad quickly separated them.[12]

After the brawl, Ilm Din was disappointed when Haji stated that he was no longer interested in seeing or speaking to him.[13] To prevent more drama from unfolding, Fatta pushed Ilm Din into a nearby *tanga* (horse carriage) and ordered the coachman to take them to the Sunheri Masjid, an eighteenth-century mosque with gilded domes in the old city. On their ride there, Ilm Din opened up to Fatta. The drama around Haji had made him want to, in his words, 'put an end to my life and his (Haji's)'.[14] Fatta snapped Ilm Din out of such violent thoughts by reminding him even if he would kill himself and Haji, 'the people would say that [Ilm Din] had destroyed [his] life for the son of a villain.'[15]

Fatta's appeal could not fully convince Ilm Din. In his own words, he had become 'tired of the world'. Then, another thought crossed Ilm Din's mind. He recalled that last year, while a friend of his was getting flyers printed to promote a wrestling match, he had shown him Arya Books, a small shop just off Anarkali bazaar, and remarked that the publisher of *Rangila Rasul* worked there. With his interpersonal drama at a boiling point, Ilm Din decided that 'if I were to put an end to my life, I should better do it to vindicate the Holy Prophet's honour by doing away with the said Hindu and then get martyrdom.'[16]

To prepare himself for this, Ilm Din woke up early the next day and went to Khalifa Gama's barbershop for a fresh trim and a clean shave. He then briefly stopped by the Data Darbar, Lahore's holiest

Sufi shrine, to pray. After that, Ilm Din walked straight to a knife stall and haggled down the price of an eight-inch blade to one rupee. Wrapping the knife in the fold of his *shalwar*, he entered Arya Books, where he saw Rajpal, the publisher of the pamphlet, tucked away in a corner reading a book. Ilm Din took the knife out of his shalwar and made a few quick steps towards Rajpal, and stabbed him eight times, cracking the right parietal bone of his head and piercing his heart.[17] Rajpal died on the spot.

Ilm Din's flight into a nearby woodshop was cut short when bystanders captured him almost immediately and, with his *kameez* still soaked with Rajpal's blood, handed him over to the arriving police constables. Because of the potentially religious nature of Ilm Din's killing, the authorities decided to quickly transport him to Mianwali jail, a recently built panoptical prison complex roughly three hundred kilometres north-west of Lahore. At Mianwali, Ilm Din was not the only idealistic twenty-something who had killed for a higher purpose. Interned in another cell sat Bhagat Singh, a Marxist revolutionary, whose strong Arya Samaj convictions had triggered him to avenge the death of Lala Lajpat Rai by killing a British police officer.[18]

A month later, a local Sessions Court sentenced Ilm Din to death by hanging. Three months on, Ilm Din was latching on to an appeal at Lahore's High Court. Convoyed by Muhammad Ali Jinnah, one of India's finest attorneys and by then the most visible All India Muslim political figure, Ilm Din dared to hope that the judge may overturn his death sentence. To hasten this process, Ilm Din had recanted all earlier admissions of guilt. He now claimed that he had nothing to do with the crime and was, in fact, merely on his way to the *sabzi mandi* (vegetable market) to buy food when a Hindu mob started beating him.[19]

To establish the veracity of Din's new statement, Jinnah impeached the witness testimony of the employees, who had seen Ilm Din kill Rajpal. In an attempt to have their testimony thrown out, Jinnah repeatedly labelled them as 'interested'.[20] Upon further investigation from the judge, this 'interest' turned out to be that they had all worked for Rajpal. A link between how such an 'interest' would impact one's ability to identify someone at close range after a stabbing incident remained unanswered. Jinnah was also unsuccessful in convincing the judge that the knife seller's identification of Ilm Din was 'untrue and improbable'.[21]

To those who knew him, it seemed somewhat out of character that Jinnah had taken on Ilm Din's case. Some argued that he was doing it for the money. There is a good argument to be made for it. Jinnah did not lower his fees and demanded a whopping compensation of ten thousand rupees, which had been painstakingly gathered through a nationwide fundraising campaign.[22] It would also be fair to say that Jinnah spent not more than three days engaging with Ilm Din's file and that is if one includes the lengthy travel time from Bombay to Lahore. Just like any barristers of note, Jinnah had worked on morally dubious criminal cases before. The infamous Bawla murder case of 1925 is one such example.[23] In the Bawla case, a wealthy Muslim merchant was driving down Bombay's scenic Malabar Hills in his car. Seated next to him was his friend, a former nautch girl of the Maharaja of Indore, who had escaped from the Raja's clutches and was now enjoying her freedom by taking 'motor trips' around India.[24] In a brutal act to recoup the woman from the merchant, the Raja had sent 'hired desperado' after them. Those goons overtook the couple's car on Gibbs Road, one of Bombay's poshest avenues, brought it to a halt, and started shooting. This shoot-out left the merchant Abdul Kadir Bawla dead, and the nautch girl's face slashed in half a dozen places from knife cuts.[25] Jinnah had defended one of the attackers.[26]

On the other hand, Jinnah also took on cases he deemed politically relevant. For instance, he had rushed to 'Lokmanya' Tilak's defence twice after the colonial government slapped sedition charges on the aged Indian freedom fighter for his activity as the leader of the Congress party's 'extremist' wing.[27] In Tilak's second defence, in 1916, Jinnah was even able to have the charges against him dropped.[28] With similar cool-headed legal acumen, in 1923, Jinnah also defended the religiously promiscuous Marmaduke Pickthall, who was then editor of the fiercely nationalist *Bombay Chronicle*, in a contempt of court case.[29] From this angle, Jinnah's attraction to the Ilm Din case likely stemmed from the religious and political entanglements he saw in it. His declared aim was to represent Indian

Muslims. With Ilm Din, he had found a topic that sparked the passion of Indian Muslims.

Despite Jinnah's spirited defence, Judge Broadway affirmed Ilm Dean's death sentence. Jinnah's plea that Ilm Din was immature and might have been influenced 'by feelings of veneration for the founder of his religion'[30] were, according to Broadway, 'wholly insufficient reason[s] for not imposing the appropriate sentence provided by the law.'[31] On 31 October 1929, at Mianwali Jail, the colonial authorities hanged and immediately buried Ilm Din. Before the hanging, Jinnah made a final appeal to the Legislative Assembly in September 1929 in which he denounced the 'damnable system of Government' for leading young idealistic revolutionaries driven by the 'the justice of [their] cause'.[32] While Jinnah linked these remarks to Bhagat Singh's arrest, he may have also included Ilm Din, when he said that such men were not 'guilty of cold-blooded, sordid, wicked crime[s].'[33]

II

Rajpal was born around 1885 in Amritsar, at a time when the city had lost much of its magnificence. Once hailed as the crown of the Sikh Empire, the city was left desolate after the British took over in 1849. It was in Amritsar where Rajpal came in contact with Dayanand's Arya Samaj teachings. At an early age, he committed himself entirely to religious service. For this, Rajpal moved to Lahore, the Arya Samaj hub, in 1905. After working a series of odd jobs at Samaj schools and temples, he opened a bookshop in the Anarkali bazaar and named it Arya Books. His entire catalogue consisted of Arya Samaj missionary literature. For this reason, and perhaps also due to its convenient central location, the bookshop soon became a fixture on the Arya Samaj map. When in Lahore, many members would stop by to buy copies of the latest newspapers and books.

Following in the footsteps the Arya Samaj's strict *mahatma*-wing, Rajpal also engaged in religious polemics. As he had little formal education, Rajpal jumped into the role of a publisher and left the writing and editing to his co-religionists. Rajpal commissioned several critical works on Christianity and orthodox Hinduism. They did not make much of an impact. Most of the books he published on

74

Islam responded to the literature that was pouring out from Qadian, but even these evaporated into thin air after a short rebuttal or counterattack from Ahmadiyya newspapers. While these books were debated between Ahmadis and Arya Samajis in the alleys and bazaars of Ludhiana, Amritsar, Lahore, and Batala, none of these works had a national impact until 1924.

Before *Rangila Rasul*, the closest Rajpal came to wider public acknowledgement was the publication of a political drama in three acts called *Khushnasib Hindustan* (Fortunate India). The play, set in 1922, celebrated the nationalist zeal of Swami Shraddhanand, Tilak, and Lajpat Rai. As was the norm in Arya Samaj circles at the time, Gandhi appeared as the villain. At one point in the play, when Tilak is just about to declare self-rule for India, Gandhi barges in and aborts the process by swinging a Swaraj flag and telling his startled countrymen that they should wait until Britain is ready to grant them self-rule. Somewhat unconnected to this line of the plot, a British Officer enters a room with a young Indian woman, says the line 'my hand is restless in order to break the bangles of your marriage', and goes on to rape her.[34] Rajpal's play was not a showstopper. But it was a little condescending when the colonial government, usually quick on their feet to jump on anything that smelled of sedition, decided not to prosecute Rajpal, for the sole reason that he was a man 'of no account'.[35] All of this changed with the publication of *Rangila Rasul*.

At the national level, Gandhi cast the first stone in the book. Already jaded with the Arya Samaj from his encounters with them in South Africa, Gandhi criticised Dayanand Saraswati's *Satyarth Prakash*, the Arya bible, accusing Dayanand of purposefully 'misinterpreting' Christianity, Islam, and Hinduism.[36] For *Rangila Rasul*, Gandhi's words were even more direct. He found the title 'offensive', the content untranslatable, and written for the sole purpose to 'inflame passions'. As works of religious propaganda, Gandhi felt that such writings had 'no value whatsoever'.[37] Gandhi's bad relationship with Swami Shraddhanand was another factor that led him to lash out against the Arya Samaj. He saw the conversion efforts of Shraddhanand as the main reason for disunity between Hindus and Muslims.[38] Gandhi prescribed publishing 'clean literature', which is to say writings that focus on the positive aspects of other religions.[39]

This formula, Gandhi hoped, would civilise the 'gutter press' and produce an atmosphere of mutual respect and tolerance.

When the local magistrate first summoned the Arya Samaj publisher in late August 1924, Rajpal feigned ignorance. He claimed to have published the book not to harm but to help Muslims. Reading the book carefully, Rajpal insisted, would help Muslims in weaning themselves away from 'polygamy, concubinage, mutaa [temporary marriage], and the gross disparity of age in marriage'.[40] Doubling down on the book's historical accuracy, Rajpal claimed that he could not be guilty under Section 153A Indian Penal Law (for inciting enmity between classes). Everything written in the book was historically accurate.[41]

This argument got the local magistrate, H.L. Phailbus, an Anglo-Indian Christian from Amritsar, thinking. Phailbus would repeatedly call upon Muslim witnesses and ask them to share their feelings about the pamphlet over the next few months.[42] He would also frequently discuss history with them at great length.[43] Phailbus was not known as the workhorse of the colonial administration. After hearings and cross-examinations, he repeatedly attempted to transfer the case to the High Court. When the High Court rejected his requests, he grudgingly complied on hearing it himself.[44] But Phailbus's superiors became severely concerned about his work ethic when, after more than a year, he had still not reached a decision in this case.[45] It went so far that Lord Birkenhead, the Secretary of State for India, pondered aloud if Anglo-Indian judges, who were neither 'the most experienced [n]or the most efficient members of the district staff,' should be given preference in trying such sensitive communal cases.[46]

To the relief of the colonial administration, H.L. Phailbus ultimately sentenced Rajpal to eighteen months' 'rigorous imprisonment' and a fine of a thousand rupees.[47] The harshness of the sentence stems, at least in part, from Phailbus wanting to appear efficient. But Phailbus also believed that a harsh punishment had better chances of getting confirmed by the higher courts in an appeal. Rajpal's legal team, which consisted of Dr Gokul Chand Narang and Badri Das, two Arya Samaj stalwarts, had already gestured that they wanted to take the case to the highest possible court.[48]

In the first stage of the appeal, in front of the Session Judge Col. F. Nicolas, Rajpal's conviction was upheld in principle, though Nicolas reduced the sentence to six months.[49] He drily observed that far too much time had passed between the publication and the sentencing and that since the book had been banned straight after publication, very few had read the pamphlet. Upon further appeal, the cases landed at Dalip Singh's desk. Singh was a recent Cambridge graduate and the youngest son of the Raja of Kapurthala.[50] Trained in applying the law without passion, an idea that most Indian judges quickly abandoned in favour of soothing local sentiments, Dalip Singh leaned towards overturning the decision as he did not see any merit in the case.

No doubt, the pamphlet was 'a scurrilous satire on the founder of the Muslim religion,' Singh observed. Dalip Singh then whisked through the possible sections of the Indian Penal Code and found none that matched the case. According to his interpretation, no law could substantiate the punishment that had been given to Rajpal.[51] If there was anything objectionable with the book that could excite her Majesty's classes, Singh reasoned, it would have turned one class against the other—not Muslims against a pamphlet. He concluded that the booklet had not generated enmity between classes, as the letter of the law demanded, but hostility towards anti-Islamic literature in general.[52]

Dalip Singh's ruling ignored the growing resentment and violence between Hindus and Muslims. Even before the judgement came out, Shraddhanand's murder had thrown Lahore into chaos.[53] In May 1927, communal riots killed and wounded hundreds of residents. For a moderately sized city of 280,000 souls, this was an issue of grave concern. While Muslims accounted for more than half of Lahore's population and could therefore elect more members to the municipality, Hindus, perhaps because of their educational advantage, had a firmer grip on public institutions. Punjab University had mostly Hindu employees. The Lahore High Court was headed by a Hindu Chief Justice, Sir Shadi Lal, who was, some Muslims claimed, systematically rejecting any permanent Muslim appointments to the highest bench.[54]

Hindu–Muslim violence flared up after two Arya Samaj newspapers, the *Milap* and the *Pratap*, published a series of nasty attacks on Islam to avenge Swami Shraddhanand's murder. Ever ready to respond to the Arya Samaj, the Ahmadis fired back with the same rhetoric through their newspapers *Paigham-e-Sulh* and *Al-Badr*. At the time, Ahmadis were in the leadership of many Muslim organs. Dr Mirza Yakub Beg ran the *Anjuman-i-Himayat-i-Islam*, Lahore's most influential Muslim cultural organisation, and Dalwar Shah Bukhari was the editor of the *Muslim Outlook*, one of the most widely read Muslim newspapers. It is not surprising that a secret police report from the time holds that Ahmadis were the 'leaders and inspirers of Muslim opinion in Lahore'. According to the same report, Hindu opinion in such matters was 'led as usual by the Arya Samaj'.[55]

When Dalip Singh announced his ruling on 4 May, more riots followed, though not all were connected to *Rangila Rasul*. A young Sikh woman from Chanhatta Wasti quarter, a working-class neighbourhood, was raped by her Muslim neighbour. She reported the incident to the police, who forwarded it to H.L. Phailbus for trial. Instead of trying this sensitive case at once, Phailbus decided to adjourn the case for several weeks. Sikhs were rightly outraged and felt the administration was siding with the Muslim rapist. Not realising that the wheels of justice in Phailbus's court turned very slowly, Sikhs took to the streets to demonstrate.

When a drunk Muslim day-labourer accidentally stumbled into one of the demonstrators, Sikhs drew blood first. Feeling that a riot was in the air, Teja Singh, one of the ringleaders of the demonstration and a police constable by profession, ran to the closest shop and phoned the police station. He told them that Muslims were attacking a Sikh gurdwara in another part of town, hoping that this would divert the authorities long enough for him to escalate the still tame demonstrations.[56] After the call, Teja Singh encouraged Sikhs to rush towards a nearby mosque and beat up any Muslims they could find. Meanwhile, at the police station, the Deputy Superintendent was desperately trying to get the deployment of a large police contingent approved. The person who needed to be informed about the measure was the city magistrate, H.L. Phailbus. After multiple attempts to call him, the Deputy Superintendent eventually gave up.[57]

Teja Singh led a sizeable Sikh crowd equipped with *lathis* and *kirpans* (daggers) towards a small mosque adjacent to the Dabbi bazaar. Muslims were slowly dribbling out of a small mosque after evening prayers. Teja Singh's Sikhs began beating them severely, and at least four Muslims died in the brawl.[58] A Hindu boy who had worn a Muslim cap for fashion purposes was also brutally beaten. He barely survived, and that only after screaming that he was Hindu.[59] Muslims were outraged by these acts of violence, and Dalip Singh's ruling further fed into their grievances.

More than seven thousand Muslims participated in the funeral procession following the mosque attack. They beat up several Sikh-looking bystanders in revenge attacks. To regain control of this steadily escalating situation, the imperial police imposed a curfew, which was announced through loud drumming at dusk and dawn.[60] Worried about his safety, Rajpal circulated a statement to 'soothe the feelings of [his] Muslim brethren.'[61] Short of an apology, Rajpal stated that he had stopped selling Rangila Rasul pamphlets as soon as he became aware that 'Muslims felt offended at its publication.'[62] Rajpal wrote that for him the episode was now closed, and he promised 'not to bring out any further edition of the book.'[63]

Rajpal's measured words did not soothe Muslim sentiments. With antagonistic newspaper articles at a historic peak, the *Muslim Outlook* fuelled conspiracy theories outright. Their editor suggested that food bought from Hindu shops had a high likelihood of containing poison.[64] In the next issue, they demanded the resignation of Justice Dalip Singh for overturning Rajpal's sentence. Dilawar Shah Bukhari, the *Muslim Outlook*'s editor, took this issue very much to heart.[65] His article in the 14 June 1927 issue contained the most direct attacks on the young judge. Bukhari scathed that Singh had displayed 'a deplorable lack of experience' and had no 'sense of responsibility'. For Bukhari, the issue was not Singh's interpretation of the law, which one should anyway 'leave to students of the law to argue'.[66] It was with Singh's inability to understand 'the spirit of the law,' which, according to Bukhari, had to protect the public interest and, therefore, ought to be guided by 'public policy'.[67] Bukhari then concluded with the following paragraph, which would swiftly land him and the publisher swiftly behind bars:

We believe that if the prerogative of independence of a High Court Judge cannot be a bar to the examination of any act of his as a public servant, and even a Governor-General may be impeached in the public interest, then there is in the present judgement a bona fide apprehension that there must have been an extraordinary cause for its patent aberration. If that is so, it is a public duty to bring it to the light of day.[68]

Judge Singh's decision was undoubtedly tone-deaf, which may have been a consequence of his inexperience. But Bukhari's insinuation that 'extraordinary' causes that had played a role in Singh's decision-making process ruffled the administration enough to see him charged with contempt of court. On 21 June 1927, the Lahore High Court heard this contempt of court case.[69] Many Muslims believed that Bukhari deserved leniency. Zafarullah Khan, who had defended Abdul Rashid earlier that year, appeared for Bukhari's defence and asked the High Court to dismiss the case on procedural grounds as it lacked the jurisdiction to rule over a contempt of court case related to a ruling by that same court.[70] Judge Broadway, who was not going to be stopped on mere procedural grounds in a case closely monitored by the colonial government, dismissed Zafarullah's view by pointing towards an old and somewhat obscure decision on such matters from the Allahabad court. Considering it 'a very serious case of contempt,' Broadway then sentenced Bukhari to 'six months' simple imprisonment and the payment of a fine of Rs. 750 or in default six weeks' single imprisonment.'[71]

One of the reasons for this rather strict punishment was, as Broadway stated openly, Bukhari's refusal to apologise. In the three other contempt of court cases that the Lahore High Court had adjudicated and that had led to more lenient punishments, the editors of the papers had acknowledged and apologised for their mistakes.[72] After consulting with Mirza Mahmud and Zafarullah Khan, Bukhari had accepted their conclusion that it was 'better to go to prison than to offer an apology'.[73] Receiving this hefty sentence now lent Bukhari a 'halo of martyrdom' and further increased the stakes of the Qadian Ahmadis in the *Rangila Rasul* affair.[74]

On 22 June 1927, Zafar Ali Khan of the *Zamindar*, a newspaper famed for its wide circulation as well as its high-brow Urdu and low-brow content, drummed together tens of thousands of Muslims in the Municipal Gardens outside of Delhi Gate to protest Bukhari's sentencing.[75] After listening to soul-stirring poems in Punjabi by Abdul Rahim Aziz, who poked fun at the weaknesses of man-made law and called Dalip Singh 'an ass in good clothes', Zafar Ali Khan proposed two resolutions.[76] Zafar Ali Khan advised the crowds first that to vote in favour of a resolution they should shout Allahu Akbar. He did not identify a way of expressing dissent. In the first resolution, the organisers denounced the attack on the Prophet Muhammad in the *Rangila Rasul* pamphlet and Justice Dalip Singh's ruling in that matter. In the second resolution, they expressed sympathy with Bukhari and the printer of the *Muslim Outlook*, who, despite Bukhari accepting all of the blame, had also been sentenced.[77] For Zafar Ali Khan, Bukhari had vindicated 'the honour of our sacred Prophet'.[78] The resolution then lamented that the law stood helpless to 'give protection to the fair name of the Holy Prophet of Islam.'[79] Well after midnight, the crowds slowly dispersed, and it was rumoured that Phailbus had attended the meeting in disguise until the very end.[80]

Two weeks later, Phailbus intervened at another gathering to protest the *Rangila Rasul* meeting and ordered the police to disperse the crowds. More than ten thousand protesters had gathered outside Mochi Gate to listen to the Hasrat Mohani, a noted Urdu poet, who had popularised the slogan *Inqalab Zindabad* (Long live the revolution).[81] Syed Habib of the *Siyasat*, a paper that sought to compete with the *Zamindar* in style and content, and Zafar Ali Khan were also seated on the podium with him. After Mohani had spoken, Zafar Ali Khan stepped up to the microphone, thinking that it was now his turn to renounce Dalip Singh's ruling. But, in a brute display of power, Syed Habib ordered him to sit down. When Zafar Ali Khan refused, Habib hurled abuse at him. 'You son of a sow, you swine, you dirty pimp!'[82] Zafar Ali Khan looked startled, paused for a bit, and then punched Habib right in the face. Before the fight could escalate further, Phailbus blew his whistle to alert the constables and ordered everyone to disperse.[83] Phailbus also imposed a ban on meetings for the next ten days. Meetings in mosques, however, were excluded from this ban. Using this loophole, Ata Ullah Shah Bukhari, who had founded the Majlis-e-Ahrar to oppose the Ahmadiyya influence in Punjab's political and cultural organisations, gave a fiery speech at Lahore's largest mosque, the *Badshahi masjid*. In his remarks, he issued the following fatwa: 'If any Hindu in any open meeting or procession uses obscene language about the Prophet, he should be killed there and then. Any Muhammadan who would not be prepared to do this is not a true Muslim.'[84]

With comments like these spreading quickly through Lahore, the colonial government was again on high alert. Malcolm Hailey, the Governor of the Punjab, even inquired from Dalip Singh if 'any admission embarrassing to [him] might have to be made', should he be questioned under oath on the forthcoming *Muslim Outlook* case.[85] Hailey asked because he was suspicious. A lawyer in his own right, he found it strange that Shadi Lal, Lahore High Court's Chief Justice, had chosen a junior judge to adjudicate this vital case.[86] Singh was Christian because of his father's conversion, but his Sikh family ties were otherwise intact. For Hailey, a Divisional Bench would have been the appropriate measure to handle the case, and he suspected foul play.[87] Singh denied this vehemently: '[T]o obviate any misconceptions, I should like to add for His Excellency's information that [...] [t]he allegations and insinuations made against me personally are not correct.'[88]

To rectify the ruling in the *Rangila Rasul* case, Malcolm Hailey had now pinned his hopes on another article that insulted the Prophet Muhammad entitled *Sair-i-Dozakh* (Trip to Hell). Published in April 1927, for the May edition of the Arya Samaj weekly *Risala-e-Vartman*, the *Sair-i-Dozakh* had striking parallels to *Rangila Rasul*: it was written by an Arya Samaj preacher in response to the Ahmadiyya publication *Unisveen Saddi ka Maharishi* (The Saint of the Nineteenth Century); it attacked the Prophet Muhammad in vile language; it was first made prominent through posters printed in Qadian and hung in town squares across North India and the Frontier; and it was proscribed almost immediately after its publication.[89] Hailey had promised a Muslim delegation headed by Muhammad Iqbal on 15 June 1927 that the *Vartman* judgement would accommodate their concerns regarding insults against the Prophet Muhammad.[90]

For this, he felt that Judge Broadway would be the best candidate. But since Broadway had already left Lahore and was about to board a steamer in Bombay, Hailey had to convince him in a lengthy telegram to return to Lahore 'in the interest of peace'.[91] He also promised Broadway that he would favourably review 'any proposal [...] for grant of leave in continuation of vacation' in the future.[92] Broadway reluctantly returned and obliged Hailey's request. Against Dalip Singh's judgement, Broadway's bench dutifully ruled that a 'scurrilous and vituperative attack on religion or on its founder' did indeed fall under Section 153A Indian Penal Code and was therefore punishable in law.[93]

Locking the printer and publisher of the *Risala-e-Vartman* away was not enough in Maulana Mohamed Ali's eyes. An Oxford graduate, Mohamed Ali had thrown himself into the Khilafat movement but had come out of it disillusioned and increasingly bitter. His relationship with Gandhi had suffered severely, especially after the murder of Swami Shraddhanand. Despite knowing that he would strain his ties to the Congress Working Committee further, Mohamed Ali had displayed a significant level of sympathy and understanding for Abdul Rashid. To make matters worse, he had visited Abdul Rashid in prison. After heavy criticism for his visit from *The Nation*, an English weekly with strong Congress leanings, Mohamed Ali penned a letter to its editor challenging that he 'had any reverence for him [Abdul Rashid]?'[94] Yet only a few mention lines later in the same letter, Mohamed Ali wrote the following:

> I had certainly told the Musalmans in the Masjid that I had heard that Abdur Rashid was alleged to have said he had seen the vision of an old and saintly man immediately after the murder, who told him he could arrange for his escape, if he so desired, but that he had refused and had said that he had done the deed in order to enter paradise and was willing to face the world to die for what he had done. I said this at least was courageous and Musalmans should imitate him in this and, if they approved of his deed, they should boldly say so and not take shelter behind outward condemnation, while approving the thing in their heart of hearts.[95]

Mohamed Ali also demanded new legislation that would provide clear guidelines to judges on adjudicating blasphemy cases.[96] Here he was following the lead of Mirza Mahmud, who, after meeting with Punjab's Governor Malcolm Hailey,[97] was the first to pitch a draft for a new blasphemy law straight to Lord Irwin, India's Viceroy.[98] The memorial Mirza Mahmud presented to the Viceroy had the purpose, as Mirza Mahmud put at the outset, to 'safeguard the honour of Prophets, Avatars and Founders of all religions.'[99] Much of the proposed blasphemy law carried Zafarullah Khan's handwriting. Zafarullah was one of the closest advisors to Mirza Mahmud and the only lawyer in the Ahmadiyya with substantial legal drafting experience.[100] Already in October 1926, well before the *Rangila Rasul* judgement, Mirza Mahmud had proposed that a 'most clear worded section should be added to the Indian Penal Code making it illegal for anyone to intentionally [..] attack [...] holy persons.'[101]

Cautious not to disrupt their pamphlet war with the Arya Samaj that had now been raging for decades, Mirza Mahmud suggested that writings that were 'merely and truly a refutation of another writing published by a member of any other Community' should not be banned.[102] It should only be 'illegal for anyone to intentionally make [...] a personal attack either in speech or in writing [...] on past Prophets or Avatars or Sikh Gurus or Founders of religions or Founders of religious sects or those holy person whom a class of His Majesty's subjects look upon as Divinely inspired religious reformers.'[103] The last section was a clear nod to Mirza Ghulam Ahmad, who had made several claims to divine inspiration. In the promotion efforts for his blasphemy law, Mirza Mahmud even travelled to Simla, where the summer sessions of the Legislative Assembly took place, to lobby for his draft. There he circulated it amongst parliamentarians to test the waters. To his delight, he found that 'almost all the leading members of all religions' were in 'full sympathy'.[104]

It is difficult to reconcile how Mirza Mahmud conceptually brought together his lobbying to introduce blasphemy law with his ongoing contentious encounters with the Arya Samaj. In 1927 alone, the colonial administration had warned Ahmadiyya newspapers 'for writing objectionable articles' on three separate occasions.[105] They had also reprimanded Mirza Mahmud for reprinting sections of the *Sair-e-Dozikh* with the sensationalist heading 'How can those who truly love the Prophet Muhammad continue to sit idle?'[106]

III

During the summer, the Indian administration traditionally moved to Simla, a leafy town in the Himalayas, to escape Delhi's scorching heat. For the Legislative Assembly and the Council of State session in 1927, all legislative questions revolved around blasphemy. It started with four Muslim members proposing resolutions that condemned Dalip Singh's ruling and asked for Dalawar Shah Bukhari's immediate release from jail. Viceroy Irwin dismissed them. The resolutions that came in through the Assembly were also stopped out of 'public interest,'[107] and the ones that came in through the upper house were dismissed as they did not relate 'to a matter which is not primarily the concern of the Governor-General in Council.'[108]

On 5 September 1927, a blasphemy bill was hastily introduced into the Legislative Assembly under the name, 'Criminal Law Amendment Act of 1927'. Muhammad Ali Jinnah and Madhan Mohan Malviya led the Select Committee to flesh out the contours of the legal act.[109] In this committee, Jinnah and his colleagues narrowed down the scale of what was to count as attacks. They argued that blasphemy should only be criminalised if insults were hurled with a deliberate intention to outrage feelings.[110] Many assembly members shared the Select Committee's vision that not every negative depiction of religion should count as blasphemy. The more secular term 'vulgarity' was made the yardstick for measuring blasphemous content. Such a yardstick weighed down more heavily upon the uneducated classes, and prevented them from expressing themselves in the public sphere.

T.A.K. Shervani, a representative of the United Provinces, supported the bill with measurable discomfort. For him, it was not the government's job to protect the Prophet but an individual ethical duty for Indian Muslims. If any publication attacked the Prophet, he argued, Muslims should write a strongly worded response. Shervani was also sensitive about where this legislation could lead in the future. He warned that there was no clear-cut definition of who counted as a Muslim. Instead, Indian Islam was split in three factions, 'Sunnis and Shiahs and Ahmadis'.[111] Once blasphemy legislation was ratified, he feared that each one of these groups could be accused by another of having insulted the Prophet Muhammad. As opposed to strengthening a Muslim political fraternity, blasphemy would entirely deplete it. Still, he decided to vote in favour of the bill as he hoped it might curtail hurtful writings from the Arya Samaj against the Prophet Muhammad. The blasphemy bill was finally adopted, with all Muslim members voting for the implementation of the following Penal Code that still constitutes Section 295-A in the legal orders of India and Pakistan:

> Whoever, with deliberate and malicious intention of outraging the religious feelings of any class of His Majesty's subjects, by words, either spoken or written, or by visible representations, insults or attempts to insult the religious beliefs of that class, shall be punished with imprisonment of either description for a term which may extend to two years, or with fine, or with both.

***

What had started as a provincial debate between Lekh Ram and Mirza Ghulam Ahmad had grown into a matter of national importance and cultivated Muslim thinking on blasphemy. With the Criminal Law Amendment Act of 1927, blasphemy had become the central concern in all debates regarding freedom of expression and free speech. In the coming decades, Muslims would frequently return to the terms set by these early debates to position themselves towards partition in 1947. Muslims feared that a united India would allow Hindus to erase their religion and culture through democratic means. Against a future spectre of Hindu Raj, thinly veiled as a liberal democracy, they would soon propose Pakistan, a Muslim homeland on Indian soil.

4

TRANSGRESSION

I

When Muhammad Ali Jinnah offered Sir Choudhary Zafarullah Khan the Ministry of Foreign Affairs and asked him to steer the nascent Pakistani state through the louring waters of post-war international relations, it was not a promotion for Zafarullah.[1] After making a name for himself defending blasphemy avengers in court and expressing outrage over Arya Samaj leaflets, Zafarullah had won a seat at the Punjab Legislative Council in 1926. In 1931, Zafarullah briefly became President of the All-India Muslim League, taking over the sceptre from Muhammad Iqbal, though he in characteristic humility would later remark that '[t]here was nothing much to it. The All-India Muslim League was not a very active or forceful organisation in those years.'[2]

From 1930–32, Zafarullah represented Indian Muslims at the Round Table Conferences, a series of peace talks held in London to determine India's constitutional future.[3] Having prepared his briefs in microscopic detail, Zafarullah was astonished to find Gandhi disrupting the meetings through oblique acts. During the last meeting, Zafarullah remembered, Gandhi lugged a portable spinning wheel to the Aga Khan's suite at the Ritz on Piccadilly, slouched on the ground and began to spin. Once his initial bewilderment turned into curiosity, Zafarullah captured the feelings of the League and Congress members in the following way: 'We began to hope that a settlement between Hindus and Muslims might emerge from the spinning wheel.'[4]

From 1935–40, Zafarullah served as one of three Indian members at the Viceroy's Executive Council, perhaps the most powerful political office in colonial India. '[We exercised almost] absolute authority over the whole vast domain, which included not only what are today India and Pakistan but also Burma.'[5] And, to bring his career in colonial India to a dignified end, retired as Sir Zafarullah to a cushioned seat at the Federal Court of India, the precursor to the Indian Supreme Court.[6] He later recalled that '[a]t the time, the Supreme Court had a limited jurisdiction [...] the Court was not overly-occupied [...] Then there was the four months' vacation in the summer'.[7]

Zafarullah took the cabinet post that Jinnah offered him. As a government official for Pakistan, he first oversaw the drawing of the Radcliffe line, together with Muhammad Munir and Din Muhammad, his junior colleague from the Lahore bar.[8] Then he briefed the UN Security Council on the escalating Kashmir issue, for which he is perhaps best remembered today.[9] After that, he devoted considerable time to pondering the meaning of Pakistan. He was not the first Ahmadi to do so. In the most extensive non-polemical elaboration on that question, F.K. Khan Durrani, a former imam of the Ahmadiyya mosque in Berlin, had already sketched out the political legitimacy and guiding principles of a Muslim homeland on Indian soil.[10]

In his 1944 book *The Meaning of Pakistan*, F.K. Khan Durrani directed much of the blame for communalism and the need to create a Muslim majority state on Swami Shraddhanand and the Arya Samaj. Their conversion campaigns had forced Muslims to ask for separation. Durrani also chastised Savarkar's Hindu Mahasabha for flushing the idea of a superior Hindu race into the political mainstream.[11] Though commonly passed over in most accounts on Pakistan's early history, Durrani's book was one of the critical texts read and cited in the years preceding partition. Rajendra Prasad, the first President of the Indian Republic, in his literary cry for unity called *India Divided,* directed his criticism of Pakistan almost exclusively at F.K. Khan Durrani.[12]

Zafarullah, more sober administrator than persuasive politician, circulated his views in academic journals. Nonetheless, he made his views explicit. On the most abstract level, Pakistan was an 'experiment of a synthesis between material progress and moral and spiritual evolution'.[13] In this way, Zafarullah counteracted the disenchanting processes of modernity with an appeal to enchant the spiritual condition of the masses. For him, religion was propelling this moral and spiritual evolution. In Zafarullah's words, Islam was 'not only a religion in the narrower sense of the term but a way of life.'[14] Turning his attention to blasphemy, Zafarullah opted for a conventional liberal line, which seemed a little disingenuous given his enthusiastic involvement in court cases that involved blasphemy. Sobered through the exposure to institutional politics, Zafarullah also wrote that 'Islam forbids Muslims the use of harsh expressions concerning idols and false gods whom others revere and regard as sacred, the principle being that those who believe in them may be as devoted to them and as sensitive concerning them as the Muslims are with regard to God and the prophets.'[15]

Resistance against Zafarullah's remarkable career, especially his appointment to the Viceroy's Executive Council in the early 1930s as the only Muslim member, spurred opposition from a small but fervent group of Indian Muslims. Ata Ullah Shah Bukhari and his Majlis-e-Ahrar were at the forefront of smearing Zafarullah's credentials and intentions. Immediately after Zafarullah's appointment, they maintained that this was a conspiracy to weaken Islam. Depending on the day, Zafarullah was scheming to preserve the British Empire, joining hands with Hindus to splinter the Muslim vote bank, or abetting a global Jewish freemasonry to suffocate the entire Muslim ummah. Perhaps it was because of these absurd accusations and Ata Ullah Shah Bukhari's swapping between them that led Sir Fazl-i-Husain, the founding member of Punjab's Unionist Party, to dismiss the Majlis-e-Ahrar altogether as the 'riff-raffs of Muslims.'[16]

There was something acutely guttural in Bukhari's attacks. In his more memorable speeches against Zafarullah, he accused Ahmadis of possessing less nationalist stamina than 'the froth of urine.'[17] Zafarullah was 'the tail-less dog of Britain [who] flatters and cleans the toes of Britain's shoes.'[18] As a group, Ahmadis constituted 'the largest batch of spies'.[19] Such insults may have given his audience some satisfaction, but they did not sustain Bukhari's critique. Instead, Bukhari's appropriation of blasphemy against the Prophet Muhammad allowed these attacks to stick. Over and over, Bukhari railed that Ahmadis were blaspheming by violating the doctrine of the finality of Prophethood. Every true Muslim believer, according to Bukhari, was compelled as a 'foremost duty to defend the honour of the Holy Prophet' from such attacks.[20] Bukhari's accusations can be easily dismissed as strategic moves to enhance his political appeal. But this would not help explain why it was blasphemy through which Bukhari sustained his criticism and not some other concept. Instead, it seems that Bukhari was trying to mirror the rise of Ahmadis by making the vulnerability of the Prophet Muhammad his central concern. By mirroring the Ahmadiyya focus on blasphemy, Bukhari hoped to be catapulted into the national limelight as many Ahmadis had been.[21]

Issues around blasphemy quickly transitioned into the primary political talking point amongst the North Indian Muslim salariat, desperately awaiting swift social uplift. In 1935, even Jawaharlal Nehru moved into the debate and questioned the exclusionary stance many Muslim leaders had taken on the Ahmadiyya. An ageing Muhammad Iqbal reprimanded Nehru for this intervention.[22] Ahmadis were threatening the Muslim community's solidarity, Iqbal maintained, as they had violated the doctrine of the finality of Prophethood by accepting Mirza Ghulam Ahmad as a prophet.[23] According to Iqbal, the most progressive solution to deal with Ahmadis, as public crucifixions like in the case of Jesus were no longer acceptable, was to bar Ahmadis from counting as Muslims through constitutional measures.[24]

Zafarullah's retreat to the Federal Court and the Second World War stalled the fury on blasphemy for a moment. Ata Ullah Shah Bukhari shifted his focus slightly to the Muslim League's Western-educated leadership. To undermine the League's claims to represent Indian Muslims, Bukhari threw in his lot with the Congress, though many of their leaders too had received a Western education. By 1943, Bukhari had labelled Jinnah an infidel, Zafarullah a stooge of the British, and Liaqat Ali Khan a traitor. He was in good company. Most of the ulema sided with the All-India National Congress in the run-up to independence and were scathing of the idea of Pakistan.[25]

II

To understand Pakistan's problems in her first seventy years, one only needs to turn to the first seven sessions of the Constituent Assembly.[26] The Assembly was the sovereign body established under the Indian Independence Act of 1947 to furnish Pakistan with a fitting constitution.[27] Sixty-seven elected members arrived in Karachi on trains, ships, cars, and planes from the two separate territorial wings that constituted Pakistan. In Karachi, they debated Pakistan's new political form and constitution. Jinnah had a rough idea of where this journey should go. If blasphemy was the 'id' of the nationalist movement and the Muslim League its 'ego,' Jinnah wanted the constitution to act as a restraining 'superego.'

After the Assembly unanimously elected him President, Jinnah gave his first speech on 11 August 1947. Somewhat surprisingly, four days before independence, he put the possibility of a united India back on the table. '[I]n my judgement it [a united India] would have led us to terrific disaster. May be that view is correct; may be it is not; that remains to be seen.'[28] Jinnah then swivelled towards some form of proto-secularism. Comparing Hindus and Muslims to Roman Catholics and Protestants in early modern England, he suggested that just like in contemporary England, India's Hindu–Muslim problems would soon disappear, and their religious identities would evaporate from politics. Faith could be adhered to freely in the private sphere. Jinnah's most cited words as a politician are from this speech. '[Y]ou will find that in course of time Hindus would cease to be Hindus and Muslims would cease to be Muslims, not in the religious sense, because that is the personal faith of each individual, but in the political sense as citizens of the State.'[29]

While Jinnah's words came startlingly close to the ideas that Jawaharlal Nehru had proposed after the collapse of the Cabinet

Mission Plan in 1946, he must have believed that separating faith from politics was easier to accomplish in a Muslim-majority country.[30] Perhaps Jinnah felt that the rigid caste structure of Hinduism would never allow the detachment of social and political life from religion. Another way to understand Jinnah's liberal assertions is to view them as direct responses to questions posed by the Congress party. Many of the early Constituent Assembly debates in Pakistan read like the continuation of negotiations with the Congress. In such a reading, Jinnah may have just wanted to force the sister-Assembly in India to grant Muslims equal constitutional safeguards. A favourable attitude towards minorities in Pakistan would, from this perspective, potentially lead to a better attitude towards minorities in India.

Yet, Jinnah showed no inclination to defend secularism beyond such sporadic public announcements. Just minutes after uttering his admittedly highly quotable words on the state's blindness towards religious identities, Jinnah found no fault with Liaquat Ali Khan, his right-hand man, when the latter pulled out a slightly modified flag of the Muslim League and proposed it as the national flag of Pakistan. When challenged on how using the Muslim League flag with a crescent moon and a star, visibly Islamic symbols, fit into the secular vision Jinnah had outlined just minutes earlier, Liaquat Ali Khan answered for him. '[M]oon and stars are as common to my Honourable friend [Dhirendra Nath Datta, a Hindu member from Bengal], and they are as much his property as mine.'[31] Determined not to let this one go, Dhirendra Nath Datta shot back that the sun, a symbol for Hinduism, should then also be added to the flag as it was common property as well. Continuing with his secular double talk, Liaquat Ali Khan responded, bemused, '[t]he only objection is that the sun's heat is scorching and moon's light is soothing. I do not want our flag to be scorching. I want our flag to give the light that will soothe the nerves.'[32] Jinnah sat through this spat unphased and did not intervene.

Early on in its tenure, the Assembly also approved a problematic concentration of power. Jinnah held the offices of the President of the League, Governor-General (the British monarch's representative), and President of the Constituent Assembly. In a heightened show of reverence, the Assembly continued to endow Jinnah with more powers; for instance, the right to suspend the membership of any parliamentarian he deemed disloyal to the state of Pakistan. Dhirendra Nath Datta labelled this as 'pure totalitarianism'.[33] He was not alone. Even the Muslim League stalwart Huseyn Shaheed Suhrawardy cautioned his colleagues against 'investing autocratic powers beyond the law' in Jinnah, which in effect would make him 'the informer, the Prosecutor, and the Judge'.[34] While both trusted that Jinnah would not misuse such powers, they were uneasy about the precedent this would set for the next leader of the League.

Since most Pakistanis resided in East Pakistan and spoke Bengali, the language issue came up almost immediately.[35] Bhupendra Kumar Datta suggested that next to English and Urdu, languages only native to 'the upper few of West Pakistan,' the Assembly should also adopt Bengali as a national language.[36] Forcing Urdu upon the entire population, Datta observed, would signal a 'tendency towards domination of the upper few of a particular region of the State.'[37] In an astounding attempt to discredit Datta's proposal, Ghazanfar Ali Khan from Punjab reasoned that Urdu had to be adopted as the sole national language to thwart the idea 'that the will of the majority must prevail'.[38] Building on this shaky foundation, Ghazanfar Ali Khan declared that Pakistan's fundamental principle was to 'take into consideration the rights of the [Urdu speaking] minority'.[39] Liaquat Ali Khan closed this debate with autocratic frankness by asserting that Pakistan's national language could 'only be Urdu and no other language'.[40]

From the moment of Pakistan's inception, many members of the Constituent Assembly remained disturbingly aloof to the havoc partition was causing around them.[41] This attitude came out most clearly when, at the height of the ghastly violence, members thought it apt to spend an entire session discussing which titles to confer upon Muhammad Ali Jinnah for his indeed historic deed of creating a Muslim homeland. They felt the need to do this because in India, Gandhi was known as 'mahatma' and Nehru as 'pandit.' After a lengthy debate, they settled on 'Quaid-i-Azam' [great leader] as the appropriate title for Jinnah.[42]

With all these issues simmering in the background, Pakistan encountered its first substantive political and constitutional crisis in 1953. The event concerned blasphemy and the Ahmadiyya. Shah Ata Ullah Bukhari had teamed up with Zafar Ali from the *Zamindar* newspaper and founded the *Majlis-e-Tahaffuz-e-Khatme Nabuwwat* (Society for the Protection of the Finality of Prophethood). Together with Maulana Maududi's *Jamaat-e-Islami* they recycled an old fatwa by the renegade Deobandi-cleric Shabbir Ahmad Usmani.[43] In that fatwa, Usmani had declared Ahmadis *wajib-ul-qatl* (worthy of killing) and emphasised that this also applied to Muslims who had recently converted to the Ahmadiyya.

Many political observers were surprised to see Shah Ata Ullah Bukhari back in public life. After Pakistan's birth, he had withdrawn into relative seclusion to Muzaffarnagar for two years. He must have felt a sense of shame for mocking the Pakistan movement and its leaders throughout the 1940s. Yet when Bukhari returned to the national political stage, he felt sufficiently emboldened to escalate his insults on the Ahmadis even further. He now claimed that Mirza Mahmud, the son of Mirza Ghulam Ahmad and the 'caliph' of the Ahmadiyya, regularly shared a bed with Mahatma Gandhi. He also maintained that the United States had bribed Zafarullah by gifting him a house opposite the one President Truman owned. This insult against Zafarullah cut especially deep because Truman lived in rural Missouri, where real estate is cheap, which meant Zafarullah must have sold Pakistan for a small sum.

Increasingly bullish, Bukhari advocated that the only way to solve the Ahmadi issue in a Muslim nation-state was to 'hang an Ahmadi from every tree-top between Qadian and Rabwah [the city where many Ahmadis had settled to avoid persecution in the urban centres of Pakistan]'.[44] He also accused Ahmadis of promoting reunification with India. This claim must have felt strange to his audience as Bukhari was loudest in denouncing Ahmadis for breaking up a united India through their separatist fantasies only a few years earlier.[45] In dozens of rallies, the Ahrar and their companions demanded that Zafarullah resign as Foreign Minister and that the Constituent Assembly must declare Ahmadis a non-Muslim minority because they had blasphemed against the Prophet Muhammad. Only by excluding Ahmadis from the political levers of power could the honour of the Prophet be re-established.

To show that he was not intimidated by these gestures, Zafarullah decided to address an Ahmadiyya convention at Jahangir Park in Karachi in May 1952. Khawaja Nazimuddin, the then prime minister, was worried about the Ahrar instigating protests and cautioned Zafarullah not to go. But Zafarullah, who had given his word to the organiser, his younger brother, offered to resign from Nazimuddin's cabinet rather than miss the meeting. Nazimuddin eventually gave in. Zafarullah's speech 'Islam: A Living Religion' came straight to the theme that divided him from the Ahrar: the emergence of prophets after the Prophet Muhammad. He argued that without divine revelation guiding humanity at every turn in history, Islam was nothing more than 'a dried up tree having no demonstrable superiority over other religions'.[46] While the Prophet Muhammad retained his position as the final Prophet, holy men in the form of prophets could continue to receive Divine guidance through revelation. Mirza Ghulam Ahmad was one such individual, Zafarullah asserted: he was 'a plant implanted by God Himself'. For Zafarullah, following Mirza's revelations was also a fruitful path to safeguard Islam from doctrinal attacks.[47]

In an immediate response to Zafarullah's proselytising speech, Ahrar sympathisers smashed windows at the Shezan Hotel and threw in bricks at Shahnawaz Motors in Karachi, two well-known Ahmadi-owned businesses. Ahrar-Ahmadi riots immediately spread to other parts of the country. Zafarullah was still the primary target of this rage. In one procession through Kasur, demonstrators staged several mock funerals of him. Not satisfied with parading around three straw bodies labelled 'Zafarullah' in a single march, the organiser also procured a donkey and suggestively wrote 'Mrs Zafarullah' on its rear.[48]

Punjab's chief minister Mian Mumtaz Daultana openly empathised with the protesters instead of calming the masses. Daultana even began to stoke fears of an imminent Ahmadi takeover of Pakistan. Perhaps he hoped that riots against Ahmadis would destabilise the central government enough to whisk him into Nazimuddin's seat. In several meetings with the Ahrar, Daultana signalled that he would not intervene in their protest marches, fully aware that such demonstrations could easily spill into violence. Daultana also ramped up government funding for struggling newspapers spewing religious hatred against Ahmadis. More than 200,000 Rupees from the 'Adult Literacy Fund', intended to educate illiterate adults, were thrust into such newspapers. When asked later, Daultana defended himself by saying he misunderstood the word 'literacy' and thought the funds had been earmarked for promoting reading in general. The *Afaq*, a daily newspaper known for its vitriol hatred against the Ahmadiyya, was one of the recipients of a particularly generous grant which made up for much of its revenue. A later investigation revealed that Daultana partly owned that newspaper.[49]

With Khawaja Nazimuddin determined to ignore the protesters, the Ahrar finally issued an ultimatum. They wanted to see Zafarullah and all other Ahmadi members in higher government positions removed. They further demanded that the Government should declare Ahmadis a non-Muslim minority. In March 1953, after Khawaja Nazimuddin refused to obey the ultimatum, the Majlis-e-Ahrar took to the streets.

In Lahore, the riots began when a boy named Ghazi Ilm Din, whose parents must have been mighty impressed with Rajpal's murderer, threw bricks at a police car. Then streams of protesters began looting and burning. Overwhelmed with the sudden chaos that ensued, the police arrested hundreds but could not quell the protesters. Newspapers printed rumours that a police constable had torn up a copy of the Holy Quran, which would be strange if true, and in a connected incident, also killed a boy. As a crown witness for both incidents, the protesters paraded around a child, who silently held up torn Quran pages as material proof.[50]

With the *Majlis-e-Ahrar* establishing control over central Lahore, outraged protesters killed several police officers near the Wazir Khan mosque. Like in colonial times, the police resorted to a curfew. Again, like in colonial times, it failed to achieve its intended purpose. Already on the first day of the curfew, the police fired at protesters who had gathered despite the order. Dozens of protesters were killed, but the looting and burning intensified further. Protesters plundered Ahmadi shops and burned down several government offices as they suspected Ahmadis worked there. With their *lathis* and self-made spears, the Ahrar declared that they would kill anyone wearing a uniform or anyone they suspected of being Ahmadi. Identifying Ahmadis, however, proved more difficult than identifying police constables. The mob killed several Muslims whom they mistook for Ahmadis.[51] Soon the riots spread across the Punjab to Rawalpindi, Gujranwala, Lyallpur, and Sialkot, all cities with a substantive Ahmadi presence and urban centres that had endured considerable violence during partition.

Khawaja Nazimuddin found himself in a difficult position. Of a conservative bent, he agreed with the substantive demands forwarded by the ulema. He had endorsed the Objective Revolutions in 1949, the preamble to Pakistan's Constitution had declared Pakistan an Islamic Republic. Nazimuddin was also reluctant to intervene because he believed that 'if ninety per cent of the Ulama agree that a believer in Mirza Ghulam Ahmad was a kafir, or that he should be stoned to death,' it was his religious duty to take such religious rulings seriously.[52]

However, Nazimuddin thought that removing Zafarullah and bowing to the protesters' demands would trigger severe international repercussions. Foreign governments would reprimand Pakistan for violating international human rights standards. Pakistan was also heavily dependent on food imports to feed its population. Nazimuddin was convinced that if he replaced Zafarullah, 'Pakistan would not get a grain of wheat from America'.[53] He also had concerns relating to India. Nizamuddin thought that India would retaliate if he removed all Ahmadis from government positions in Pakistan by removing all Muslims from higher government posts in India as a precedent had now been set on the other side of the border. Trained as he was in religious and legal discourse, Nazimuddin understood the complexity of finding a working definition of the term 'Muslim': a definition that would legally carve out Ahmadis but keep all the other sects embedded within the fold of Islam.[54]

Though blasphemy agitations were causing a 'complete breakdown of the administrative machinery and total collapse of civil power', Khawaja Nazimuddin could only reluctantly bring himself to declare the country's first martial law on 6 March 1953.[55] He also finally ordered the arrest of the leading ulema involved in the agitations. What led to his decision was reframing the riots as a law-and-order problem and not a religious one. Therefore, he did not ask the police to arrest anyone spewing hatred against Ahmadis but only those who were actively involved in the destruction of property.

Apart from law-and-order concerns, Pakistan's Governor-General, Ghulam Malik Muhammad, may have also pressured Nazimuddin into putting an end to the riots. A former businessman and bureaucrat, Ghulam Malik Muhammad had an affinity for regional loyalties that transcended religion. He saw Zafarullah primarily as a Punjabi from Daska. His potential removal was a threat to the Punjabi representation in Nizamuddin's increasingly Bengali cabinet. Ghulam Malik also wanted to keep satisfied the army, whose higher officers, still entirely British trained, looked at religious agitations with suspicious curiosity.[56]

Declaring martial law was the first capitulation of Pakistan's civilian government. The finality of Prophethood and blasphemy had brought down the existing legal order of Pakistan just a few years after it had come into existence. And with the army out of the barracks, it would take some convincing to lure them back into the cantonments.

III

Twenty years later, the tenth Session of the Pakistan National Assembly took place from May to August 1974 in Islamabad's State Bank Building. It was marked with short bursts of thrilling euphoria, which seamlessly transitioned into long bouts of existential grief. The parliamentarians had plenty of reasons to mourn. Older members were still coming to terms with the blood-soaked separation from India in 1947, which had birthed a Muslim homeland leaving as many Indian Muslims out of Pakistan's territories as were huddled within them.[57] Others lamented the loss of East Pakistan, after a cruel civil war three years earlier, which was triggered by, amongst other things, military incompetence and Zulfikar Ali Bhutto's hesitation to accept the sweeping electoral victory of Sheikh Mujeeb-ur-Rehman's Awami League.

In Pakistan's first general elections in 1970, Mujeeb's party had won 161 of 300 parliamentary seats. Bhutto's Pakistan Peoples Party

(PPP) stood at a distant second with 81.[58] Yet, Bhutto considered himself victorious. He reasoned that the Awami League had not secured any seats in the West and only won constituencies in East Pakistan. Bhutto stuck to this view even after the civil war, writing in his 1972 book *A Great Tragedy* that if Pakistan had remained united under Mujeeb, he would have used the 'brute force of his majority inside the Assembly' to punish West Pakistan for its economic exploitation of the East.[59] To nip Bengali majoritarian fantasies in the bud (one may well call them democratic), Bhutto boycotted the National Assembly and proposed two transfers of power, in which he would be appointed as the leader for West Pakistan. At a rally in Lahore, he threatened that if any democratically elected members from West Pakistan were thinking about attending the Assembly in Dhaka, he would make sure that they had 'no legs to stand on' once they returned.[60] Such threats were necessary because Bhutto was losing the goodwill of the majority in the West as well. While the PPP had emerged as a sizeable force in West Pakistan, Bhutto's party had only received 6.1 million votes out of the thirty-three million cast.

One way in which Bhutto attempted to overcome his potential legitimacy deficit was by interpreting votes that the electorate had cast against his party as really being cast for him. Bhutto argued that the masses were ignorant of a 'Hegelian understanding of the State'. They also knew nothing of 'Austin's concept of sovereignty'. Therefore, they were susceptible to adopting a false consciousness.[61] In what many of his supporters hail as Bhutto's intellectual brilliance, he reasoned that those who voted for the Awami League had in fact wanted to cast their vote for him. According to Bhutto, this logically followed from the fact that the vote was an outcome of 'the ruthless exploitation which he [the common man] suffered, first under the Hindus before 1947 and then by the Hindus who remained behind and the West Pakistani capitalists'.[62] Thus, a vote for the Awami League was a vote against capitalism. Since he also stood against capitalism and not the Awami League, all the votes were his for the taking.

Another way to plaster over the fact that he lost Pakistan's first democratic elections was by ridding himself of any responsibility for the events surrounding the creation of Bangladesh. In one such move of disassociation, Bhutto remarked to Nixon and Kissinger at the White House: 'The experience of 1971 was a freak. There were a couple of morons in power in Pakistan.'[63] Yet another way that Bhutto adopted to perform democratic legitimacy was to stage public votes at his rallies. It is unclear if Bhutto saw them as gimmicks to keep those attending entertained or if he seriously thought this was how to attain legitimacy from an Austinian or Hegelian perspective. For instance, at a meeting in Karachi's Nishtar Park, Bhutto, now Chief Martial Law Administrator, posed the question of whether the elected prime minister of Pakistan, Sheikh Mujeeb-ur-Rehman, should be released from jail:

> I have come here to put an issue up for vote. I am a democrat and like to let the people decide. [...] Should I release Mujeeb-ur-Rehman from jail? Raise your hands. Do you agree with me that we should release him? [loud screaming] Thank you, thank you. You have lifted a heavy burden from me. Karachi is a big city. The opinion in Lahore, Rawalpindi and Gujranwala cannot be different from what you have just expressed. We are one people. We have can only have one view.[64]

His family and upbringing may hold some clues to Bhutto's autocratic leanings. Bhutto was born into a zamindari household in the early 1920s, with substantial landholdings in the barren Sindh province but limited political clout. The Bhuttos are a rather unusual political dynasty in South Asia as they have no stake in the nationalist movement. When involving himself with political questions, Shah Nawaz Bhutto, Zulfikar's father, spent his time writing diligent petitions to the British Government. He asked them to install telegraph lines in Sindh,[65] pleaded for lower taxation for big landlords,[66] and repeatedly urged them to award him a permanent seat in the provincial council.[67] Thinking him too irrelevant a figure, and alas Sindh too irrelevant a region, the colonial Government rejected all his demands.[68]

Shah Nawaz's standing with the colonial government increased significantly with his opposition to Gandhi's non-cooperation movement.[69] For his backing of the colonial state at this crucial juncture in Indian history, the Government awarded him several non-hereditary titles. First Khan, then Khan Bahadur, and ultimately a knighthood.[70] But his political demise was sealed when elections entered Indian politics. He promptly lost the Larkana seat in the Sindh Assembly elections of 1937 to Shaikh Abdul Majid, a recent Dalit convert to Islam who ran on the sole message of moving away from Sir Shah Nawaz's feudal pro-Government line.[71] His brief stint as the Prime Minister of Junagadh, a small Princely State with a coastline to the Arabian sea, resulted in disaster, though greater nation-building forces were at play. After the Nawab of Junagadh acceded to Pakistan, a state with which Junagadh had no direct border, the Nawab fled to Karachi, leaving his state in utter disarray. With Indian troops mounting at Junagadh's borders, Shah Nawaz soberly invited the Government of India to take over Junagadh's administration to avoid senseless bloodshed.[72]

Sometime in the 1920s or '30s, Shah Nawaz had married Lakhi Bai, a Poona-born Hindu woman.[73] Both drilled into their son the importance of English, as Shah Nawaz felt the lack of modern education had held him back from his goal of becoming a serious political contender. Yet it was ultimately good fortune that brought the Bhuttos into politics. His second wife's cousin was married to General Iskander Mirza. After General Iskander Mirza removed Malik Muhammad Ghulam in a military coup, a young Zulfikar Ali Bhutto bombarded him with flattering letters. In 1957, Bhutto wrote to Iskander Mirza: '[w]hen the history of our Country is written by objective Historians, your name will be placed before that of even Mr. Jinnah.'[74]

Bhutto's rise to the top echelons of Pakistani politics was not solely facilitated through his family ties but a result of his modern education. As a man with degrees from military colleges alone, Iskander Mirza was heavily impressed with Bhutto's civilian academic credentials from Oxford and Berkeley and heaved him straight into a cabinet position. For Bhutto, this post was a colossal jump. His only work experience until then had been lecturing international law to undergraduates at the University of Sindh. Outside of the student body, the only people who knew him were those who witnessed his libationary exploits at Karachi nightclubs.[75]

When General Ayub Khan snatched power from Iskander Mirza in 1958, he kept Bhutto in the new cabinet. Bhutto was now Minister of Commerce, an unusual placement for a lawyer, especially one with no policy experience. To make himself at least formally eligible to hold a cabinet-level position in Pakistan, Bhutto quietly withdrew his application for Indian citizenship.[76] Until his appointment to the cabinet, and even a few weeks into it, he had a pending appeal at the Supreme Court of India, in which he swore to have never taken up Pakistani citizenship and that he considered himself fully Indian.[77] As proof of his ties to India, Bhutto argued at some length that he had continued to travel on an Indian passport to the United States after partition; that he intended to take up a teaching fellowship and settle permanently in the United Kingdom; that his wife was 'a girl from Iran'; that whenever he had visited Pakistan in the early fifties, he had also spent a considerable amount of time in India; that he was financially independent from his father, who had taken Pakistani citizenship; and that he did not live permanently in either Karachi or Larkana.[78]

Bhutto partly went to these great lengths because he wanted the Indian state to return his former house in Bombay that had been seized after partition. He conveniently forgot to tell the Indian authorities that he had already bagged the monetary compensation for leaving property behind in India from the Pakistani authorities.[79] Thinking that the communication between India and Pakistan was patchy, Bhutto continued to pursue both his title to the property in Bombay and the compensation payment for evacuees in Pakistan. The Bombay value of the property for which Bhutto was willing to renounce his Pakistani citizenship was 140,000 rupees, which roughly equals 1.4m USD today.[80]

Unaware of Bhutto's ongoing engagements at Indian courts, Ayub appointed him Minister of Foreign Affairs. When he found out, Ayub was stunned. In a diary entry of 1967, a bitter Ayub called Bhutto 'unscrupulous and soulless' for claiming Indian citizenship—attributes that in subsequent years have applied to Ayub himself for mounting a military coup against Iskander Mirza.[81] But by the late sixties, Bhutto's cabinet position had exposed him to the international stage, where he began to cultivate a politically marketable persona successfully.[82] Perhaps to cover up his attempt to acquire Indian citizenship, Bhutto's attitude towards

India turned hawkish, and his political vocabulary more and more infused with Islam.

In 1965, he pushed for Kashmir's 'liberation', thinking that the population would rise in joy at the sight of Pakistan's army marching in. But what Bhutto had identified as a fledgling uprising turned out to be a damp squib. Most of Kashmir's political leadership was languishing in Indian jail cells, and the Kashmiri people, overwhelmed with Bhutto's liberationist zeal, decided to observe Pakistan's military manoeuvres cautiously from their homes. Instead of catalysing an ongoing uprising, Pakistan's army found itself helplessly outnumbered. Bhutto refused to take responsibility for the ensuing military fiasco. Instead, he doubled down on patriotism in a series of fiery speeches he gave while zigzagging across West Pakistan.

Ayub Khan ended the war expedition and signed a ceasefire agreement with India. Bhutto interpreted this bilateral deal as a significant defeat for Pakistan's self-interest. He reacted similarly to the Tashkent Declaration signed a year later, in which India and Pakistan declared 'their firm resolve to restore normal and peaceful relations between their countries and promote understanding and friendly relations between their peoples.'[83] In Tashkent, the two states also reaffirmed 'their obligations under the Charter not to have recourse to force and to settle their disputes through peaceful means.'[84] For Bhutto, Ayub Khan had sold out the country by signing this declaration. Politically minded Indians were also in uproar against the government for signing the deal, claiming that it had given overly favourable terms to Pakistan. On hearing about these protests, Lal Bahadur Shastri, India's prime minister, died of a heart attack while still in Tashkent.

Ayub removed Bhutto from the cabinet because he found that 'demagogy [had] become his [Bhutto's] stock in trade.' Ayub also alleged that Bhutto had 'started drinking himself into a stupor' and was ruining Pakistan's international reputation by giving provocative speeches and assigning ambassadorships as personal favours to his friends.[85] Soon after his removal, Bhutto began publicly trumpeting the ills of the Tashkent Declaration.[86] When his message failed to take off, Bhutto looked for ways to transform his image. First, he portrayed himself as a political outsider who would trim order into the 'flat and flabby generals'.[87] Then Bhutto swapped the bespoke suits he had worn since childhood for a rugged trench coat, donned a worker's hat, and started preaching socialism. Many of the slogans he used were lifted directly from the leftist student uprisings of the late sixties.[88]

With the army exhausted and discredited after the military debacle in Bangladesh, Yahya Khan, the then military dictator, appointed Bhutto as the first civilian Chief Martial Law Administrator and as President of Pakistan in December 1971. Already in 1972, Bhutto came under pressure to deliver on his socialist promises. Strangely, he decided to purge the leftist elements from his party instead. Bhutto began to fill the upper ranks of the PPP with big landowners and former Ayub-allies, perhaps to consolidate his position at the helm of the state. Moving away from his party's socialist ideology, he openly flirted with Maulana Maududi's Jamaat-e-Islami. As a first step to fostering this new relationship, Bhutto gave them free rein on the college campus across Pakistan, which became breeding grounds for religious activism.[89] During these Bhutto years, Islamist student organisations like the *Jamiat-i-Taliba* considerably swelled in size and grew to national prominence.[90]

There had been no fresh elections after the civil war. For this reason, Bhutto received substantial pushback from the parliamentarians, many of whom felt betrayed by his accommodation of religious parties. Others loathed his authoritarianism. A lengthy military expedition into Baluchistan to quell an insurgency and keep the opposition in check through a newly established Federal Security Force further tarnished Bhutto's democratic reputation.[91] In 1974, religious parties ultimately increased the pressure on Bhutto to engage with the issue of the finality of Prophethood and to constitutionally exclude Ahmadis from counting as Muslims. By then, Bhutto had already lost much goodwill from his former socialist and liberal supporters. That the religious parties could use the Ahmadiyya issue and their constitutional treatment as Muslim citizens to challenge the legitimacy of Bhutto's government at least indicates that theological concerns around blasphemy and Prophethood had become entwined with the right to rule. Blasphemy had entered the political mainstream.

IV

On 22 May 1974, more than a hundred Nishtar Medical College students, clad in white coats, khaki pants, black shoes, and grey Jinnah caps, travelled from Multan to Peshawar on a college trip funded by the *Jamiat-i-Taliba*.[92] Their train stopped in the Ahmadi town of Rabwah. Steeped in the rhetoric tradition of Maulana Maududi and Zafar Ali, by then revered religious figures and campus heroes, the students disembarked and shouted abuses at Mirza Ghulam Ahmad and his followers. Some of their slogans seemed antiquated. 'Zafarullah Khan, *murdabad* (death)' was still popular, though Zafarullah had left Pakistan and was now President of the International Court of Justice in The Hague.[93] On their return, their train stopped in Rabwah again. According to an eyewitness account, though there is undoubtedly some exaggeration at play, the students stripped out of their uniforms and nakedly 'danced at Rabwah railway station and wanted to outrage Ahmadi girls'.[94] In a later investigation, the students claimed that they were sitting quietly in their train compartments when Ahmadis entered and distributed flyers for proselytisation. Whichever incident occurred, it ultimately led to a big brawl between Ahmadi youths and the students.

Thirteen of the college students were injured. As such, there was nothing noteworthy about the event. But after newspapers sensationalised the fight and spoke of several deaths amongst the college students, large-scale riots ensued, leaving dozens of Ahmadis dead, hundreds of their shops looted, and thousands of Ahmadi homes burnt.[95] Punjab's Chief Minister, Muhammad Hanif Ramay, reacted promptly and set up a judicial inquiry. However, he limited the investigation to merely resolving who had thrown the first punch during the so-called 'Rabwah incident'.[96] As the inquiry report has yet to be released, the Rabwah incident has been elevated to almost mythical status in political debates. After keeping a tactical calm for months while Punjab was burning, Bhutto sensibly attempted to keep the flames of religious antagonism outside parliament. 'This is hardly the time to debate it [the Ahmadiyya] if you want to make any contribution to the solidarity and integrity of Pakistan,' Bhutto asserted in parliament before going on to reframe the demonstrations and violence against Ahmadis as primarily a 'law and order problem'.[97] Eventually, he gave in to the *Jamaat-e-Islami*, and acknowledged that the issue of Ahmadis blaspheming by denying the finality of Prophethood was 'a national problem' and, plunging straight into conspiracy theories, that it was happening 'according to a [foreign] plan [with] ulterior motives.'[98]

Bhutto's initial stalling of the issue evoked severe reactions from religious parties as well as the PPP.[99] Muhammad Hanif Ramay, a close associate of Bhutto, declared that 'The Peoples' Party had promised to build a society reminiscent of the period of Hazrat Omar [the second Caliph after the Prophet Muhammad].'[100] Sahibzada Ahmad Raza Khan Qasuri, who had entered parliament on a PPP ticket, felt betrayed by Bhutto's tiptoeing around the issue and repeatedly disrupted one of Bhutto's parliamentary speeches. In their infamous spat, Bhutto shouted him down: 'You keep quiet. I have had enough of you; absolute poison. I will not tolerate your nuisance.'[101] Qasuri shouted back that he was not 'subordinate to [anyone] in this House'.[102] To clarify what he thought of Bhutto as a human being, Qasuri also called him 'that monkey'.[103]

A day before this verbal tussle, Qasuri had loudly proclaimed himself the 'defender of the finality of Prophethood'. He had also threatened parliamentarians with the words, 'it is now time for all of you to be killed. Your time is up. Run for your lives. I can see all of you hanging from your necks. [...] Be afraid! Be afraid!'[104] A few months later, the Federal Security Force, a paramilitary unit Bhutto had established for his personal protection, sprayed Qasuri's car with bullets. The attack killed his father, who was riding in the passenger seat, but left Qasuri himself uninjured. When the police reluctantly took his first information report at the hospital, Qasuri, still in shock, insinuated that Bhutto might have ordered the attack. Thinking about the circumstances some more, Qasuri doubled down on his claim that this was Bhutto's doing. Only someone in a position of state authority could have switched off the road lights and created the roadblocks that led to the shooting. He also witnessed a police constable making suspicious flashlight signals when his car passed by seconds before the shooting. Qasuri also claimed that the bullets used in the shooting were only available to Bhutto's private militia, though he later failed to prove this assertion in court.[105] Since Qasuri was also the only PPP member who had gone to Dhaka to attend the National Assembly on 3 March 1971, he was able to connect a motive, however tenuous, to Bhutto.[106]

V

In 1974, Pakistan's Parliament debated to have the Arya Samaj bible, Dayanand Saraswati's *Satyarth Prakash*, banned as hate speech, and to constitutionally exclude Ahmadis from calling themselves Muslims. Removing a sect that considered itself Muslim from Islam through parliamentary means was an unprecedented step, but one closely linked to the religious impulses that had fuelled Pakistan's creation. As the state had rested itself substantially on the claim of shielding the Prophet Muhammad from blasphemy, whoever held up that shield acquired at least some political legitimacy.[107] Mirza Ghulam Ahmad had been one of the first to speak out on this issue. Ninety years later, the ulema had transformed his ideas that emerged during his feud with the Arya Samaj. In the new Muslim-majority state, these arguments were now levelled against Mirza's followers.

Much of Punjab was in flames when Bhutto introduced the Ahmadi issue in the National Assembly in 1974. He set up a full-house inquiry committee, which on the insistence of the left, was also going to hear the Ahmadiyya perspective from Mirza Nasir, the grandson of Mirza Ghulam Ahmad. Mirza Nasir answered questions that ranged from Islamic doctrine to mysticism in a marathon inquiry over fourteen days. For the most part, Yahya Bakhtiyar, Pakistan's Attorney General and one of Bhutto's closest allies, led the cross examination.

Once the two men had acquainted themselves with the inquiry committee's formalities, Yahya Bakhtiar began a line of questioning that sought to push Nasir Ahmad to concede that there was nothing objectionable for a Muslim state to exclude a group it considered outside the pale of Islam. But there was a profound disconnect between the two men that ran throughout the entirety of the cross-examination. Bakhtiar's hypothetical examples were, for the most part, taken up by Mirza Nasir at face value and treated as if they required any immediate moral judgment.

Yahya Bakhtiar: We have got a lot of Hippies these days.

Mirza Nasir Ahmad: Are they human?

Yahya Bakhtiar: Of course, I hope you will not deny them that right?

Mirza Nasir: I did, in England, and...

Yahya Bakhtiar: These Hippies?

Mirza Nasir Ahmad: ...they accepted my version.

Yahya Bakhtiar: These Hippies declare, announce, proclaim that they are Christians of Hippy sect, and then they further announce...

Mirza Nasir Ahmad: Have they been punished for this?

Yahya Bakhtiar: Nobody can punish them.

Mirza Nasir Ahmad: Then the question is quite clear.[108]

Yet very little was clear. During most of the cross-examination, Mirza Nasir and Bakhtiar talked across each other. Despite this, they managed to shed light on three critical issues. First, the question of whether Ahmadi doctrine considered Mirza Ghulam Ahmad a prophet. Second, if Mirza Nasir considered those who had rejected Mirza Ghulam Ahmad's claim to be *kafir* (infidels). And third, if an Islamic Republic had the right to utilise constitutional means to solve theological questions and exclude those it deemed outside the fold of Islam. Mirza Nasir dodged the first two questions and came down with a hard 'no' on the last.

On the first point, Mirza Nasir distinguished between law-bearing Prophets, like the Prophets Moses and Muhammad, who brought new rules to their people, and non-law-bearing Prophets. Jesus, for instance, would be a non-law-bearing Prophet according to this logic as he came to reform the Jewish faith and not with a new set of divine laws. Like Jesus then, Mirza Nasir argued, Mirza Ghulam Ahmad was a non-law-bearing prophet who had come to restore the Muslim faith. Mirza Nasir claimed that such shadowy prophethoods would not violate the finality of Prophethood.

On the second issue, things got blurrier. Mirza Nasir accepted that he considered Muslims who had not accepted his grandfather's messianic message as *kafirs*, but only in the narrow Arabic sense of the word as 'deniers'. Since these Muslims had denied someone he considered a prophet, he was entitled to call them *kafir*. But in his conceptual architecture, he also saw them as Muslims still. Bakhtiar then confronted him with a saying of his father, Mirza Mahmud, which depleted much of Mirza Nasir's apologetic firepower. Mirza Mahmud had said that 'anyone who believes in Moses but does not believe in Jesus, believes in Jesus but does not believe in Muhammad, believes in Muhammad but does not believe in Mirza Ghulam Ahmad, is a kafir, a big kafir and outside of the pale of Islam'.[109] Mirza Nasir said his father had approached this point from a purely theological sense. According to the Ahmadiyya belief, Mirza Nasir maintained, Allah would consider such Muslims outside the pale of Islam, and Mirza Mahmud had merely reiterated that position.

On the last point, Mirza Nasir stressed that nobody had the authority to exclude him from Islam. As a political *millat* (community), he argued, Islam had to accept anyone who professed allegiance and count them as Muslim. However, in a religious sense, one could draw differences in the *umma*, which Islamic scholars had done for hundreds of years. There has indeed been a big tradition of *takfir* (excommunicating) in Islam, maybe because there is no central authority to rule over such decisions. Hence, such assertions of *kufr* relied heavily on discursive elements. But Pakistan was treading on unmarked territory as a state that increasingly saw itself as one where religion and politics overlapped and mutually enforced one another. Here, Bakhtiar pushed Mirza Nasir to explain why the Ahmadis would stop their girls from marrying into the wider Muslim community. To this Mirza Nasir responded that cross-sectarian marriages always end in tragedy. On the follow-up, why Ahmadis would allow their men to marry outside of the community, Mirza Nasir answered that their organisation would take pride in caring for women who belonged to other faiths.

In this context, Bakhtiar also brought up the *janazah* (funeral prayer) issue. He asked Mirza Nasir why Zafarullah Khan had not prayed with the rest of the Muslim congregation at Jinnah's funeral. On this, Mirza Nasir replied that Jinnah was a Shia. Strangely, this seemed acceptable to the audience. Several religious leaders now comfortably seated in the Assembly had boycotted Jinnah's funeral for the same reason. While the committee staged itself as an impressive spectacle of orderly procedure, its fine-grained formalistic approach went above the heads of large swathes of parliamentarians. Until the very last day, Committee members kept demanding that 'the witness' should be interrogated more strictly, only to be told repeatedly that this was not a court hearing and that there was no witness. Members also insisted that they were ready for a ruling, though there was no ruling to give.

This suggests that many parliamentarians had already made up their minds on how they were going to vote, well before the inquiry proceedings started. For them, the invitation to Mirza Nasir was not meant to deduce some insightful knowledge about the theological form and structure of the Ahmadiyya. Inviting him was a way to accommodate the secular and left-wing forces within the PPP, whose natural inclination was to leave such a question outside of parliament. Bhutto did not attend a single day of the sessions, perhaps due to his close ties to Mirza Tahir, another grandson of Mirza Ghulam Ahmad, who had poured roughly three million rupees into Bhutto's election campaign in 1970 and briefly acted as his advisor for the Punjab region.[110]

Some of the questions Bakhtiar put to Mirza Nasir were plainly unfair. Repeating phrases from Mirza Ghulam Ahmad that he had developed during an all-out pamphlet war with the Arya Samaj and were entirely out of place in the sterile confines of the National Assembly. Not mentioning the recipients of Mirza Ghulam's writings, much of the substance of these conversations was also lost. They make for very odd reading. The theological changes Mirza Ghulam Ahmad had ushered in through his discovery of the Prophet's vulnerability were now absorbed by a legalistic counter-revolution. As counter-revolutionaries often do, the ulema felt that the first guard had betrayed eternal first principles and ideals.

On 7 September 1974, the National Assembly passed the second amendment to the Constitution of Pakistan, which categorised Ahmadis as a minority for election purposes. They did this by amending Article 106, which obliged 'persons of Quadiani group or the Lahori group (who call themselves "Ahmadis")' next to Christian, Hindu, Sikh, Buddhists and Parsees to contest reserved seats only.[111] Then parliamentarians enacted further that 'for the purposes of the Constitution or law', any person 'who does not believe in the absolute and unqualified finality of the Prophethood of MUHAMMAD (Peace be upon him)' was not a Muslim.[112] Mirza Nasir's view that Muslims had the full right to exclude any group from the *ummah*, the transnational body of all followers of Islam, but they could not exclude any group from the *millat* was rejected. Yet parliamentarians were uneasy about claiming theological authority on religious issues. Therefore, many of them thought of the Second Amendment as a mere political solution to a pressing problem of law and order.

There has been plenty of speculation as to why Bhutto promoted the Second Amendment. Apart from Bhutto himself, nobody has argued that he had a Muslim awakening. If personal conduct is to be a measure for someone's Muslimness, Bhutto may not have scored very highly. More than the drinking and the womanising for which he was famed in his younger years, it was Bhutto's inability to reflect on his shortcomings that made an inner conversion unlikely. Scholars have therefore looked for other potential pressures that may have compelled Bhutto.

Several scholars have pointed to King Faisal of Saudi Arabia. They argue that Faisal wanted to exclude Ahmadis from performing the Hajj to Mecca. Since many Ahmadis arrived in Saudi Arabia on Pakistani passports, which stated their religion as 'Islam', there was no way for Saudi authorities to distinguish Ahmadis from Muslims. There is some weight to this argument. Saudi Arabia had been pumping petrodollars into madrassas with a Deobandi bent across Pakistan from the 1960s onwards. There was also proximity in spirit to some of Pakistan's leading ulema, like Maulana Maududi. However, the finality of Prophethood remained a very subcontinental pre-occupation that was driven more from the Barelvi groups than the Deobandi ones. Saudi Arabia's involvement would also make it difficult to square why King Faisal had invited Zafarullah to stay in his palace and perform the Hajj as late as 1967.

Several of Bhutto's close associates have suggested that religious parties had blackmailed him into the Second Amendment. With much of the country in turmoil over the Ahmadi issue, Bhutto wanted to appease the religious factions through symbolic acts. Next to 'solving the ninety-year-old problem of the Qadianis', as Bhutto liked to put it in countless speeches, he declared Friday a public holiday; banned alcohol and nightclubs; stopped the lottery system for the allocation of Hajj (now everyone with enough money could go); invited heads of Muslim majority countries to Lahore to find a common political platform; and set up a centralised *Ruet-e-Hilal* Committee responsible for moon sightings to determine Eid festivals. It seems that by the mid-1970s, Bhutto had wholly identified with his self-assumed title Quaid-e-Awam (the leader of the people) and lost his drive to implement large-scale infrastructure projects, let alone socialist reforms or educational and economic uplift of the poor.

Bhutto's woes were not limited to the Ahmadi issue. He had ushered in widespread disenchantment through his violent crackdown on leftist student movements. His popularity abroad tanked. In 1975, his daughter Benazir, then at Oxford, led a campaign to award her father an honorary doctorate. Here Bhutto again made history. He was the first person to have a Council-approved proposal for an honorary doctorate rejected by Oxford's general congregation.[113] There was a low bar for such approvals. President Truman had his degree conferred a few years earlier despite dropping nuclear bombs on Hiroshima and Nagasaki. Partly, Bhutto's unpopularity stemmed from his mishandling of the separation from Bangladesh. Yet to a large extent, his authoritarianism made him increasingly unpalatable to a global audience.

In 1977, with the first democratic elections only months away, even Bhutto's security forces could no longer silence the public demonstrations against him. Though his popularity was at its nadir, Bhutto managed to win the elections in a landslide. The opposition claimed with some validity that PPP workers and the FSF had stuffed ballots, intimated opposition parties and voters, and outright captured polling stations. One polling agent from Sind reported that the local landlord, a PPP candidate, threw him out of the polling station with the words: 'You bastard! You call yourself a polling agent. Has a peasant ever been a polling agent?'[114] When the opposition took to the streets to protest the fairness of the election result, Bhutto imposed 'partial martial law', but this refuge to extra-constitutional measures was frustrated by the High Court.

Despite the country being in disarray, Bhutto was caught off-guard when Zia-ul-Haq, his hand-picked chief of army staff, declared martial law in July 1977. As the new martial law administrator, Zia pledged that he would guide the country towards Islamic principles. For this position, he received enthusiastic support from the *Jamaat-e-Islami* and a large section of the population, who were disillusioned with Bhutto.

Ostensibly as a step to curb favouritism in the judiciary and the police forces, Zia reopened the investigation into the killing of Qasuri's father. Bhutto was arrested on conspiracy to murder charges, but Justice Samdani of the Lahore High Court released him after ten days as the evidence the prosecutor had marshalled against him was contradictory and incomplete. Zia swiftly arrested Bhutto again. This time, the prosecution charged Bhutto before a full bench of five justices, who found Bhutto guilty. As the reason for their decision, the justices cited the testimony of several people, who had participated in the murder and who would go on death row with Bhutto, that the former prime minister ordered the killing of Qasuri.

After more than two years in jail, seven Supreme Court justices heard Bhutto's appeal. Bhutto argued that he had nothing to do with the murder and that Zia had only thrown him into prison to keep him out of office. Bhutto was correct that Zia had an interest in keeping him out of politics. The two men had developed something of a personal vendetta. When in power, Bhutto had humiliated General Zia in public more than once. For instance, Bhutto asserted his dominance over the General by making him wait for hours in the anteroom of his private house. Once a guest noted that General Zia was waiting outside and Bhutto simply shrugged it away: 'F*** him!'[115]

Zia's political motivation to remove Bhutto from office did not produce the murder charge, however. Several high-ranking government officials were not surprised at his use of extra-judicial measures to silence opponents. As early as 1972, General Ayub Khan had suspected that Bhutto was ordering killings of his opponents.[116]

If the evidence put before the Supreme Court was enough to support the death sentence awarded by the Lahore High Court, however, it will remain questionable until all the evidence that went into the ruling is made public in its entirety.

Like many second-generation leaders of countries with a recent colonial past, Bhutto wrestled with issues of identity, culture, and democracy throughout his life. With his rule cut short by Zia, we will never find out how a more balanced and mature Bhutto would have fared as a politician. It is no exaggeration, however, that towards the end of his life, Bhutto had understood the most critical shift that had taken place in the history of subcontinental Islam and Muslim politics. When fighting against the High Court's charge that he did not live up to the ideals of conduct prescribed for Muslims in Islam, Bhutto immediately responded that he had rendered a better service to Islam than any of the previous rulers of Pakistan, as he 'was instrumental in solving the age-old Qadiani-problem'.[117]

Zulfikar Ali Bhutto was hanged at Rawalpindi jail on 4 April 1979. Zia-ul-Haq had made elaborate preparations to quell public uprisings on the next day. To his surprise, there were no protests.

5

PUNISHMENT

I

In August 1988, Arnold Raphael, the American ambassador to Pakistan, reached Bahawalpur to give his condolences to a grieving Catholic community, and to sell military equipment. A few days earlier, Sister Susan Wojciechowski, a thirty-six-year-old American nun teaching at the local Catholic school, had taken two of her students for dinner to a nearby restaurant. On their way back to the convent, a man suddenly jumped out from behind the bushes, tried to snatch their handbags, and when Sister Susan resisted, shot her in the back of the head.[1]

After expressing his sorrow at Bahawalpur's St. Dominic's Church in the morning, Raphael drove to a strategic military base near the Indian border and extolled his latest tanks. U.S. foreign aid had sent General Zia-ul-Haq, Pakistan's military dictator, on a buying spree of military wares.[2] According to America's grand strategy, or at least its cynical spectre haunting the late eighties, all means were acceptable to stem the Red Menace. After the catastrophic military engagement in Vietnam, American intelligence had identified Afghanistan as the most critical front-line state in an all-consuming battle against communism. In undignified haste, Zia offered Pakistan as a proxy state to funnel mujahideen and weapons into Afghanistan to fuel the resistance against the Soviets.[3] With Khomeini removing the secular Shah of Iran from his throne in 1979, America embraced Pakistan, at first with hesitation and then uncomfortably long and firm, as their primary tactical partner in the region.

After the trade show, General Zia, Raphael, and Pakistan's top military brass hopped into PAK ONE, a modified Lockheed C-130 Hercules plane, to commute back to the army headquarters in Rawalpindi. It was a hot and dry day. Their plane wheeled off the runway smoothly, gained height, stuttered, and abruptly plunged nose-down into the ground, exploding into a massive fireball.[4] Everyone on board died. An inquiry commission, staffed with several U.S. aviation experts, ruled out a mechanical failure and speculated that someone had downed the plane through a 'criminal act of sabotage perpetrated in the aircraft'.[5] Experts later reinforced these findings when they discovered traces of odourless nerve gas in the cockpit. They speculated that someone might have stored it in a bottle of soft drink or perfume, which had leaked after take-off and incapacitated the pilots.[6]

Speculations about the cause of Zia's death were rampant. Some suggested that Zulfikar Ali Bhutto's radicalised son Murtaza with his terrorist group 'Al-Zulfikar' had brought down the plane.[7] Others suspected India, China, the KGB, Arafat's PLO, some fringe Afghan paramilitary unit unhappy with their cut of U.S. funding, insurgency movements, Shia hardliners, or even disgruntled Sandhurst-trained army officers bickering with Zia's Islamisation.[8] Zia had many enemies. Surprisingly, he also had many friends. More than a million people turned up to his funeral in Islamabad. 'Control your emotions! Control your emotions! Control your emotions!' Azhar Lodhi stammered during the live broadcast of the funeral on PTV, before breaking down and sobbing uncontrollably for five minutes.[9] When fake, such emotional outbursts are usually reserved for living dictators.

If Bhutto's driving force in politics was feudal narcissism and self-hatred, as supporters of Zia never fail to mention, then Zia's was utter self-righteousness. For this reason, Zia's desire to punish any transgression corresponded to Bhutto's search for redemption through punishment. Both men were deafeningly hypocritical.

Beyond occasional lip service, they had little regard for the Constitution.[10] There were more similarities between them. Both had all but ignored the Pakistan movement. They had both toyed with religion to decrypt the political system of Pakistan and repeatedly tapped Western nations and Saudi Arabia for financial help. Both men also betted that developing a nuclear programme was the best insurance policy against foreign attacks.[11]

There were also many differences. Trained in the military, Zia was more attuned to taking advice from those around him. Yet the fact that he remained at the helm of the state for eleven years was not entirely due to developing lasting relationships with senior bureaucrats. Zia was incredibly fortunate. Just a short while after his putsch, Pakistan's geopolitical location turned it into a central state for the U.S. when Soviet tanks crossed the Hindu Kush into Afghanistan. Bhutto's large-scale nationalisation efforts had also pushed many professionals and blue-collar workers, who found themselves out of a job in Pakistan, to migrate to the Gulf states. From there, they were sending home remittances that filled Pakistan's coffers with much needed foreign exchange. Pakistan also experienced consecutive record harvests. Combined with Zia's staunchly neo-liberal economic policies, these factors led to impressive yearly GDP growth of six per cent almost throughout Zia's tenure.

However, the long-term price that Pakistan paid for this economic miracle was steep. In his later years, servicing the enormous debts that Zia took on to keep the economy afloat had begun to eat heavily into Pakistan's budget. His foreign policy to house and train Afghan mujahideen for their battle against the Russians, tore grave fissures in Pakistan's social fabric. In hindsight, Zia's most durable contribution to the idea of Pakistan was arguably Ordinance XX—his 1984 promulgation that stripped Ahmadis of the right to perform their faith publicly and his codification of blasphemy as well as the broader Islamisation of laws.

II

Almost anywhere in the world, when protesters occupy public spaces to get their political message across, they like to hold up demonising caricatures of their opponents. When people took to the streets against Zia-ul-Haq, they often just held up his picture. Zia had a short stocky build, hooded eyes, a black moustache, oiled hair parted in the middle and combed back, and gleaming white teeth. Upon encountering him for the first time, a British diplomat observed with the whiff of early twentieth-century racism that Zia's physical traits gave him 'the distinct look of the villain in a Victorian melodrama'.[12]

Bhutto picked Zia as Chief of Army Staff in 1976, thinking him uncharismatic, dim-witted, narrowly focused on Islam, and, most importantly, without ethnic or social ties to other senior army officers. He also liked that Zia had strong family connections outside of Pakistan, which would make him, Bhutto hoped, a more pliable Chief of Army Staff (COAS). Zia's wife, the daughter of Indian doctors, was born in Tanzania and grew up in Uganda. His son studied in the United States, and his daughter lived in London.[13] Bhutto also thought that promoting him well above more senior officers in the force would keep Zia fully occupied with the internal matter of the armed forces and keep him away from developing an interest in politics. Bhutto was wrong. Zia staged a coup d'état in July 1977 and soon afterwards arrested Bhutto on conspiracy to murder charges and refused to bow to international pressure for amnesty.[14]

The reason Zia could get away with the coup was middle-class angst and a changed understanding of what Islam had come to mean in the late twentieth century. Bhutto's gestures towards socialism—while at the same time guarding the rights of big landlords, many of whom were his party allies—had alienated him from the growing urban middle class. With a series of martial law ordinances from 1972 onwards, Bhutto had also made massive inroads into the economy. The most famous of Bhutto's reforms, and the ones that impacted Pakistan's economy most severely, was the nationalisation of banks, insurance companies, large industries, and schools and colleges. Bhutto also established public-sector enterprises to manufacture essential foods to prevent starvation. While on paper, many of these projects looked viable and noble, the implementation was disastrous. To bring about his dream of Fabian socialism, Bhutto put people into leading positions based on loyalty and not their ability to administer funds or staff. Many of them came from feudal backgrounds and were entirely out of place in any professional setting. As often happens in large-scale economic restructuring, corruption flourished, and productivity plummeted. Private fixed investment fell to a record low in the first years of Bhutto taking power.[15]

On top of his economic policies, Bhutto had also dismantled the Civil Service of Pakistan, an elite cadre of bureaucrats and one of the few functioning organs Pakistan had inherited from the British. Without the civil servants acting as a regulating buffer and managing state policies, Bhutto's implementation strategy relied solely on his local party workers. They had little to no experience in administering large-scale projects and predictably failed to advance productivity. Instead, their involvement led to the politicising of all economic decisions: from the national to the village level.

Under the banner of socialism, Bhutto had also swept many big landlords into political power. With the civil service dismantled, there was no institution to challenge their decisions effectively.[16] After the election results of 1977, which many considered rigged, this anger against Bhutto's reforms came into public view. Religious parties galvanised this middle-class rage and mixed it with sectarian messages to further entice street rallies against Bhutto. Thousands of protesters began to burn down cinemas and breweries, rightly or wrongly identified as the two hallmarks of secularism and the move away from religious faith.[17] In many ways, Zia's coup absorbed this moralist rage for order.

In addition to naked instrumentality, Zia's move towards Islamisation was an outcome of his early development. Born in Jallandhar in 1924—the year Muhammad Ali Jinnah reorganised the Muslim League as a viable electoral force—Zia was unlikely to embark on a career in politics and the army. Just a decade earlier, his ethnic background and social status would have severely hampered his prospects of climbing up the army ranks, let alone acquiring political power on a national level. Zia excelled in school. In 1940, he gained admission to St. Stephen's College, one of India's most prestigious universities. With the support of his entire family, especially his father 'Maulvi' Akbar Ali, a religiously minded clerk in the colonial administration, Zia scraped together thirty rupees a month to finance his B.A. in History. He spent eighteen rupees on tuition and the rest on food and cigarettes. Sometimes he would top up his income by selling the League's newspaper *Dawn*. Later in life, Zia half-jokingly recalled this event as his 'quite revolutionary' contribution to the Pakistan movement.[18]

Zia's was not a life of luxury or revolutionary zeal. Religion helped him cope with the anxiety about his future and kept him from swinging the Muslim League banner like his more radical contemporaries. In his term breaks, Zia would travel back home to Jalandhar and attend religious gatherings. After graduation, Zia found employment in the Raj's officer corps and underwent a brief crash course at the Indian Military Academy in Dehradun. From there, he was deployed to South-East Asia to fight against the Japanese.

Zia did not switch sides, like thousands of freedom fighters who had swapped their colonial uniforms for the Indian National Army and now continued the battle on the side of the Japanese. After World War II, when India became engrossed in communal violence, Zia's parents moved to Peshawar. Zia made his way to the Muslim homeland by train. On his journey to Lahore, he witnessed the gruesome violence that accompanied the birth of Pakistan. 'It was a civil war', Zia recalled for *Christian Science Monitor* in 1983, 'we were under constant fire, the country was burning [...] Life had become so cheap between Hindus and Muslims [...] mutilated bodies of men and women [were] lying along the rail trail.'[19]

Prevention of civil war became his guiding motive. It was perhaps for this reason that Zia willingly assisted King Hussein in mowing down the Palestinian Liberation Movement during Jordan's bloody civil war in 1970. General Yahya had dispatched Brigadier Zia and a handful of other aspiring officers to the Hashemite Kingdom for strategic consultancy. When Syrian forces backing the PLO advanced into northern Jordan, King Hussein requested Zia to give him undiluted reports from the front. Zia telephoned his assessment back soon afterwards: 'I'm shitting green'. Harrow-educated and entirely detached from American jargon that Zia may have picked up during his two-year stint at Fort Leavenworth in Kansas, King Hussein had to request his American aide to decipher Zia's message. 'Things are very bad', another advisor hesitantly translated.[20]

When General Tikka Khan's term as COAS ended in 1976, Bhutto wisely skipped his protégé Lt Gen Akbar Khan for the promotion. Instead, he went with Zia, which at the time seemed a fair strategic bet. Zia had shown little interest in politics and the heart conditions of one of his daughters, who was also diagnosed with Down syndrome, kept him occupied. What also spoke for Zia was that unlike Akbar Khan, who had fought insurgencies in Baluchistan, Zia had not commanded any troops through a real battle. Finally, selecting Zia over the heads of the other older Corps Commanders would also trigger their resignation, which was very much in Bhutto's interest. As had become the unwritten norm by then, Bhutto rewarded such resigning officers with plush ambassadorships. To ensure that Akbar Khan would not interfere in domestic politics, Bhutto dispatched him to Pakistan's embassy in Mexico, perhaps the farthest posting available.[21]

Despite his professed apolitical nature and piety, signs of Zia's consolidation of institutional power within the armed forces were almost immediately visible. His senior colleagues had barely reached their far-flung embassies when Zia retired nearly sixty senior army officers, allegedly on the grounds of inefficiency. Amongst them were Major Generals, Brigadiers, and full Colonels.[22] There was another pattern to Zia's early retirement scheme. Most of these officers had served in Dhaka in 1971. All of them had a close relationship with either Tikka Khan or Akbar Khan. It seems that Zia was not worried about inefficacy so much as he was about loyalty and the danger of a rebellion with the senior army leadership exerting influence. The forced retirement also allowed Zia to appoint dozens of young officers to senior positions. In this way, Zia created a loyal group of senior officers around him, who felt personally indebted to him for their advancement.[23]

Opening the officer ranks to junior staff also had the added benefit of closing the chapter of 1971. By clearing the force from those who remembered the large-scale atrocities that soldiers witnessed and committed against the civilian population in Bangladesh, and soldiers who had served in the British Indian Army, the so-called 'Rankers', allowed Zia to start afresh. Zia suspected that anyone who had gone through either of these two experiences would have problems accepting him as the Chief of Army Staff. To gain a broader acceptance in the force, Zia then began to recruit people from non-traditional military backgrounds, which allowed him to break the reliance on a handful of Punjabi districts for new recruits. He was also willing to lower the bar to admission. At military academies, the entry requirement of fluency in the English language was removed, a bar that had left many aspiring candidates from more poor backgrounds disadvantaged.

When he declared martial law and promoted himself to the position of Chief Martial Law Administrator (CMLA), Zia had no straightforward political program. A flat joke from the barracks went that as an acronym, CMLA stood for 'Cancel My Last Announcement.' Islam mixed with technocratic governance could only partly plaster over the gaping holes in Zia's political ideology. For this reason, Zia struggled to produce a tangible political outlook for Pakistan. Even years into his military rule, when he had long abandoned his initial promise to hold 'elections within three months', Zia mostly appeared surprised when asked why he had chosen Islamic laws as a solution to Pakistan's pressing economic problems.[24]

In most cases, when Zia spoke of Islam, it appeared as an afterthought to power. At times, his call for moral uplift through Islam was coupled so closely with establishing political power that it became painfully obvious. For instance, when discussing public flogging, which Zia introduced early on, he justified it in the following way: 'Nobody was going to give me any loyalty unless I demanded it by right [Zia clenches a fist]. And by establishing some of these severe punishments, the basic aim was to establish authority and to make them [the Pakistani people] feel that if they do something wrong, they will be punished and they will be punished severely.' And then, almost as an afterthought, '... it is also an Islamic punishment.'[25]

Employing Islam for political legitimacy soon plunged Zia into the same problems that Muslim thinkers had wrestled with for much of the last two centuries. Whose Islam? Zia approached this question in the following way. As immoral impulses always prevailed within society and politics, the population needs to be put under permanent tutelage. This tutelage would restrain greed and force semblance of morality into the population. Without proper supervision, society would always disintegrate into civil war. As the army, in Zia's view, was the only institution that could prevent society from reverting into the state of nature, it needed to base itself on higher values. Because Pakistan was a homeland for Indian Muslims, these values had to be Islamic. From Zia's perspective, it was easy to suspend the Constitution as the impotence of the law had failed to stop partition violence in 1947. Yet, it remains challenging to understand how Zia made sense of the role of Pakistan's armed forces during the secession of Bangladesh, a case where an army not only didn't restrain civil war but also actively stoked it. Most likely, Zia just ignored such complications.

One factor for Zia's longevity in office was the economic upswing that Pakistan experienced. His early years saw record harvests, which in primarily agricultural countries can make or break a political tenure. Bhutto's economic policies had largely failed to bring about socialism and instead left Pakistan paralysed. Not knowing much about economics himself, Zia outsourced the decisions to dedicated technocrats. This approach gave some relief. By taking on state debt, Zia's economic measures lifted millions out of abject poverty. During one of his budget sessions of the Majlis-e-Shura, a renamed and emasculated version of the National Assembly, Zia told the handpicked members to tighten their belts. After his programme for poverty alleviation, state coffers were empty:

> Countries much smaller than ours have a lot more money than we do. They save money. We don't save money. Some of you have told me that we don't have a habit of saving money in Pakistan. Well, I say, that's not a problem. Just start. It's like your first cigarette. First, you borrow it from a friend. Then you buy your own pack and smoke it while hiding. Finally, you just go out and smoke in public. That's how you develop a habit for saving as well.[26]

Driven by both personal piety and the preservation of political power, Zia planned to reform the higher judiciary, a colonial inheritance that had mostly remained unaltered. He suggested bringing the entirety of the legal system into closer proximity with the legal system of the Prophet Muhammad, the *Nizam-e-Mustafa* (System of the Prophet

123

Muhammad). That Zia chose the same slogan for his Islamisation of laws that conservative groups of the Pakistan National Alliance had employed to rage against Bhutto's regime is not a coincidence. In the early stages after his coup, Zia actively tried to portray his military rule as a direct consequence of these agitations, hoping that it would lend legitimacy to his coup.[27]

Zia primarily thought about the institutional changes to spur Islamisation. The content of these laws sometimes came as a stray afterthought. In September 1978, upon Fazl Elahi Chaudhry's end of term, Zia additionally assumed the role of President. As if the only problem with him taking over the office was the added workload, Zia disarmingly assured the press that his presidential duties 'will not take me more than three hours a week.'[28] A.K. Brohi, the minister of law, also jumped to Zia's defence and lectured the crowd that there was nothing wrong with Zia assuming the presidency, as Zia already possessed absolute power: '[T]he President, as such, has no power,' Brohi concluded his argument.[29]

Zia now held the offices of President, CMLA, COAS, and the portfolios of Cabinet Division, CMLA's Secretariat, Defence Production, Foreign Affairs, Atomic Energy, and Planning Commission. This stark accumulation of power was perhaps the main reason that none of his promised projects took off. For instance, Zia decreed the establishment of Sharia courts without determining which school of jurisprudence these courts would follow. Doctrinal differences predictably led to immediate conflict. Schools of jurisprudence vary significantly in interpreting Sharia law, especially in their prescription of punishments, which range from amputating limbs to a mere soft tap with a stick for the same crime. Zia's Hudood Ordinance introduced in 1979 to Islamise the laws did little to provide a clear guideline to the judges either.[30]

In addition to this, even religious hardliners like Mufti Mahmud, the president of the PNA, who had happily endorsed Zia when he began publicly whipping child molesters, were unsure about implementing hand-chopping in theft cases or public stoning for adultery.[31] They held that an Islamic system, albeit perfect as it was revealed from Allah, would fail to reach its aims when imposed on a population unfamiliar with Islamic norms.[32] Some politicians took this indecisiveness of religious scholars a step further and used it to push for their own agenda. Mir Ghaus Bakhsh Bizenjo, the former Governor of Baluchistan, toured the country and declared the very idea of Muslim nationality dead. He began promoting a maximum of provincial autonomy. 'The concept of a Muslim nation did not exist on earth, and similarly there never was, and there is no such thing at present as Pakistan ideology,' Bizenjo announced at Lahore's Press Club.[33]

Larger geopolitical constellations further complicated Zia's domestic politics. Afghans fleeing their war-torn country crossed the open border to Pakistan in droves to settle along the Khyber Pass. Many brought their sheep, yaks, and cattle and, to minimise their impact on what was often their only source of livelihood, preferred to stay close to the border. Their numbers quickly swelled to over two million. Zia propagated this moment as Pakistan's great sacrifice as a bulwark against communism to the global community. Internally, however, things looked different. With a porous if not altogether open border to the north, weapons and drugs flooded into Lahore, Karachi, and Quetta, a process that severely strained the already weak solidarity between Pakistanis.[34] Zia's solution to this problem was to shore up foreign aid. One way he did this was to emphasise the strategic importance of Pakistan in the conflict between the two superpowers. In an interview with a Thai newspaper editor in Bangkok, for instance, Zia stressed that, in the Afghanistan question, 'the very survival of the post-war international order' was at stake.[35]

Zia eagerly scouted an agreeable meeting ground between the ulema that could give normative shape to Islam and solidify a feeling of unity amongst Pakistanis. Zia first burned his fingers on the introduction of *zakat*, a mandatory two per cent tax for redistribution amongst the poor, and *usher*, a ten per cent tax on agricultural production. He then flexed his presidential muscle, barely a week after Fazal Elahi Chaudhry left the office, to amend election laws.[36] Like Bhutto before him, Zia turned to the Ahmadis and the issue of blasphemy. He brought back separate electorates, a system first introduced on the insistence of Muslims under British rule to acquire a fixed parliamentary representation in Hindu majority areas. But while in the early twentieth century, the motivating factor for separate electorates was fear of an overwhelmingly Hindu majority, in Pakistan, they came to signify the suppression of minorities.[37] Separate electorates became a strong institutional manifestation that only Muslims had the right to full citizenship.

After Zia's military coup in 1977, Pakistan's higher judiciary also addressed the blasphemy issue. Elaborating on the meaning of Bhutto's second amendment, the High Court of Lahore held in *Abdur Rahman Mobashir v. Amir Ali Shah*, a civil law case decided in 1978, that while Ahmadis were not Muslims according to the constitution, they still enjoyed the constitutional right to freedom of religion. In this case, Ahmadis had argued that Article 260(3), which excluded them from Islam, did not apply to them. It only targeted those groups, they held, who believed in a prophet who had appeared after the ratification of the constitutional amendment in 1974. They concluded that since Mirza Ghulam Ahmad had made his claim to prophethood in the late nineteenth century, their community still counted as Muslims under Pakistan's constitution.

As the intention of parliament was explicitly to target Ahmadis, the Court did not follow the Ahmadi defence. However, they sided with the Ahmadis on the issue of erecting mosques, calling the Azan from their minarets, and performing prayers in the same manner as Muslims. These Islamic religious terms, according to the bench, were not protected through intellectual property law. Therefore, in the words of the Court, 'there is no positive law investing the plaintiffs with any such right to debar the defendants [the Ahmadis] from freedom of conscience, worship, or from calling their places by any name they like.'[38]

From a civil law perspective, there was little Zia could do to stop Ahmadis from conducting religious rituals. He therefore turned to penal law and issued Ordinance XX in 1984 to criminalise acts where Ahmadis employed Islamic terms or gestures. Ahmadis could now no longer act as Muslims. The following code captures well how blasphemy against the Prophet Muhammad turned into the primary marker for determining Muslim citizenship in Pakistan.

298-B Misuse of epithets, descriptions and titles, etc., reserved for certain holy personages or places:

(1) Any person of the Quadiani group or the Lahori group (who call themselves 'Ahmadis' or by any other name) who by words, either spoken or written, or by visible representation,— (a) refers to or addresses, any person, other than a Caliph [successor of the Prophet] or companion of the Holy Prophet Muhammad (peace be upon him), as 'Ameer-ul-Mumineen' [commander of the faithful], 'Khalifa-tul-Munineen' [Caliph of the faithful], 'Khalifa-tul-Muslimeen' [Caliph of the Muslims], 'Sahaabi' [companion of the Prophet] or 'Razi Allah Anho' [may God be pleased with him] [...]

(2) Any person of the Quadiani group or Lahori group (who call themselves 'Ahmadis' or by any other name) who by words, either spoken or written, or by visible representation, refer to the mode or form of call to prayers followed by his faith as 'Azan' [Muslim call to prayer], or recites Azan as used by the Muslims, shall be punished with imprisonment of either description for a term which may extend to three years, and shall also be liable to fine.

298-C Person of Quadiani group, etc., calling himself a Muslim or preaching or propagating his faith:

Any person of the Quadiani group or the Lahori group (who call themselves 'Ahmadis' or by any other name), who directly or indirectly, poses himself as a Muslim, or calls, or refers to, his faith as Islam, or preaches or propagates his faith, or invites others to accept his faith, by words, either spoken or written, or by visible representations, or in any manner whatsoever outrages the religious feelings of Muslims, shall be punished with imprisonment of either description for a term which may extend to three years and shall also be liable to fine.

Criminalising religious practice was an enormous legal and political step. It signalled the departure from two centuries of colonial jurisprudence, where religion had overwhelmingly been considered as a private law matter. Zia forwarded three main reasons to justify this departure from these longstanding legal principles: First, that he was merely defending the constitution which, while excluding Ahmadis from Islam, had failed to criminalise their behaviour for 'posing' as Muslims. Second, that the government had to step in and defend the Prophet Muhammad's honour, which could only be upheld if the Islamic principle on the finality of Prophethood was sufficiently protected. And third, and somewhat conspiratorially, Zia argued that the Ahmadis had been receiving funds from foreign actors to destabilise Pakistan. In short, to keep the country together, especially to maintain a bond amongst all its Muslim members and improve foreign relations to other Muslim countries, Pakistan had to implement more stringent penal rules against Ahmadis.[39]

Zia also further elevated the punishment for offences against the Prophet Muhammad. Through the Criminal Law Amendment Act of 1986, section 295C of the Pakistan Penal Code, any words uttered against the Prophet Muhammad could now be 'punished with death', though the death penalty for such acts was not mandatory. Judges had the option of punishing the perpetrator with imprisonment for life.

III

By the time Zia's plane shattered into pieces near Bahawalpur, prosecutors had issued more than a thousand charges against Ahmadis under Ordinance XX.[40] This is not surprising because it had become impossible for Ahmadis not to get entangled in criminal activity. Greeting someone with 'salaam' already constituted an attack on Islam, an attack that could warrant a lengthy prison sentence. Zia's sudden death paved the way for a renewed glimmer of democracy in 1988. Yet over the past three decades, trust in democracy only continued to spiral downward. Only forty per cent of the electorate bothered going to the polls, a substantive decrease from the voter turnout in 1977.[41] Bhutto certainly did his part to disillusion the public confidence in democratic elections. In his final act before his hanging, and what many still consider a betrayal of the socialist values he preached, Bhutto had bequeathed the Pakistan Peoples Party to his wife. Nusrat Bhutto dutifully transferred it to her eldest daughter Benazir.

Just weeks before Zia's plane crashed, Benazir's place in Pakistan's political landscape looked gloomy. Her eight-party alliance to oppose Zia, the Movement for Restoration of Democracy, had lost one of its most vital members, the Pakistan National Party. But after the crash, her position improved dramatically. Exhausted by eleven years of ruling the country, Pakistan's military establishment set general elections for November 1988. With Benazir as the new face of the election campaign, the PPP emerged as the largest party, leaving her rival Nawaz Sharif, who had been lifted into politics by Zia to promote urban industrialists, far behind in most constituencies.

During Zia's reign, Benazir had promised Western diplomats that hers would be a secular and liberal regime to their liking. When the interim President Ghulam Ishaq Khan swore Benazir into office as Pakistan's first female prime minister, she could not keep this promise in any meaningful way. In one of her first acts in office, Benazir asked Ghulam Ishaq Khan to release political prisoners who had been sentenced in military courts. However, she was not asking for a general amnesty, but only for those with party ties to the PPP.[42] Many saw this as an early blow to her political reputation, which, at least for a short window, held the potential to transform Pakistan into a more stable democracy. In other ways, too, Benazir appeared more like a meticulous accountant rather than a reconciliatory political figure. Whoever had crossed her father was now punished. Those who had remained loyal to him received key political posts. She appointed Tikka Khan, the former Chief of Army Staff, and widely known as the 'Butcher of Bengal' for his excessive use of force during the military campaign in East Pakistan, as Punjab's Governor.

Barely six months later, at the 1989 Harvard Commencement Speech in Cambridge, Benazir portrayed herself as a champion of human rights and democracy. Wrapped in a brown Pashmina stole with delicate hand-embroidered borders and a bulky pair of spectacles, Benazir recounted the following story:

> I arrived here from a country that in my lifetime had not known democracy or political freedom. As an undergraduate here, I was constantly reminded of the value of democracy by the history of freedom that permeates this place. [...] My Harvard years, 1969 to 1973 coincided with growing frustration over U.S. policy in South East Asia. This was particularly true in the campuses where students were in the forefront of those protesting the Vietnam

war. For me there were demonstrations on Boston Commons and in Washington. Mass Meetings at Harvard Stadium.[43]

A week after this speech on morality and values, Bhutto allegedly opened two shell companies on the British Virgin Islands to receive kickbacks for awarding government contracts to specific firms.[44] Going against the spirit of the words in her Harvard speech, Benazir also became the first democratically elected representative to welcome Li Peng, the Chinese premier, into her country. Li Peng had become a pariah for most liberal democratic states after he ordered soldiers to fire at student protesters at Tiananmen Square. Within Pakistan, Benazir made life a lot worse for Ahmadis. During multiple rallies, she highlighted Zulfikar's role in excluding the Ahmadis and repeatedly called it 'the great service my father did for Islam'.

Benazir was also quick to clarify that her government would not make 'any concession to Qadianis' and that 'they will remain non-Muslim'.[45] According to Mirza Tahir, a grandson of Ghulam Ahmad who had fled to London during the later Zia years, Benazir was even planning to further sharpen the constitutional measures already in place against the Ahmadis. Once installed in the prime minister's seat, Benazir also began to ban books. Removing Salman Rushdie's *The Satanic Verses* from the shelves could still be explained away through the potential threat it posed to public order. But Benazir went much further than that. She also banned Martin Ling's *Muhammad: His Life Based on the Earliest Sources*, a work regarded as a stellar contribution to scholarship, for blasphemy. Just a few years earlier, Zia had awarded Martin Ling state recognition for the same book.

On 6 August 1990, after just twenty months in office, President Ghulam Ishaq Khan ordered army troops to surround Benazir's residence, take over all radio and television channels, and occupy the foreign office. He then dismissed her government, dissolved the National Assembly, and replaced the Governors of Sindh and Punjab.[46] Benazir rightly labelled this act as a 'constitutional coup d'état'. She then asserted that corruption charges against her, on the basis of which the President had dissolved the government, were entirely 'politically motivated'.[47] President Ghulam Ishaq Khan installed a provisional government to oversee new elections. After the *Islami*

Jamhoori Ittihad, a broad alliance of conservative parties opposed to the PPP, emerged victorious, Ghulam Ishaq Khan transferred power to their leader, Mian Nawaz Sharif.[48]

During Nawaz Sharif's rule, the *Jamaat-e-Islami* petitioned the Federal Sharia Court to increase punishment for insulting the Prophet Muhammad from life imprisonment to a mandatory death penalty. To make this case, the government lawyers argued that, according to the Quran and the Sunnah, it was obligatory for Muslims to punish blasphemy with the death sentence—though scholarly opinions on this issue diverge widely. Yet it came as a surprise to many when the Federal Sharia Court, through a full bench of five justices, unanimously ruled that the softer penalty of life imprisonment was 'repugnant to the Injunctions of Islam as given in the Holy Quran and Sunnah'.[49] In their opinion, 'the penalty for contempt of the Holy Prophet [...] is death and nothing else.' They also placed an injunction on the legislature to amend Section 295C until 30 April 1991. In case the legislature failed to act, the words 'or punishment for life' would 'cease to have any effect on that date'.[50]

Less than three years later, President Ghulam Ishaq Khan dismissed Nawaz Sharif's government on charges of corruption and mismanagement. During this period of political instability and tumult, Ahmadis launched judicial appeals against Zia's Ordinance XX. One of these cases, *Zaheerudin v. State*, reached the Supreme Court of Pakistan in 1993. Mujeeb-ur-Rehman, a veteran human rights lawyer, argued for the release of all Ahmadis arrested on blasphemy charges. He held that it was impossible to bring Ordinance XX into accordance with the fundamental rights guaranteed in the Constitution of Pakistan—especially freedom of religion enshrined in Article 20 and with the international human rights treaties that Pakistan had signed.

His basic premise was that Islamic laws could not reduce the scope of fundamental rights laid out in the Constitution. The counsel for the Federal Government countered his legal assertations by reading out an excerpt of Muhammad Iqbal's essay on the Ahmadis. Iqbal had argued that there were two basic tenets in Islam, *tawhid* (oneness of God) and *khatam-e-nabuwwat*, the finality of Prophethood. Since Ahmadis were violating the latter, the maintenance of solidarity amongst the Muslim nation hinged upon their punishment.[51] Iqbal's position on the Ahmadiyya, the government's counsel argued, 'would justify the constitutional amendment'.[52] Apart from one dissenting opinion, the Supreme Court found such an argument compelling and rejected the Ahmadi appeal.

In their ruling, the justices refrained from citing Muhammad Iqbal outright. Instead, they backed their decision with secular copyright law. Justice Abdul Qadeer Chaudhary, leading the majority opinion, found that Pakistan, as an Islamic state, held the exclusive rights to all things related to Islam within its sovereign boundaries. Through simple religious activities like praying, calling the Azan, or greeting someone with 'salaam', Ahmadis were infringing upon copyright. It was, therefore, the state's responsibility to stop them, just like corporations safeguarding their work product. To visualise this argument further, Chaudhary analogised Pakistan to the Coca Cola Cooperation and Islam to the soft drink it produces. In the words of Chaudhary:

> For example, the Coca Cola Company will not permit anyone to sell, even a few ounces of his own product in his own bottles or other receptacles, marked Coca Cola, even though its price may be a few cents.[53]

From a constitutional perspective, Chaudhary also oddly stirred together religious practice to commercially driven activity. His reasons become more explicit in his second argument, which weighed in on public safety. If Ahmadis behaved like Muslims, he reasoned, real Muslims would necessarily lose 'control of himself'.[54] In scenarios where an Ahmadi was permitted to 'chant in public', the state was to blame for making 'a Rushdi [sic] out of him.'[55] Chaudhary was thus earnest when he wrote that to permit Ahmadis to hold religious processions would be 'like permitting civil war'.[56]

Chaudhary backed his argument with tangentially related precedent from U.S. Supreme Court rulings.[57] That Chaudhary felt the need to rely on transnational law, in a decision that international NGOs regarded as a remnant of an archaic past, shows his desire to couch the removal of fundamental rights in a broader, global landscape. Pakistan, according to Chaudhary, was going to implement this globalisation on its terms. Tossing at least two centuries of colonial jurisprudence out of the window, he concluded that:

> [E]very man-made law must now conform to the Injunctions of Islam as contained in Qur'an and Sunnah of the Holy Prophet (p.b.u.h.) [peace be upon him]. Therefore, even the Fundamental Rights as given in the Constitution must not violate the norms of Islam [...] Anything, in any fundamental rights, which violates the Injunctions of Islam thus must be repugnant.[58]

With this ruling, Chaudhary did not transform Pakistan's higher judges into mullahs overnight. Yet, his ruling now permitted judges to apply Islamic law drawn from the Sunnah and the Quran directly, without consulting any other source of law. From a purely legal perspective grounded in statutory law, this move was a radical shift in the self-understanding of the judiciary. Judges quickly caught on to the Supreme Court's guidelines. For instance, building on the *Zaheeruddin* decisions, the Lahore High Court soon ruled that blasphemy laws should not be limited to the Prophet Muhammad. '[A]ll the prophets of Allah mentioned in the Koran', the judges found, fell under the protection of the blasphemy laws. This decision effectively rendered the roughly one million Christians—who, in contrast to the Quran and Muslims, believe in the divinity of Jesus— as blasphemers under the law.[59] Such rulings closed the door to the judiciary that minorities had gravitated towards for protection.

In the general elections that followed Nawaz Sharif's removal in 1993, only half of the electorate went to the polling stations. Benazir's PPP came out as the strongest party, and she was again sworn in as prime minister for her second term. Hopes that Benazir would usher in a new leadership style were dashed soon after she took over. More hard-nosed about the constitutional intricacies, Benazir appointed Farooq Leghari, a pliant man and PPP member, as President and moved into an alliance with the Islamic parties.

Her governance began to lose the veneer of any progressive political vision. Benazir indulged in several vanity projects in infrastructure and building that drained public resources. On state costs, Benazir ordered the building of a polo ground next to her official residence in Islamabad, converted her family's formerly

133

humble graveyard into a gigantic mausoleum, and some believe that she even ordered the police to gun down her brother Murtaza so he could not enter politics.

Benazir also pumped state funds into the Taliban, an amateur militia with recruits drawn from the Afghan refugee camps, to keep the religious parties she allied with happy. She was the first to recognise the Taliban government as the legitimate government of Afghanistan at a time when the Taliban had just conquered a few patches of land around Kabul. In 1997, President Leghari dismissed Benazir's government for mismanagement and corruption and called an election that brought about another stint for Nawaz Sharif. Sharif's tenure, equally marred with vanity projects and alleged gross corruption, was cut short in 1999 when General Musharraf declared martial law and brought the army back into the driving seat of state affairs. A decade of experimenting with democracy had only worsened the living condition for minorities. Zia's Ordinance XX looked comparatively soft against the increase in scope of punishment ushered in through Benazir and Nawaz Sharif.

With the military, the government, the legislature, and the judiciary outdoing each other to prevent blasphemy, ordinary bureaucratic tasks acquired a new significance. Every citizen now had to sign the following declaration to run for parliament; enter the government service; enrol in government schools and colleges; or simply to apply for a passport:

(i) I am Muslim and believe in the absolute and unqualified finality of the prophethood of Muhammad (peace be upon him) the last of the prophets.

(ii) I do not recognise any person who claims to be a prophet in any sense of the word or of any description whatsoever after Muhammad (peace be upon him) or recognise such a claimant as prophet or a religious reformer as a Muslim.

(iii) I consider Mirza Ghulam Ahmad Quadiani [sic] to be an imposter nabi [prophet] and also consider his followers whether belonging to the Lahori or Qadiani group to be Non-Muslim. Signature & thumb impression (with name in block letters of applicant in indelible ink).[60]

This declaration is a manifestation of how Islam and blasphemy had become inextricably linked and that it was no longer possible to claim Muslimness without considering 'Mirza Ghulam Ahmad to be an imposter'. For the Pakistani state, declaring another person blasphemous had become constitutive of being Muslim.[61]

The reasons behind Pakistan's failure to entrench a stable form of democratic governance for much of the 1990s were partly structural.[62] As his most enduring legacy, Zia had instilled a deep distrust of civilian politicians into the military. For this reason, the army continued to feel entitled to limit civilian authority in national security matters. Such interferences made democratic governance difficult for both Benazir and Sharif. To weaken resistance, General Zia had also all but hollowed out Pakistan's already frail civilian institutions. These conditions proved insurmountable stumbling blocks for Pakistan's political leaders.[63] The other reason Pakistan's democracy failed to flourish after the collapse of the Soviet Union—when the political climate briefly looked hospitable for liberal democracies—was its inexperienced political leadership, which could not live up to democratic aspirations.

Trust in democratic institutions was at a minimum when General Parvez Musharraf declared martial law in 1999 and ousted Prime Minister Nawaz Sharif from office. A high unemployment rate, mounting foreign debt, glaring social inequality, and an economy spiralling downwards plagued the country.[64] This might explain why there was little public resistance against Musharraf's putsch. General Musharraf's rule was also stabilised through a major military campaign of the United States against Afghanistan to flush out the plotters of the 9/11 attacks.[65] The U.S. campaign was part of the greater 'war on terrorism'. Islamist militant outlets, often closely associated with Deobandi and Middle Eastern Salafi denominations, the same groups the United States and Pakistani secret agencies had assisted with weapons and cash to stem Soviet expansionism in the 1980s, were now turning against them. During much of Musharraf's rule, militant outlets wreaked havoc in large cities through terrorist attacks.

General Musharraf's alignment with the U.S. war efforts against the Taliban won him few domestic friends. The wound of Zia's foreign policies in Afghanistan, which had turned Pakistan into a tool for U.S. Cold War interests, had not healed yet. Musharraf paired this renewed reliance on the U.S. with a firm resolve to bring about 'enlightened moderation' in Pakistan, a system that sought to link religious reform to social uplift. As he told the United Nations General Assembly at its 58th Session in New York, this enlightened moderation consisted of seeking out, on the one hand 'science and technology, higher education and human resource development'.[66] On the other, Pakistani Muslims had to 'eschew extremism and confrontation'.[67] Some of Musharraf's activism also had an impact in Pakistan's legal sphere, where he attempted to curb Hudood laws. It was Musharraf, for instance, who changed the procedural code for rape cases to be heard exclusively at civil courts by amending the Hudood Ordinance 1979 with the Women Protection Act 2006.[68] In the past, female rape victims had regularly failed to provide evidence that met the high standards of Sharia courts and had their accusations of rape turned into adultery cases on them instead.[69]

Musharraf's 'enlightened moderation' also meant stifling Deobandi military outlets. One way in which Musharraf hoped to reduce Deobandi influence on the public was to promote Sufi Islam by recruiting primarily Barelvi clerics to work in state-funded mosques. These clerics followed the teachings of Raza Ahmed Barelvi, who embraced local traditions against the Deobandi influence on Indian Islam. As opposed to espousing a doctrinal and legalistic interpretation of Islam, Ahmad Raza Khan Barelvi levelled affinity to the motherland and rootedness as the core concepts according to which Muslims should structure their lives. During his lifetime from the mid-nineteenth to the early twentieth century, Raza Khan Barelvi had defended the folk traditions of saint worship and an inclusive attitude towards heterodox social practices. Musharraf further formalised the relationship between the state and Sufism through the establishment of institutions. One such institution was the National Council for the Promotion of Sufism. Through this Council, Musharraf attempted to begin a Sufi publication offensive that would, in the words of the first appointed chairman Choudhry Shujaat, 'propagate the message of Shah Abdul Latif Bhittai, Shah Hussain Sachal Sarmast and Allama Iqbal'.[70]

After a botched attempt to remove the Supreme Court Chief Justice, Musharraf ultimately resigned and left the country in November 2008. With the army back in the barracks, Pakistan's second democratic moment began, with the Pakistan Peoples Party winning the elections after the assassination of Benazir Bhutto. Asif Ali Zardari, Benazir's husband, who took over the party, forged a political alliance with the *Jamiat Ulema-e-Islam*, a Deobandi outlet founded by Mufti Mahmud's son, Maulana Fazal-ur-Rehman. His sidelining of Barelvi clerics that had gained a prominent footprint in the administrative structure of the state directly led to the creation of a new radical Barelvi political party, the TLP [*Tahreek-e-Labaik Pakistan*]. This party would anchor Pakistan's political system even more deeply within the finality of Prophethood and blasphemy discourse. That Sufism and romantic dwelling in the love of the Prophet Muhammad could have severe political consequences and spill into violence just as easy as a jihadist militancy of the Deobandis revealed itself painfully in decades to come.

6

REDEMPTION

I

Berlin still had to rise from its winter slumber in March 2006, when Aamir Cheema, an unassuming Pakistani student in his late twenties, boarded the U6 subway going south. Affectionately nicknamed Orient Express for linking Wedding to Kreuzberg, two boroughs with substantial Turkish and Arab populations, the U6 rumbled underneath the Spree river and squeaked to a halt at Checkpoint Charlie, a former crossing point in the Berlin Wall and now a cherished tourist hotspot. Aamir Cheema disembarked, rushed to the exit, sprinted up the two dozen stairs, ignored the photo ops with men clad in Soviet uniforms, and walked towards Axel Springer Haus, a tall building roughly three hundred metres to his right. Cheema entered the lobby of the building, pulled out a kitchen knife that he had earlier taken from his sister's breakfast table, and asked, in broken German, where he could find Roger Köppel, the Swiss chief editor of the conservative *Die Welt*.[1] Security personnel hired after Köppel's decision to reprint the derogatory Danish *Jyllands-Posten* caricatures of the Prophet Muhammad overwhelmed Cheema without much effort. One security guard later recalled that Cheema appeared so amateurish that he first thought the attack just a poorly staged prank.[2]

Security handed him over to the police, where Cheema first unsuccessfully tried to intimidate the officers. Then he quickly folded and told them about his plan. As the German weekly magazine *Der Spiegel* reported, he had entered the premises because 'every Muslim had to punish Köppel for insulting the Prophet.'[3] While convinced of his homicidal conviction, Berlin's Staatsanwaltschaft (public prosecutor) was uncertain about bringing the case to trial.[4] Cheema was still many steps removed from putting his attack into motion. He had been ill-equipped and appeared non-threatening. Thus the prosecutor's office scrapped attempted-murder charges. Instead, the prosecutors merely indicted Cheema for coercion and resistance. With a pliant judge, Cheema was looking at six months with the possibility to continue studying for his Master's degree in textile management in Mönchengladbach once released. Cheema must have felt intense shame for his failure to execute Köppel and feared what would happen to him after lengthy interrogations with agents from the Bundesnachrichtendienst, Germany's Federal Intelligence Service. Shortly after his arrest, he hanged himself under the window grille of his prison cell in the Moabit penitentiary.[5]

It quickly became apparent that Cheema had no connections to any terrorist cell, a fact that worried German security officials immensely.[6] Such lone-wolf attacks, as incidents where an individual operates detached from any larger terrorist network are known, are notoriously difficult to predict for security experts.[7] After questioning Cheema's friends, his sister, and his fellow students at the University of Applied Science, the police were met with astonishment throughout. 'He was a devout Muslim', his housemate Saood remembered in an interview given after the attack, 'but he was not interested in politics and, unlike many of us, never spoke disparagingly about America.'[8] His professors were baffled by Cheema's actions. 'For an attack like this one, he lacked the necessary drive', one of them commented later.[9]

Cheema's story received a very different reception in Pakistan. Barelvi clerics took up Cheema's suicide as a case of modern-day martyrdom.[10] 'We will seek revenge from these sons of Hitler', Khadim Hussain Rizvi, one of the imams at Lahore's Data Darbar shrine, announced.[11] Angry mobs burned German flags.[12]

Conspiracy theories that German police had tortured and killed Cheema were discussed in Pakistan's Parliament. A motion with the name 'The Killing of a Pakistani (Mr Aamir Cheema) in Germany' was tabled to press German authorities for answers. Speaking out against the motion was made difficult by Moulana Abdul Akbar Chitrali, who linked Cheema's death to the protection of the honour of the Prophet Muhammad. 'This is a matter of utmost importance [...] as it involves a matter concerning the humiliation of the Holy Prophet Muhammad, peace be upon him.'[13] Chitrali also noted his dissatisfaction over news outlets calling Cheema's death a suicide.[14] There was widespread support for a self-censorship of the press.[15] Even the former cricketer Imran Khan, who had founded a technocratic party, dubbed Cheema's death a clear case of martyrdom.[16] Imran Khan even visited Cheema's parents to assure them that 'the whole nation is with them and shares their grief and sorrow'.[17]

Because of this high-level involvement, senior police officers stood on the tarmac to receive Cheema's body, which was then moved into a government helicopter and flown to an airbase at the Rahwali cantonment. From there, it was only a short drive to Saroki, Cheema's hometown.[18] All shops in the region remained shut to grieve during Cheema's funeral.[19] Despite the government's aim for a quiet event, the turnout at the funeral measured in the tens of thousands.[20] During the functions surrounding the *Janazah* prayer, Pir Afzal Qadri narrated glorified accounts of Cheema's martyrdom. Cheema's action, he said, 'would be sufficient to teach the entire West a lesson about the courage and reverence of Muslims for their Holy Prophet'.[21]

Most speakers compared Cheema to Ilm Din and Abdul Rasheed, the two early twentieth-century assassins of the Arya Samaj publisher Rajpal and Swami Shraddhanand.[22] Such assertions reflected how the modern Muslim genealogy of martyrdom was deeply entwined with the long-running Arya Samaj–Ahmadiyya dispute. None of the present speakers mentioned Cheema's apparent suicide, a sin in Islam as in most monotheistic religions, which ought to have precluded Muslims from attending Cheema's funeral prayers in the first place. Instead, their narratives coalesced around severe torture, often described in minuscule fictive detail, as the real reason for

Cheema's death.[23] More incoherent facts clustered around Cheema. He was said to have severely wounded or even killed Köppel. The message that an outspoken group of radical Barelvi *pirs* propounded was clear: any act committed in defence of the Prophet transcended adherence to narrow Islamic doctrines or issues of historical facts. The main currency in their gatherings was emotive responses to a perceived heroic act.

Another important effect of the massive turnout at Cheema's funeral was the promotion of the idea that action in the name of the Prophet immediately led to memorialisation on an enormous scale. It also demonstrated that historical truth was no longer a guiding stick to determine the validity of such action. That Cheema's attack failed, the post-mortem report showed no signs of torture, and that he had likely committed suicide, had surprisingly little impact on his memorialisation.

A narrow historicist reading would thus swiftly conclude that the Barelvi discourse is empirically flawed.[24] Yet, such a view would overstate the importance of historical accuracy in vindicatory genealogies that seek to cultivate emotions geared towards ethical self-perfection. Even to a layperson receiving all their information from radical Barelvi clerics, it is evident that their stories do not respond closely to any material notion of truth. For one, many narratives shared by the Barelvi ulema touched on direct conversations between deceased people and Allah, which they could not have been privy to.

It is much more likely that the framing of a particular event in a way that arouses emotions for the love of the Prophet is itself regarded as a noble ethical act.[25] In contemporary Barelvi thought, it seems that the ability to bridge what is historically verifiable with constructed narratives serves as the primary measurement of faith.[26] A fitting example for this is Khadim Hussain Rizvi's tale that when Neil Armstrong first stepped on the moon, he heard the Azan [Muslim call to prayer] and later in life had converted to Islam.[27] Inventing and circulating such narratives has the potential to heighten one's moral status. In Pakistan, where religion and sovereignty are intertwined, the behaviour towards such assertions has immediate consequences for citizenship.[28]

All these tropes and patterns soon played out on a much grander scale through Muhammad Malik Mumtaz Qadri, a police officer in his early twenties from a modest Punjabi background. His action would fuel the rise of the *Tahreek-e-LabaikYa Rasul Allah* [I am here to serve You, Oh Prophet of God], a rowdy movement that promises to uphold blasphemy laws, ban Ahmadis from political participation, and kill anyone who insults the Prophet Muhammad.

II

One of Pakistan's most discussed blasphemy incidents concerned Asia Naureen, a mother of five and a member of Pakistan's increasingly small Christian community.[29] In the summer of 2009, Asia Naureen was plucking *phalsa* (berries) in a field thirty miles east of Lahore when she got into a fight with two Muslim women, who later accused her of having insulted the Prophet Muhammad.[30] A few days later, local Muslim clerics accused Asia of blasphemy. According to Section 295-C of the Pakistan Penal Code, insulting prophets is a criminal offence that carries a mandatory death sentence. Within a few days, the police investigated Asia's case and quickly decided that Asia had blasphemed, despite her vehement denial that she had in any way insulted the Prophet Muhammad.[31]

The Sessions Court in Nankana Sahib, where Asia's blasphemy case was first heard, suspected that a much larger Christian conspiracy was at work in her case, with the purpose of painting a negative image of Muslim countries for mistreatment of minority rights. The judge gave the following explanation as to why he believed the two Muslim women's testimony and not Asia's:

> In our society, normally, the ladies avoid to indulge [sic] in criminal cases even as complaint or witness, particularly the parents of the unmarried and young girls never allow their daughters to go to the police stations or to appear before the Police Officers or in courts in order to record their statements or to face the ridiculous questions of the advocates. But in the instant case, the ladies (PW-2 and PW-3) took all the steps as they could not bear the blasphemy.[32]

Though Asia had never admitted to her guilt, the judge concluded that she had. For him, an exchange of 'hot words' could only be regarded as a euphemism for blasphemy: 'Hot Words should had [sic] not been other than the blasphemy'.[33] With this line of argumentation, Asia was sentenced to death by hanging.

Roughly two years later, in late 2010, Salman Taseer, a businessman turned Governor of Punjab, entered Sheikhupura's district jail with his daughter and wife to collect Asia's thumbprint for a presidential pardon.[34] Governors are not often seen in prison. In a case involving insults against the Prophet Muhammad, most politicians would have avoided such public exposure.[35] Taseer, however, was a different kind of politician. As a young man, he had worked in Zulfikar Ali Bhutto's Pakistan Peoples Party, and later penned an authoritative biography of his former party chief. One of the points that Taseer bickered over regarding Bhutto was his timid stance against the ulema on the question of excluding Ahmadis from the fold of Islam. Taseer believed that Bhutto had unnecessarily ceded ground to the religious factions when he could have defended Pakistan's religious minorities.[36]

Now in his late sixties, and with a constitutional position endowing him limited sovereign power, Salman Taseer sought to rectify the line his party had taken under Zulfikar and Benazir. To do so, he first turned around from the wooden chair from which he was addressing the gathered journalists in Sheikhupura jail, leaned on a vast table draped in green cloth with miniature flags to his left and an array of microphones pointing in his direction, and verified that the fully veiled woman behind him was indeed Asia. Then he asked her to put a thumbprint on the appeal for pardoning and went on to give the following short speech:

> I want to begin in the name of Allah who is merciful. I have come here to meet Asia Bibi. She has been in jail for two and a half years and has been sentenced to death. I believe that her death sentence is an exaggerated and cruel punishment. Asia has just filed an appeal to the President of Pakistan, Asif Ali Zardari, asking him for clemency. I hope the President will accept her appeal out of humanitarian reasons.

I just want to add one thing. In Qaid-e-Azam Muhammad Ali Jinnah's time there was no such law [blasphemy law]. It would have been impossible for such a law to pass the legislature or be applied in courts during Jinnah's time. Our religion obliges us to take minority rights seriously. Pakistan's founder added a white stripe to the flag to signify the protection and recognition of minorities. Therefore, I believe, that the verdict against Asia Bibi is in contradiction to humanitarian values. As the Governor of Punjab, I am the constitutional head of this state. That is why this appeal has come to me first. I will now submit it to the President. *Inshallah* [God willing] her sentence will be waived soon. Ninety-nine percent of our population is Muslim. With this many Muslims, it is clear that nobody can attack the honour of the Prophet. I have studied the file and am convinced that no such incident took place. This is a poor woman. She had no legal representation during her trials. It would have been difficult for her to finance lawyers, given that she is poor.[37]

A few months later, at a meeting with students from Government College Lahore, Taseer stressed that he did not want to go into a theological argument of what the punishment for a *gustakhi* [insult] against the Prophet ought to be in Islamic jurisprudence. Rather, his was an appeal for Asia's release based on humanitarian grounds [*insaniyat*]; enlightened and progressive thought [*roshana aur taraqiyaafta khiyal*]; and ultimately due to several procedural failings evident in her case as Asia had been without proper legal assistance during her first trial.[38] Since the implementation of Sharia law had resulted in her punishment, and Sharia law was part of state law, Pakistan's President could pardon Asia.[39]

His statement caused friction with clerics for several reasons. During a protest meeting against Taseer's plea for clemency at the Lahore Press Club, the firebrand Khadim Hussain Rizvi and Pir Afzal Qadri thundered that any alteration to the blasphemy laws itself constituted blasphemy.[40] They demanded that the Chief Justice of Pakistan immediately depose Taseer.[41] Lawyers from the bar associations in Sheikhupura, Nankana, and Ferozewala amplified Rizvi's views. 'The court has found her [Asia] guilty of blasphemy offences. How could the Governor declare her as innocent?' roused one of their ring leaders.[42]

More established Barelvi ulema criticised the line of reasoning that Rizvi had taken. These ulema were less concerned with Taseer's plea for the annulment of Asia's punishment. Instead, it was Taseer's refuge to humanity and secular enlightenment reason that was the source of their problem with his statement. Such an assertion would highlight, they argued, a tension of competing universalities.[43] '[S]o-called NGOs were opposing the [blasphemy] law on behalf of America.'[44] Tasser, they alleged, had painted Islam as inhumane and liberalism as the saviour of humanity.[45] This juxtaposition formed the nub of their problem. Ameer Hamza of the *Tehreek-e-Hurmat-e-Rasool* captured this sentiment succinctly when he alleged that the Western framing of Taseer's view of Islam was a form of 'intellectual terrorism'.[46] None of the ulema acknowledged that Taseer was not talking about Islam when he uttered the word 'cruel' but rather the institution of the death penalty.

Other orthodox Sunni clerics identified scope for improvement on the procedural side regarding Asia's case. While the courts had meted out the death penalty to Asia following scriptural requirements, some clerics suggested that the procedural demands in Islamic jurisprudence for such measures are a lot stricter than what the Penal Court had probed. In Asia's case, the judge had taken the witness accounts at face value. Asia thus had to prove ulterior motives to shake the validity of their testimony. A Qazi, however, would have probed the witnesses' statement according to a much higher standard. Had it not been for this procedural slip up of secular law, these scholars claimed, the establishment of truth in Asia's case could have led to her release based on insufficient evidence.

Other Barelvi pirs like Tahir-ul-Qadri, the founder of Minhaj-ul-Quran, an NGO funded overwhelmingly by the Pakistani diaspora in Scandinavia, argued that by siding with Asia the Governor had not blasphemed against the Prophet, yet.[47] Taseer's view that Asia's violation of the Prophet's honour should not result in the state taking her life could not itself constitute blasphemy. Tahir-ul-Qadri suggested that there were conflicting opinions regarding punishment in the classical works of Islamic jurisprudence. Taseer's statements asking for more lenient sentencing were entirely compatible with Islamic legal thought. Yet Tahir-ul-Qadri condemned Taseer and emphasised that he continued to support the death penalty for Asia because she had committed blasphemy.[48]

Taseer's colleagues in the PPP did not speak in one voice to circumvent the death penalty for Asia's alleged acts. Addressing journalists at the Lahore Press Club, Jehangir Badar, the PPP's secretary-general, for instance, clearly distanced himself from Taseer's statements.[49] As the Governorship was not a party office and Taseer's membership had been resting for the time of his appointment, Taseer's actions were not the responsibility of the party.[50] It helped that General Musharraf had appointed Taseer as Governor and not Zardari. The interior minister of Pakistan, Rehman Malik, outspokenly endorsed Asia's punishment and underlined that he would shoot and kill any blasphemer himself (though he later recanted that this was just an allegory, and he was merely referring to the 'bullet of the law').[51] Babar Awan, the law minister, declared that 'no one should think of finishing' blasphemy laws.[52] Sherry Rehman was among a handful of politicians who backed Taseer publicly. She even tabled a private member's bill in parliament to remove the death penalty for blasphemy, though she had to withdraw it under severe pressure shortly after its introduction.[53] Taseer's plea to Zardari was circumvented by the Lahore High Court, which banned Zardari from pardoning Asia. Taseer used this moment to clarify that he had not sought an outright abolition of blasphemy, nor did he consider it a 'black law'. Instead, his only argument was that the law had been misused, and that politicians had to find a way to tame it.[54]

Despite these attempts at clarification, Taseer was facing increased pressure on multiple fronts. In early January 2011, to express their dismay over Taseer's statements on blasphemy laws, the Mall Road Traders Association called for a complete strike, leaving most shops in Lahore closed.[55] The *Majlis-e-Tahaffuz-e-Khatme Nabuwwat*, one of the primary organisational vehicles for plotting the 1953 Lahore riots, called for a nationwide general strike. Modelling their intervention on the Mall Road Traders Association's enthusiasm, they brought Karachi and many other cities to a standstill.[56] During another demonstration of the newly founded *Tehreek-e-Tahafuze-e-*

Namoos-e-Risalat Pakistan, led by Allama Razai Mustafa Naqashbandi in Bahawalpur, an effigy of Salman Taseer was burned.[57] While all these protests were going on, Taseer found some distraction at a charity event at the Lahore Polo Club, where, in a breath-taking sixth chukker, Master Paints scored the seventh goal for a close victory against Diamond Paints.[58]

On 3 January, Taseer arrived in Islamabad. The next day, he went for a hearty French onion soup and a plate of spicy masala prawn at an expat bistro called Table Talk in Kohsar market.[59] Leaving Table Talk, he walked a few steps to his car parked just outside the restaurant. Taseer was travelling with a heavy security protocol. More than a dozen armed 'Elite Force' commandos, a unit of the Punjab Police established to fight terrorists and conduct VIP security duties, were milling around him.[60] When Taseer was about to open the door to his vehicle, one of his security men pointed an AK-47 assault rifle at him and fired the entire thirty-round magazine.[61] Taseer fell to the ground and died immediately. Mumtaz Qadri, the twenty-five-year-old shooter, slowly put down his empty rifle and kneeled to the ground with his arms raised. He was then arrested by his colleagues.[62] Later, at the local police station, Mumtaz Qadri submitted the following statement to justify his murder:

> On the faithful day, I being member of the Elite Force I was deployed as one of the member of the Escort Guard of Salman Taseer, the Governor Punjab. In Koh-i-Sar Market, the Governor with another after having lunch in a restaurant walked to his vehicle. In adjoining mosque I went for urinating in the washroom and for making ablution. When I came out with my gun, I came across Salman Taseer. Then I had the occasion to address him, 'your honour being the Governor had remarked about blasphemy law as black law, if so it was unbecoming of you' Upon this he suddenly shouted and said, 'Not only that it is black law, but also it is my shit'. Being a Muslim I lost control and under grave and sudden provocation, I pressed the trigger and he lay dead in front of me. I have no repentance and I did it for 'Tahafuz-i-Namoos-i-Rasool' [Protection of the Prophet's Sanctity] Salman offered me grave and sudden provocation. I was justified to kill him.[63]

Qadri's attempt to justify his actions as a response to a 'sudden and grave provocation' very much conformed to the legal language used in courts to defend religiously motivated murders. Its use is deliberate and goes to show that Qadri had thought about the issue of his legal defence at some length. The image of Taseer dining in an exclusive restaurant while his bodyguard used the local mosque to urinate excmplified more than just flagging class disparities. Qadri juxtaposes exclusive secular pockets of leisure against inclusive religious spaces of necessity. Building on this, Qadri also argued that 'Taseer had proved himself as an infidel'. To substantiate this claim, Qadri marshalled evidence from the semi-autobiographical novel of Taseer's son. In the book, Taseer's son had outlined the Western habits of his father. Citing those paragraphs at some length, Qadri insisted that the prosecution should now first prove that Taseer had been a pious Muslim before they could move on to punish him for Taseer's killing.[64] If the prosecution failed to show that Taseer had been a believer, Qadri maintained that he had merely exercised his Islamic duty for killing an apostate.

It is unlikely that a tell-all book written by Taseer's estranged son in English had roused Qadri's condemnation.[65] It must have been transmitted to him through other ways. Qadri had been a regular visitor at gatherings of the extremist Barelvi group *Dawat-e-Islami*, whose preachers frequently evoke 'Ghazi' Ilm Din and 'Ghazi' Abdul Rashid. In these meetings, the notion of sacrifice for the Prophet Muhammad's honour was highlighted as the highest spiritual achievement. Unlike the Deobandi movement's attempt to regard the Prophet as a mere human who died a human death, Barelvis see the Prophet as part human and part light [*nur*]. According to one Barelvi doctrine, the Prophet Muhammad existed in some primordial form well before humans inhabited the planet and continued to exist well after his bodily demise. Barelvis ascribe the knowledge of the unseen to the Prophet Muhammad, which is to say that he possesses a universal intellect derived directly from God. They also call him *Hazir-o-Nazir* [present at multiple places at the same time], an attribute Deobandis reserve solely to Allah. Barelvis, on the other hand, favour a departure from the supremacy of enlightenment reason and promote a romantic drowning in *ishq* [obsessive love] through the remembrance of the Prophet Muhmmad. In this way, Barelvis aim to actively depict the hollowness of both enlightenment reason and the Deobandi notion that the Prophet Muhammad can be confined to the category of man.

Shortly before Taseer's murder, Qadri attended the sermons of Hanif Qureshi.[66] Qureshi had trained at the Barelvi madrassa *Jamia Rizwia Zia-ul-Uloom* in Rawalpindi and was a frequent speaker at religious gatherings. Like many other wandering clerics of his generation, Qureshi had matured on stage, performing hymns with glittering fairy lights in the background. His voice drowned well in echo, an essential requirement for future stars.[67] Ever since Taseer had spoken in favour of Asia's release, Qureshi had developed a segment in his speeches that would vilify the Governor. Qureshi went so far as to advocate for Taseer's killing openly.[68] For this reason, he was amongst the first arrested after Taseer's death, though the police released him on bail almost immediately.[69]

Many of Qadri's sermons at the time followed a strictly rehearsed pattern. Qureshi would begin by glorifying Ilm Din's murder of Rajpal and Abdul Rasheed's killing of Swami Shraddhanand. Then Qureshi would emphasise how Ilm Din and Abdul Rasheed, though entirely illiterate, managed to affirm their faith through acts of killing.[70] Qureshi would then go on to claim that he and the audience were the rightful heirs of the legacy these martyrs had left.[71] At this stage of his sermons, he would frequently become possessed by some intense form of emotional fervour and either start crying or suddenly stand up, drum his chest, and make exaggerated gestures.[72] In his most memorable meeting, held shortly after Taseer's press conference with Asia, Qureshi performed the following:

> We are the heirs of Ghazi Ilm Din Shaheed. We are the heirs of Ghazi Abdul Rasheed Shaheed. [...] [shoving the microphone to one side, Qureshi stands up and, overcome with emotions, begins gesticulating widely] If our country begins to pardon those charged for insults against the Prophet Muhammad under Section 295-C, then it should be known that Allah has given us the courage to take matters in our own hands. We know how to shoot guns. We know how to fire bullets. And we know how to slit the throats of those who have insulted the Prophet.[73]

Qureshi employed emotions to lay an authoritative claim to a history of martyrdom.[74] Having clarified the genealogy of Ilm Din and Abdul Rasheed to Pakistan's blasphemy laws, Qureshi stressed that Muslims were no longer able to control themselves once confronted with insults against the Prophet Muhammad. Murder for Qureshi was an automatic response that followed blasphemy.

> We are very polite [he uses the English word] people. We are peaceful people. But I swear by the honour of Allah that when someone insults and dishonours the Prophet Muhammad it feels like [at this stage Qureshi bursts into shouting] our chests are pierced through with bullets. That is why we cannot bear to see anyone alive who has insulted the Prophet. I say without hesitation, even if the government is listening to these words, write them down. Release the dog [Taseer] from your protection, and you will witness how even his dead body will not be recognisable. Let him out. How can someone insult the Prophet and still be alive in Pakistan? Will he die from your prayers alone or through your bullets? [Crowd cheers: Through bullets]. Tell me how will he die? [Crowd: Through bullets] Yes, he will die through bullets.[75]

Such interludes become less impressive when one considers that Qureshi performed them with equal gusto when speaking about women wearing nail polish.[76] By framing Muslims as 'polite' and 'peaceful people', Qureshi was already hinting at what constituted the exception: the moment when they stop being polite. For Qureshi, if triggered with the right provocative stimulus, in this case, insults of the Prophet Muhammad, Muslims were entitled to fire bullets. In other meetings, Qureshi emphasised how Taseer had strayed from Islamic norms and may well have been an agent of a foreign force that sought to disintegrate Pakistan. He suspected this force of taking orders from the Jewish freemasonry.

> Today these despicable oppressing devils are running their tongues against the Prophet Muhammad, funded by the Jews. Our shameless Governor is an apostate [murtad]. In his intoxication [with alcohol], he is yelling out rubbish against

the Prophet. 'What does it matter if someone has insulted the Prophet?' *Astagfirullah* [I seek forgiveness from Allah] [...] Let me tell him that even a person who insults the shoes that touched the Prophet's feet is an apostate and deserves to be killed [*wajib'ul qatal*].[77]

To condition the appropriate emotive reaction to insults of the Prophet, Qureshi frequently disrupted his speech with cheers to incite the crowd for participation. 'The only appropriate punishment for blasphemy against the Prophet is [crowds screaming in response: 'death']'.[78] Qadri may have drawn from this emotional and conceptual architecture to respond to Taseer's alleged blasphemy with the immediate intention to kill. In the aftermath of Taseer's murder, Asif Ali Zardari withdrew from Asia's case and left it to the judiciary. Like many other PPP leaders and most clerics, he also avoided Taseer's funeral prayer. According to *The Economist*, even Pakistan's army chief hesitated to condemn the killing for fear that his troops may side with Qadri.[79]

An Anti-Terrorism Court in Rawalpindi sentenced Qadri to death for murder in October 2011.[80] Such Anti-Terrorism Courts were originally installed in 1997, under Nawaz Sharif's rule, to deliver speedy justice in cases that involved terrorism.[81] The term was defined in the broadest possible way to encompass any act that could potentially 'strike terror in people'.[82] Qadri had admitted to the killing, but objected to the charge of murder under sections 302 and 109 of the Pakistan Penal Code. Despite his acknowledgement of the killing, the prosecution still rallied fourteen witnesses and placed a report from the Forensic Science Laboratory before the Court to prove that Qadri was indeed the shooter.

During Qadri's early days in prison, hundreds of madrassa students began demonstrating daily outside the jail where he was kept and loudly demanding his release. After Qadri was moved to death row in Adiala and awaited his appeal hearing at Islamabad High Court, the protests grew in size and even involved some coordination efforts between otherwise rival Barelvi madrassas. Disparate militant Barelvi groups joined forces with Khadim Hussain Rizvi and Pir Afzal Qadri in the *Tahreek-e-Rehai Mumtaz Qadri*

[Movement for the Liberation of Mumtaz Qadri]. After receiving death threats for openly criticising blasphemy laws, Pakistan's only Christian cabinet minister, Shahbaz Bhatti, published an article in which he exclaimed that 'I was told that if I continued the campaign against blasphemy law, I would be assassinated. I will be beheaded. But forces of violence and extremism cannot threaten me'.[83] Four gunmen wielding Kalashnikovs killed Bhatti in March 2011.

III

In October 2014, Judge Muhammad Anwaarul Haq and Judge Syed Shabaz Ali Rizvi confirmed Asia's death sentence at the Lahore High Court.[84] Framing Asia as a 'Christian Preacher', they went into some detail about her alleged insults to the Prophet Muhammad. Then the judges determined that Asia's two fellow workers were credible witnesses. They also held that Asia could not prove they had acted based on 'previous enmity, ill will or ulterior motive of the eye witnesses'.[85] Asia's defence team had argued that these witnesses should be vetted according to Islamic Law, where the principle of *Tazkiyah al Shuhood* [mode of judicial inquiry] lays out truthfulness criteria.[86] Witnesses often fail to live up to the high standards required therein. While acknowledging that an application of Islamic legal standards may have led to a different decision, Judges Rizvi and Haq suggested in their verdict that the Government of Pakistan should take up this issue and amend the procedural laws accordingly. Until then, they could only confirm the Sessions Court's death sentence.[87]

There was considerable pressure on the Lahore High Court to uphold the death verdict. Khadim Hussain Rizvi, Pir Afzal Qadri and Hanif Qureshi, the leading lights of a burgeoning Barelvi militancy, mobilised thousands of their followers to take to the streets. Fearing that the decision of the Lahore High Court may overturn the death sentence of the lower courts, as was traditional convention in such cases for decades, a dozen lawyers of Attaullah Shah Bukhari's *khatam-e-nabuwwat* movement were present in Court.[88] Together with the *Tahreek-e-Rehai Mumtaz Qadri,* they celebrated the ruling as a great victory for their cause of protecting the Prophet's honour.

Emboldened by this victory, Khadim Hussain Rizvi, wheelchair-bound after a car crash in 2009, further increased his street presence to have Mumtaz Qadri released. A gifted orator, able to seamlessly change from Iqbal's Persian verses to Punjabi expletives, Rizvi's *Tahreek-e-Rehai Mumtaz Qadri* quickly grew in size. Much of its membership consisted of the lumpen-youth and the politically disenfranchised. Rizvi gave them a purpose and an institutional vehicle to demand political rights. In the name of the Prophet Muhammad, the widespread feeling amongst his devotees went, the poor masses could hold those in leadership positions to account and, going further, even stake their claim for political participation.[89] And at the same time, they could also have some fun burning tyres during street rallies.[90] Yet, Rizvi's reach extended beyond such disenfranchised groups. His constant exploration of the philosophical and historical background of the Pakistan movement and the role of Prophet Muhammad therein made him palatable to senior civil servants, army officers and lawyers.

Despite Rizvi flexing his street muscle, the bench at Islamabad High Court dismissed Qadri's appeal. Qadri had received an impressive defence, counting two retired judges from the Lahore High Court in his team. They argued that Qadri had acted in the heat of the moment. Thus his actions would not warrant the death penalty. Nazir Ahmed Ghazi, one of his lawyers, claimed that Qadri had also acted to defend the honour of the Prophet and in such cases, the perpetrator would always be overcome with rage, which constituted grounds for a sentence reduction.[91] Nazir Ahmed also complained that Qadri's indictment suffered from irredeemable procedural error as it should have been brought before an Anti-Terrorism Court.[92] But Nazir Ahmed's most crucial contribution was his evocation of deep history that laid bare the roots of the grievance:

> In the interviews that [Taseer's] son and daughter gave, we got to know what Taseer was about to do [next]. His next step was to undo the constitutional ban of Qadiani's from the Muslim fold. This was his plan. When I was touring Europe somebody said that Taseer's daughter has also come here. A young engineer

reported this to me. And he said that the entire function she participated in was organised by Qadianis. Ninety-five percent of the people at her talk were Qadiani.[93]

For the movement defenders of Qadri, the creation of Pakistan was a reward from Allah for the great sacrifice of Ilm Din. Nazir Ahmed fleshed out this point in detail at a later speech at the Shah Ahmad Noorani Convention, a gathering organised by the Jamiat Ulema-e-Pakistan to remember the religious and political contribution of Noorani, especially his efforts to declare Ahmadis non-Muslim. Here Nazir Ahmed said the following: 'Ghazi Ilm Din Shaheed gave his sacrifice in 1929. Allah said that you have sacrificed yourself for my beloved Prophet. March on People! For the deeds of the Prophet of Arabia and the deeds of Ghazi Ilm Din Shaheed, I will give you a *Mumlikat Khudadad* [God-gifted Dominion]. Pakistan is the fruit of this.'[94]

By 2015, around the time Islamabad High Court dismissed his appeal, Mumtaz Qadri had become a household name.[95] To determine whether one was 'secular' or 'religious' in one's stance towards Qadri, the question was no longer if one considered him a murderer. In an increasingly self-censoring public sphere, it moved to whether one thought Qadri had the right to take the law into his own hands. Qadri owed his fame partly to the high profile of Salman Taseer. Partly, however, his fame was due to the charismatic orations of Khadim Hussain Rizvi, who spun hagiographical tales around Qadri's sentencing that anchored themselves in the evocative dispute between the nineteenth-century legal scholar Khairtabad and his disagreement with Shah Ismail Dehlvi.[96] Rizvi also argued that Qadri's killing was in accordance with the sunnah, the teachings and practices of the Prophet Muhammad:

> [With their verdict to uphold Qadri's death sentence] these judges have erected an idol. And they are now demanding that we obey and pray to this idol. They themselves have failed to obey the ruling of my beloved Prophet Muhammad. We have five Divine rulings that the *sahaba* [companions of the Prophet Muhammad] killed women and men. Then when they came to report their deeds to Huzur [Honourable term to refer to the

Prophet Muhammad]. [Rizvi goes on to stage a conversation between one of the *sahaba* and the Prophet Muhammad]

[Sahaba:] Huzur, I have killed my sister.

[Prophet Muhammad:] Why did you kill her?

[Sahaba:] She insulted the glory of my Master [the Prophet Muhammad].

[Prophet Muhammad:] Then go, her blood has no value![97]

From his jail cell in Adiala, a small village next to the garrison-town Rawalpindi, where Bhutto had also spent his last days, Qadri sporadically recorded and shared devotional songs on the exalted status of the Prophet Muhammad. As a free man, Qadri was a regular at *Dawat-e-Islami* gatherings showcasing his vocal talent and correspondingly his devotion. In one such event, he had even worn the Elite Police uniform with an AK-47 draped around his torso while chanting one of the most popular Barelvi hymns, '*Ya Rasul Allah Tere Chahne Walo ki Khair* [Oh Prophet, blessings be on those who like You].'[98] Immediately after his arrest, Qadri offered another melodic interlude by repeating the same *naat*, though with his hands cuffed behind his back and tied to a chair.[99]

In 2015, the Supreme Court of Pakistan heard Qadri's final appeal. The three Justices, headed by Asif Saeed Khan Khosa, reduced the legal implications of this case to a single point: whether vigilante action against alleged blasphemers triggered by insults on the Prophet Muhammad, should constitute mediating circumstances. The Justices answered with a resounding no. They reasoned that following such a rationale would allow any individual to become the 'complainant, prosecutor, judge and executioner'.[100] For the Justices, there were also no grounds for reducing Qadri's sentence. '[T]he appellant had acted cruelly and brutally' and therefore deserved no 'sympathy to be shown to him in the matter of his sentence'.[101] Qadri's only path to avoid the death penalty was a clemency appeal to President Mamnoon Hussain. This was not an avenue that Qadri wanted to take. Standing in his jail cell, in front of a wall plastered with images of Arabian mosques, Qadri announced that he considered a request for clemency to be against the principles of the Sharia:

I have not appealed to the President for mercy. I have not applied and will not apply. I consider it against the Sharia. Here I follow the opinions of the learned scholars Hazrat Allama Hafiz [all honorific titles] Khadim Hussain Rizvi, Hazrat Allama Dr Ashraf Asif Jalali, and Mufti Hanif Qureishi Qari and those who argue for justice. [Then kissing his thumbs and placing them on his eyes, Qadri begins to recite a poem.] The servants of Muhammad are not afraid to lay down their lives. They are not concerned with their head remaining attached to their body or cut off from it. We love Allah and his Prophet. In both worlds, our boat will cross to the other side. In service of the Prophet, we accept death. Mumtaz Qadri is prepared, *insh'Allah*.[102]

While Qadri did not appeal for clemency himself, his father filed a request on his behalf. But the appeal was swiftly rejected, and Qadri eventually hanged.[103] Khadi Hussain Rizvi visited Qadri's body in Rawalpindi and rubbed his turban against his feet to signal respect. Rizvi then led a huge funeral procession with over one hundred thousand people to Liaquat Park and its surrounding streets.[104] Most religious leaders came out in support of Rizvi or decided to remain silent on this issue. Only a handful came out against the celebration of Qadri's martyrdom. One of these scholars, Javed Ahmad Ghamidi, deeply entrenched in traditional *fiqh*, pointed out that there was no scope in Islamic jurisprudence for either blasphemy laws or killings in defence of the Prophet's honour. Arguments to the contrary, Ghamidi observed dryly, could not anchor themselves in a single Quranic verse and were, at best, relying on feeble Hadith that former ulema had frequently dismissed as weak.[105]

Despite failing in its political cause to save Qadri's life, let alone free him, Rizvi's *Tahreek-e-Rehai Mumtaz Qadri* had won the most potent political symbol on the Indian subcontinent: a martyr. With this martyrdom in tow, Rizvi entered electoral politics. He did this by first renaming his movement *Tahreek-e-Labaik Ya Rasul Allah* and soon after establishing a dedicated political wing, the *Tahreek-e-Labaik Pakistan* (TLP). Its twenty-point manifesto appears to have been put together in haste and only acquires meaning when viewed through the lens of Rizvi's longstanding anti-Ahmadi agenda. As its ultimate objective, the TLP seeks to defend Pakistan's blasphemy laws and to ban Ahmadis from calling themselves Muslim. Rizvi also promised that he would protect the honour of the Prophet Muhammad globally through all available means. Such vows to protection include the usage of nuclear weapons to prevent insults against the Prophet Muhammad. When the Dutch anti-Islam politician Geert Wilders announced a cartoon competition on the Prophet Muhammad in 2018 and again in 2019, Rizvi roared that the appropriate response would be 'to drop an atom bomb on Holland'.[106]

With controversial statements like these, Rizvi's popularity soared. He began to think bigger. In early October 2017, the ruling Pakistan Muslim League Nawaz (PML-N) bulldozed an Election Act through Parliament to secure a political afterlife for the corruption-tarred Nawaz Sharif. Shortly before parliament passed the Election Act, the Supreme Court removed Nawaz Sharif from office for dishonesty in financial matters. As the PML-N had put together the Act in great haste, it contained what looked like a clerical error. In Form A of the Election Commission, which all Muslim candidates must sign to run for office, section (iii) had been modified. Here the words 'I solemnly swear' had been cut, though it still featured the obligatory declaration on the finality of Prophethood and that the candidate applying to run was not an Ahmadi.[107] It is reasonable to assume that softening blasphemy laws was not any of Nawaz Sharif immediate political concerns.

After this error came to light, Nawaz's law minister Zahid Hamid tabled an amendment that fixed the mistake and reverted the declaration to an oath.[108] All of this happened within two weeks. Yet, Rizvi interpreted Nawaz's action as a full-fledged attack on the Prophet Muhammad and the principle of the finality of Prophethood. He demanded that Zahid Hamid, who had introduced the controversial changes into Parliament, be prosecuted on blasphemy charges and hanged. Alternatively, he could also resign. Rizvi also claimed that Hamid was a closeted Ahmadi.[109] To emphasise that he was serious about Hamid's resignation, Rizvi occupied the Faizabad interchange, one of Islamabad's main entrance and exit points. Only a few hundred men were with him. Right at the beginning of this dharna (sit-in/protest), Rizvi lifted Qadri's seven-year-old son on stage. While Rizvi was rhythmically moving his hands, Qadri's son, wearing a decorated green turban and a white *shalwar kameez*, sang '*inqilab laye ga, khoon mere papa ka*', the blood of my father will usher in a revolution.[110] As the state did not intervene in the protests, more men joined the dharna, and it soon ballooned to several thousand people.

Rizvi had a keen understanding of politics. His dharna virtually paralysed Islamabad and Rawalpindi, the twin cities that house most state institutions. Emergency vehicles could not get to hospitals, and many commuters could not reach their schools, colleges, and universities. Several opposition parties sought to associate themselves with the TLP to vent their grievances against the government. Imran Khan's *Pakistan Tehreek-e-Insaf*, for instance, participated in the protest through audio messages.[111] After the government failed to disperse the protesters, they requested the army to step in.[112] Before the situation could escalate, Zahid Hamid resigned. Rizvi had fought with the state and emerged victorious. Through the media exposure that he had received, the TLP had become known throughout Pakistan.[113] That a sit-in mixed with speeches whipping up religious sentiments around the Prophet Muhammad had led the state to falter enticed Rizvi to give up all semblance of modesty. In his last sermon at the Faizabad dharna, Rizvi told the gathered crowds: 'if you want to conquer Kashmir, just organise two of my speaking events there.'[114]

IV

On 31 October 2018, the Supreme Court ordered Asia's release.[115] The Justices ruled that the witnesses had not been credible and that there was no other evidence to prove Asia had committed blasphemy. In principle, they upheld the tenets on which blasphemy legislation rests. They referred to Ilm Din with the honourable title 'Ghazi' and 'Shaheed'.[116]

Only months earlier, the TLP had shown an impressive electoral performance in the 2018 general elections, bagging over 2.2 million votes, which made them the fifth largest political party in Pakistan and the third in the crucial Punjab province. Imran Khan's Tehreek-e-Insaf won the largest vote share, and Khan took the oath as Prime

Minister. During his time in opposition Imran Khan had rallied hard to uphold the blasphemy laws and defend the finality of Prophethood.[117] Once in power, it briefly looked like Khan was reverting to a more liberal attitude that one would assume given his Aitchison and Oxford education. He appointed Atif Mian, a Princeton professor and an Ahmadi convert, to his economic council.[118] However, after a tiff with the TLP, he quickly withdrew his support for Mian.[119] Taking this as a precedent, TLP leaders also pressured Imran Khan to halt Asia's release. Pir Afzal Qadri alleged an elaborate conspiracy that involved Jewish agents, the United States, and Ahmadis. He also declared all three Justices who had participated in the ruling had become *wajib-ul-qatl*. 'If you kill them you will become Ghazi Ilm Din Shaheed. You will become Ghazi Mumtaz Qadri,' he extolled to a cheering crowd in Bahawalpur. 'General Bajwa [the Chief of Army Staff] should also leave the army and take all the other Qadianis with him.'[120]

Rizvi even outdid Pir Afzal Qadri by calling on the armed troops to rebel against the military elite. Despite such announcements, the government negotiated a deal with the TLP in which they agreed to review Asia's case and ban her from leaving the country. In return, the TLP called off their 'march of millions' to Karachi. Soon afterwards, however, the police locked up Pir Afzal Qadri and Rizvi. To keep calm public sentiments about these arrests, Pakistan's information minister Chaudhary Fawad Hussain tweeted that their arrests had 'nothing [to do] with Asia Bibi case [sic].'[121]

With the two most outspoken critics of her release detained on treason charges, and protests of hard-line Barelvis gradually winding down, the government facilitated Asia's escape to Canada. Meanwhile, the state intensified pressure on the TLP to backtrack on their statements regarding the killing of Pakistan's three highest judges and, perhaps more importantly, the accusation that General Bajwa was an Ahmadi. In late April 2019, Afzal Qadri resigned from all TLP office and apologised. 'I suffer from heart failure, stroke, kidney problems, diabetes, and high blood pressure. For these health reasons, I was overcome with emotions when I heard the ruling in the Asia case. I now apologise to my government, the judiciary, and to the Chief of Army Staff for what I said in that moment.'[122]

Rizvi was more resilient. After his release, he ducked public attention for a while but emerged with a revamped social media presence and videos highly critical of Imran Khan's domestic and foreign policy. Rizvi's solutions never matched the problems he sought to tackle. For instance, he proposed that Pakistan's reliance on foreign debt could be ended by paying government employees less. Regarding foreign policy, he was blatantly hawkish. He believed that Imran Khan should threaten India's Prime Minister Narendra Modi with open warfare. This threat alone would suffice, Rizvi thought, perhaps extrapolating from his own dharna experience, to resolve all their thorny foreign policy disputes.

Despite an Anti-Terrorism Court ruling against 86 TLP workers in January 2020 for their disruptive protests in the aftermath of the Supreme Court releasing Asia, Rizvi continued to celebrate the killings of blasphemers.[123] Ilm Din served as the primary conceptual vehicle through which Rizvi articulated his new vision for Pakistan. Throughout dozens of sermons, Rizvi attached more glorifying tales to Ilm Din. In tandem with the adoration of Ilm Din, Rizvi attacked Mirza Ghulam Ahmad.[124] When a Pashtun teenager shot dead an Ahmadi man accused of blasphemy in a Peshawar courtroom, Rizvi exclaimed in front of an enthused audience: 'This man said that he was a Prophet. What else could Ghazi Khalid [the shooter] have done but slaughter him.'[125]

***

Come spring 2020, with Covid-19 cases surging in Pakistan and around the world, Rizvi and other hardline clerics vehemently denied the existence of the disease. They opposed government orders to close down mosques to contain the spread. While not medically trained, Rizvi confidently asserted that pious Muslims were immune from contracting and succumbing to the disease. Narrating a saying from the Prophet Muhammad, where he hinted that he liked sweets, Rizvi also claimed that no Muslim could catch diabetes from excessive sugar intake. Rizvi had gone far beyond what the state once hoped would constitute a 'softer' Sufi Islam to counteract jihadi militancy. With a carefully curated genealogy that understood Pakistan's existence as a divine gift for the deeds of Ilm Din and Abdul Rasheed, Rizvi had instead challenged the state's monopoly on the use of force. Rizvi openly proposed a new militancy that endorsed individuals to kill to defend the honour of the Prophet Muhammad.[126]

The heroes of these new militants are 'Ghazi' Aamir Cheema, 'Ghazi' Mumtaz Qadri, 'Ghazi' Faisal Khalid, and after his death of respiratory issues during his second Faizabad dharna, 'Ghazi' Khadim Hussain Rizvi.[127] Rizvi had staged his last dharna to force Imran Khan's government and the military leadership to 'get out the atom bomb and declare jihad on France,' after French President Macron's comments on Islam following a string of attacks carried out by Islamic extremists.[128] 'Let us all die! At least death will spare us the shame on judgement day for having failed to defend the honour of the Prophet Muhammad,' were among Rizvi's last words.[129]

After hearing of Rizvi's death, both the Chief of Army Staff and Imran Khan tweeted their condolences.[130] Amid the raging pandemic, Rizvi's funeral drew more than two hundred thousand mourners to Lahore. It was one of the largest in the city's history— some of Rizvi's followers claim that the funeral was surpassed in size only by Ilm Din's in 1929.[131]

CONCLUSION

Over at least the past 150 years, blasphemy against the Prophet Muhammad has stirred Muslims towards political activism. In India, this activism has included the cry for divine intervention, the desire for legislation and constitutional amendments, and individual acts of killing. These events have sculpted and propelled Muslim nationalism in the mid-twentieth century and defined the citizen–state relationship in Pakistan ever since. They continue to have an enormous impact on Pakistan's ethical, legal, and political landscape today.

In the first three chapters, this book has contextualised the emergence of the trope of the Prophet Muhammad's vulnerability as rising in tandem with a distinctly Hindu political consciousness spurred by the Arya Samaj and later the Hindu Mahasabha. These groups also tilled the soil and planted the seed of Hindu nationalism.[1] Departing from the conventional canon, chapter one has rooted the birth of Hindu nationalism in Pandit Lekh Ram's charged encounters with Mirza Ghulam Ahmad. Their debates on history, community, politics, and the Prophet Muhammad's role therein, constituted modern figurations of Hindu–Muslim conflict and the need for political forms that could mediate such conflict.

Through the colonial state's introduction of religion-based electorates through the Indian Councils Act 1909 (Morley-Minto Reforms), the Arya Samaj–Ahmadiyya debate escalated to national importance. As chapter two has mapped, Swami Shraddhanand, a devout follower of Lekh Ram's *mahatma*-wing of the Arya Samaj and a critical member of the Hindu Mahasabha, spearheaded large conversion campaigns in North India. Against Gandhi's principle of *ahimsa*, a Buddhist rejection of violence, Swami Shraddhanand embraced violence in politics and in so doing constructed a Hindu political outside of the All-India National Congress.

Threatened by this vision of a looming Hindu Raj after independence, Indian Muslims increasingly politicised issues over blasphemy from the 1920s, as chapter three revealed, which manifested in killings and demands for changes in the legal framework. This politicisation continued even after partition, though Muslims were now a majority in Pakistan. Issues relating to blasphemy repeatedly pressed Pakistan's successive governments to declare a state of emergency and assert sovereignty. The last three chapters have mapped how blasphemy became one of Pakistan's most crucial political currencies.

Taken together, these chapters have suggested that Pakistan's blasphemy fixation started as a debate between two North Indian revivalist movements to pursue spiritual supremacy. They have shown that Mirza and Lekh Ram's defence of their respective religions, which often transgressed the boundaries of their own faith, later provided the central reference points in debates around blasphemy in Pakistan. Rather than framing these early debates as separate theological discourses, this book has read Hindu and Muslim revivalism in tandem and traced how tensions between these movements produced a novel legal and political grammar with profound impacts for Pakistan.

This book has provided a new perspective for looking at blasphemy's effects on the political and legal development in Pakistan and offered new angles on how religion has come to inform and dominate politics and law in South Asia more broadly. It has also provided the first comprehensive sketch of the role of blasphemy in Pakistan's legal and political history.

More recently, during a passionate speech at the United Nations General Assembly in 2019, Pakistan's prime minister Imran Khan identified insults against the Prophet Muhammad as 'the most important thing' fuelling the global phenomenon of Islamophobia.

'Every two or three years, someone would malign our Prophet—may peace be upon him—and Muslims would react, which led to Islam being labelled an intolerant religion.' According to Khan, Western societies had to understand what the Prophet Muhammad signified to Muslims in order to break this cycle of insult and outrage. '[T]he Prophet lives in our hears', Khan lectured from the rostrum in New York, '[w]hen he is ridiculed or insulted, we feel the pain.' Similar to Western restrictions on freedom of speech regarding Holocaust denial, because such statements would 'cause the Jewish community pain', Imran Khan analogised that freedom of speech should be circumscribed for people who 'insult the [H]oly Prophet and cause us [the Muslim world] pain.'[2]

Imran Khan spoke for many when he projected Pakistan, the first Islamic Republic in modern history, as spearheading the global defence against attacks on the Prophet Muhammad. Internally, this role has allowed Pakistan to control dissent and restrict freedom of expression in all fields of society. It has also enabled the state to tailor a definition of who a good Muslim really is, which increasingly relies on righteous anger as the primary index of one's faith. Externally, this process has exacerbated relationships with states who refuse to curb freedom of expression for blasphemy, and it has also placed Pakistan as a recurring feature in the global news economy for the most spectacular performances of outrage.

This book concludes with a sketch of how Arya Samaj ideas remained salient in Hindu nationalist thought in a short epilogue.

I

On the morning of 27 January 1948, two editors of the *Hindu Rashtra*, a Poona-based Marathi newspaper with strong Hindu Mahasabha leanings, boarded an Air India flight from Bombay to Delhi.[3] Once the plane landed, the two men hopped onto the afternoon train to Gwalior, the erstwhile royal seat of the Scandia dynasty. In Gwalior, they purchased a Barretta M1934 from Jagdish Prasad Goel, a petty arms trader who had stocked up on handguns when British officers were shedding their belongings.[4] With the gun securely hidden in their luggage, the two trotted back to Delhi on the morning train and finally, after covering two thousand kilometres in two days, slept off their travel fatigue in a 'retiring-room' at Delhi's central railway station.[5]

A little after five pm on 30 January, Mohandas Karamchand Gandhi, with his hands resting on his two nieces' shoulders, inched towards the prayer platform in the sprawling gardens of Birla House. A large crowd awaited his arrival, and they opened a narrow lane for Gandhi to pass through. When Gandhi had moved about seven paces into the crowd, one of the *Hindu Rashtra* editors, Nathuram Godse, stepped into the lane and bowed to Gandhi with his hands folded in a ritualistic gesture of deference. Then, obscuring the lines between reverence and revolt, Godse brought out the pistol from Gwalior, aimed at Gandhi, and fired three shots from close range. Gandhi uttered a last 'Hei Ram' before he collapsed.[6]

During the murder trial, Nathuram Godse offered a long list of grievances that had motivated him to kill Gandhi.[7] The main reason was that Godse blamed Gandhi for allowing Indian Muslims to create their own homeland in Pakistan. He also accused Gandhi of misreading and hijacking Indian politics. Godse elaborated that Gandhi had thrown Indian politics into disarray for three decades by uncritically applying political ideas he had developed during his twenty-year-long struggle for civil rights in Africa. As Indians were a minority in South Africa, Godse argued, it was much easier for Gandhi to rally Hindu–Muslim support behind him. Hindu–Muslim interests in South Africa were aligned, Godse reasoned, as they had the same complaints.[8] Their problem was that the 'Boer and the British' treated all Indians as 'door mats', irrespective of their religion.[9] Therefore, Hindu–Muslim unity could serve as the launchpad for the Gandhian political dictum of communal friendship.

In India, however, the British had already undermined solidarity between Hindus and Muslims. Through a 'sinister policy of communal favouritism', the colonial state had pitted Hindus and Muslims against each other. At its most visible, this crystallised in the form of separate electorates.[10] Gandhi's insistence on representing both communities, for Godse, was therefore like 'accepting the generalship of an army divided against itself.'[11] Instead of finding Hindu–Muslim unity, Gandhi's policy of granting Muslims more and more concession in return for their loyalty to accept him as a political leader had sparked 'a huge slaughter of the Hindus, numerous forcible conversions, rape and arson.'[12] For Godse, Gandhi's message of Hindu–Muslim unity as a starting point for Indian nationalism had only produced more communal violence.

Godse showered praise on Swami Shraddhanand, the Arya Samaj leader and reluctant politician. He regarded Shraddhanand as an authoritative and sober countermodel to Gandhi's (non-violent) non-cooperation programme. Godse blamed Gandhi's attack on the writings of the Arya Samaj in the 1920s, labelling them selectively as 'reactionary', 'gutter press', and 'hate speech' for triggering 'a Muslim youth to murder Swami Shraddhanandji within a few months.'[13] A Mahasabha member of a generation that still credited the Arya Samaj for having etched out Hindu politics, Godse lamented the empty shell the Samaj had become after the death of Swami Shraddhanand. '[T]he lure of office and leadership has induced numerous Arya Samajists to play the double game of claiming to be Gandhite Congressmen and Arya Samajists at the same time,' Godse grumbled.[14]

Returning to Dayanand Saraswati, the founder of the Arya Samaj, Godse applauded his doctrine of radical equality by emphasising that they had promoted 'the abolition of untouchability long before the birth of Gandhiji'.[15] For Godse, Dayanand Saraswati's revolutionary reform efforts made it possible for Hindus to think of themselves as a single political force; a force that would not splinter according to a caste logic.

With Gandhi dead, the Nehruvian state clamped down on communal organisation. Within a week, the central government had declared the Rashtriya Swayamsevak Sangh [RSS], a Hindu paramilitary group formed after splintering from the Hindu Mahasabha, 'an unlawful association'.[16] For Jawaharlal Nehru, banning communal organisation from public view was convenient given the looming national elections. It was also a way for the Indian Republic to assert its authority over the former Princely States, who were still figuring out their place in a new India. A large part of the blame for the ban must be shouldered by the RSS as well. 'The R.S.S. in Patiala state,' wrote one incensed member of the state's assembly, 'has celebrated the occasion of Bapu's [Gandhi] death by holding entertainment parties and distributing sweets in various parts of the state.'[17]

The RSS was founded in 1925 by Keshav Baliram Hedgewar, who increasingly felt frustrated with the Hindu Mahasabha's orthodox section and desired to create an institution for Hindu social uplift without any immediate political face.[18] In the Sabha, Hedgewar argued, the early social radicalism of the Arya Samaj leaders like Swami Shraddhanand had given way to a more orthodox caste-affirming philosophy.[19] To counter this development, as one of its early leaders, R.N. Padhye, declared during the Dussehra celebrations of 1939, the RSS's main principle was to 'organise the Hindus of Hindustan irrespective of caste, colour or creed.' Only this unity would 'create in them [Hindus] a sense of solidarity', which would lead them 'to defend the honour of the Hindu religion and nation at any price.'[20]

That the Sangh's split from the Maha Sabha was a return to the principles of the iconoclastic and caste annihilating principles of the Arya Samaj was always in plain sight.[21] Their belligerent stance towards Muslims was a return to the teachings of Pandit Lekh Ram. Already in 1939, Narayan Damodar Savarkar, the brother of the Mahasabha's President Vinayak and RSS founder Ganesh, announced in Nagpur that he saw the RSS mission as allies to the 'Arya Samaj in the fight against the enemies of Hinduism', which for him manifested in 'the British Government, the Muslims and the Congress'.[22]

Golwalkar took over the Sangh's reign as 'commander-in-chief' in 1940.[23] He stood for a more muscular form of nationalism and argued that India could not achieve self-rule 'by begging it from foreigners'.[24] Instead, Indians had to claim *swaraj* through violence. In Golwalkar's evocative words, RSS volunteers should 'worship the goddess of war not by flowers but [only] by sacrifice of lives.'[25] As a political form, Golwalkar favoured dictatorships over democracies, which was in line with the authoritarian structures that pervaded the RSS. It was a blend of European technofascism and Arya Samaj revivalism. A glance over the books the Sangh distributed in 1942 to its twig organisations dotted around the country illustrates this point well. Next to 'Life of Mussolini' and the 'Life of Hitler', the Sangh published and distributed 'Life of Shraddhanand', 'Life of Dayanand Saraswati', and 'Life of Lajpatrai', all Arya Samaj leaders.[26]

Underlying the Sangh's ideology is the unshakable belief that all institutional forces are conspiring to help Muslims win the upper hand over Hindus. Viewed from this angle, the Khilafat movement, an Indian mass movement after the First World War to force the British to uphold the Sultan of Turkey as 'caliph', looked like Muslims pledging allegiance to a political leader outside India. To the Sangh, Gandhi's concession to win Muslim followers for the Congress party looked like a betrayal of Hindu interest. Sangh members thus believed that they had to stay alert, both physically and mentally, spot the danger and be prepared to stand up and fight to prevent harm to the Hindu interest.

While no longer a formal member of the Sangh by the time he shot Gandhi three times in the stomach, Godse had imbibed many of the old Arya Samaj position. His outright return to Swami Shraddhanand in his legal defence further substantiates this link and positions him firmly in the Maha Sabha's social-reformist wing.[27] Vinayak Savarkar endorsed many of these positions as well. Perhaps, for this reason, the government ordered his immediate arrest after Gandhi's killing though he was released soon after. Aged sixty-five and with little direct contact to Godse, the court found that the prosecution's suggestion that 'Savarkar is the person who got the deed done through Nathuram V Godse' was baseless.[28]

A Brahmin from Maharashtra, Savarkar came from the non-Arya Samaj wing of the Hindu Mahasabha and signified the shift that Hindu nationalism took in the 1920s, from northern to central India. His most significant contribution to Hindu nationalism was that he subsumed it under the conventional nationalist pattern of 'Blut, Boden und Kultur': race, territory, and culture. Savarkar began this process well before his notorious 1923 work *Hindutva*, where he celebrated a cultural Hindu-ness, that encompassed all those of Indian ethnic stock regardless of their religious background if, and this is critical, they were willing to acknowledge Hindu civilisational supremacy.[29] While training as a barrister in London in 1906, Savarkar penned *The Indian War of Independence of 1857*, a passionate plea to consider the uprising as a revolution against British rule rather than a sepoy riot.[30] His next book project, in 1907, was a Marathi translation of Mazzini's autobiography, whom Savarkar regarded as an incarnation of the sixteenth-century Hindu saint Ramdas.[31]

By 1911 Savarkar had not just written history but made it. No longer content to look for mere scholarly distinction, Savarkar packed twenty Browning pistols into the luggage of a friend returning to Bombay to help the revolutionary cause. His brother Ganesh picked them up and another co-conspirator, enthused with Savarkar's Marathi translations of Mazzini, shot dead a British collector at a theatre play in the city of Nasik.[32] In a pamphlet accompanying the pistols, Savarkar had made his political ambitions clear: 'Terrorise the officials, English and India, and the collapse of the whole machinery of oppression is not very far. [...] Martyrs will soon cripple the British Government in India.'[33]

For abetment to murder in the 'Nasik conspiracy', the Bombay High Court sentenced Savarkar to transportation for life.[34] Savarkar fought the case from London, but after exhausting his legal remedies, Winston Churchill, then the Secretary of State for Home Affairs, ordered his return to India. Together with two constables, Savarkar boarded the P&O steamship 'Morea'. When the ship docked in Marseilles, Savarkar asked to be taken to the toilet, squeezed through the porthole, swam ashore, sprinted past some dock labourers, and screamed 'Police! Police!' before he ultimately ran into the arms of a French officer.[35] Overwhelmed with the responsibility of caring for an Indian man with water-soaked trousers and no vest, the French officer handed Savarkar over to the British officers who had come running after Savarkar. They took him back to the ship and reached Bombay as scheduled.[36]

A few weeks after the incident, France demanded from the British to hand over Savarkar.[37] For France, the British officers had violated their sovereignty by arresting Savarkar on French soil. This dispute snowballed into the 'Savarkar Case of 1911' at the Permanent Court of Arbitration in The Hague. After careful deliberations on the right to political asylum, the notion of sovereignty, and how Dayanand Saraswati's Arya Samaj had ignited the demand 'l'Inde aux Hindous' (India to the Hindus), the tribunal issued an award. They acknowledged Britain's violation of international law.[38] Yet, the tribunal still ruled that Savarkar could remain in an Indian jail cell.[39]

Imprisoned in the Cellular Jail at Port Blair on the Andaman Islands, a tropical island group in the Bay of Bengal, Savarkar submitted several mercy petitions to the British, promising that he would not engage in political writings again. He even offered to 'volunteer to do any service' for the British.[40] After more than a decade in jail, Savarkar was released in the early 1920s on the condition that he would not comment on politics again. His tract *Hindutva*, written while still imprisoned, would set the tone of a more exclusionary political vision that Savarkar began to harness against Indian Muslims.

In 1924, Savarkar's writings brought him into conflict with the colonial authorities again. The incident that triggers the renewed dispute with the colonial state, began with Pir Jamaat Ali Shah, a Sufi saint who was then in his early nineties. As a scholarly observer Jamaat Ali Shah had witnessed the Mutiny of 1857, opposed the foundation of the Deoband seminary, written books against Mirza Ghulam Ahmad, Dayanand Saraswati, and Pandit Lekh Ram in their lifetime, and now, in the 1920s, had shifted his focus to converting non-Muslims to Islam.[41] In 1924, after the Friday prayer at Haji Bahadur mosque in Kohat, a tribal town in the Muslim-majority North-West Frontier Province, Jamaat Ali Shah welcomed a Hindu shopkeeper with great pomp into Islam.[42] Within a week, this man, now called Sheikh Abdul Rahman, had declared 'holy war' [*ghaza*] on Jai Ram, a rivalling shopkeeper after the latter refused to covert to Islam. 'You have become a "Chura" [untouchable], do you want to make me one too?' Jai Ram allegedly replied to Sheikh Abdul Rahman's conversion efforts, who went on to kill him. He also fired two bullets at Jai Ram's wife, shaved their children's hair, and made them recite the *kalima* (Islamic profession of faith). An inquiry into this matter revealed that Sheikh Abdul Rehman was having an affair with Jai Ram's wife and that '[a]fter he became a Mohammadan apparently [Jai Ram's wife] would not have anything more to do with him.'[43]

Omitting that Sheikh Abdul Rehman was a recent convert to Islam from Hinduism, Savarkar saw this as evidence of Hindu weakness and

Muslim bullying. He wrote an article in the *Maratha* claiming that Islam encouraged Muslims to wage 'Jahad to capture woman married to a non-believer, whether Christian or Jew or Hindu.'[44] Savarkar even cited a surah from the Quran to strengthen his point: 'chapter 4, Ayat 25 [...] in the opinion of several commentators support[s] this claim.'[45] Savarkar's belief that Islam was an alien religion that had infected India and required prompt removal found resonance in the Mahasabha, where Arya Samajis like Bhai Parmanand were intimately familiar with 'Pandit Lekhram's works.'[46]

***

Partition, riots, and the Kashmir crises catapulted Hindu nationalist positions to the political mainstream. These events also strengthened the idea that the liberal wing of the Congress party, with Nehru at its helm, was too weak to threaten Pakistan. In the weeks before Gandhi's murder, Vallabhbhai Patel, the home minister from the Congress's Hindu traditionalist wing, even flirted with the idea of integrating the Mahasabha and the RSS into the Congress party. At a speech given in Lucknow on 6 January 1948, Patel pleaded to the RSS to 'strengthen the hands of the Government and assist in maintaining peace' and invited them 'to join the Congress' outright.[47] After calling Pakistan 'a baby of yesterday,' Patel went on to 'appeal to the Hindu Mahasabhaites to join the Congress' as well.[48] He concluded his speech with the observation that 'RSS men are not thieves and dacoits. They are patriots.'[49]

Gandhi's murder turned the tide against Hindu-oriented groups like the Mahasabha and the RSS. It arrested their dream of any swift institutional ascent through the Congress or a democratic mandate through a general election.[50] But this was only short-lived. Already in 1949, the Mahasabha and the RSS began regrouping and resuming their political activities.[51] Nehru's negotiations with Liaquat Ali Khan, Pakistan's Prime Minister, over the rights of minorities and the facilitation of movement of migrants in 1950, reignited the fear in Congress's traditionalist wing that India was mum towards Pakistan. Attacking the Liaquat-Nehru Pact, the former president of the Hindu Maha Sabha and a minister in Nehru's cabinet, Syama Prasad Mukherjee, proclaimed that the pact was 'bound to give rise to fresh communal and political problems in India'.[52] He resigned in protest.

In 1951, Mukherjee wedded the Mahasabha to the RSS and formed a new party, the *Bharatiya Jana Sangh*. After a period of ideological promiscuity and conventional interest politics, the party refashioned itself as the *Bhartiya Janata Party* (BJP) in 1980.[53] Much of the ideological parameters that the Arya Samaj brought into the political field have been rethought, betrayed, and transformed. Yet it remains intriguing to see that Narendra Modi, a former RSS worker and the current Prime Minister of India, is at pains to establish ideological proximity of his remodelled BJP to Dayanand Saraswati and the Arya Samaj. More than just the past of Indian nationalism, Modi regards Dayanand as India's future. Standing on a saffron-drowned stage to commemorate Dayanand's birth anniversary in 2016, with an enormous poster of the Arya Samaj's founder in the background, Modi stimulated the crowd at Delhi's Jawaharlal Nehru Stadium with the following words:

> Former centuries have shown that whenever humankind has ventured on the path to knowledge, India has been at the forefront of this process. [...] The twentieth century is foremost a knowledge century and Swami Dayanand Saraswati is our repository of all knowledge [gyan marg].[54]

NOTES

INTRODUCTION

1. *'Mujaddid'* has been translated as spiritual reformer. YouTube. MrShfaq 'Tahir Naseem ahmadi views #he_claimed that he is prophet #naoozubilla' uploaded July 30, 2020 [0:08] https://www.youtube.com/watch?v=T68fTvm5H4g. Accessed December 15, 2020.
2. YouTube. Khan Zahid 'Debate between Prophet Khan, Germany, and Prophet Naseem, USA Part 3 (Ger sup)' https://www.youtube.com/watch?v=MOq4roSO9BA uploaded May 24, 2018 [1:45] Accessed December 15, 2020.
3. Ibid.
4. YouTube. 'Ghazi Khalid Khan Interview' https://www.youtube.com/watch?v=CwmIsgDXfHY uploaded July 30, 2020 [1:46] Accessed December 15, 2020.
5. National Assembly of Pakistan, August 12, 2020. http://www.na.gov.pk/uploads/documents/1599641007_458.pdf p.110 Accessed December 15, 2020.
6. YouTube. 'Peshawar ghazi Khalid Khan first hearing in court || Ghazi khalid came in court first time || latest' uploaded August 4, 2020 https://www.youtube.com/watch?v=5JAGanH6ypc [0:46] Accessed December 15, 2020.
7. Twitter. @IhsanTipu https://twitter.com/IhsanTipu/status/1290341263615680514 uploaded August 3, 2020 at 7:38pm, Accessed December 15, 2020.
8. YouTube. 'Rally in favour of Khalid/Faisal Ghazi in Peshawar' https://www.youtube.com/watch?v=NoQ7hJxxrlk uploaded July 31, 2020 [7:15] Accessed December 15, 2020.

9. U.S. Commission on International Religious Freedom, Violating Rights: Enforcing the World's Blasphemy Laws, https://www.uscirf. gov/sites/default/files/2020%20Blasphemy%20Enforcement%20 Report%20_final_0.pdf, p. 17, Accessed December 15, 2020.

10. U.S. Commission on International Religious Freedom, Violating Rights: Enforcing the World's Blasphemy Laws, https://www.uscirf. gov/sites/default/files/2020%20Blasphemy%20Enforcement%20 Report%20_final_0.pdf, p. 8.

11. Shah Ismail Dehlvi (1779–1831) was a Sunni revivalist and a grandson of the famed Shah Waliullah (1703–1762). Other reasons for issuing the fatwa include that Shah Ismail, in his book *Siraat-ul-Mustaqeem* (the straight path), had stated that it was always better to err on the side of *tawhid* (unity of Allah). Hadhrat Maulana Muhammad Ismail Shaheed Marhoom, *Siraat-ul-Mustaqeem* (Lahore: Malik Siraj-ud-Din, 1947), 85; For his role as the godfather of South Asian jihad, see: Ayesha Jalal, *Partisans of Allah: Jihad in South Asia* (Cambridge, MA: Harvard University Press, 2008) 80.

12. Philip J. Stern, *The Company-State: Corporate Sovereignty and the Early Modern Foundations of the British Empire* (Oxford: Oxford University Press, 2011).

13. For a biographical sketch of Fazl-e-Haq Khairabadi (1796-1861), see: Iqbal Hussain, 'Fazle Haq Khairabad: A Scholarly Rebel 1857', *Proceedings of the Indian History Congress, 1987*, Vol 48 (1987) 355–65.

14. Jamal Malik, 'Letters, prison sketches and autobiographical literature: The case of Fadl-e Haqq Khairabadi in the Andaman Penal Colony', *The Indian Economic and Social History Review*, Vol 43, 1 (2006) 75.

15. There is a longstanding debate in Islamic jurisprudence (fiqh) on how to adjudicate insults against the Prophet, which are called *sabb* or *shatm al-Rasul*. All four madhhabs, the jurisprudential schools that determine one's interpretation, distinguish between non-Muslim and Muslim insulters. They broadly agree that non-Muslims insulting the Prophet Muhammad should receive lighter sentences. Abu Hanifa, the founder of the Hanafi madhhab, which is prevalent in South Asia, held non-Muslims should be exempt from the death penalty. For a large fraction of scholars, Muslims who insult the Prophet Muhammad commit a form of apostasy, for which the mandatory punishment (*hadd*), if the blaspheming Muslim refuses to repent, is death. Compare, Yohanan Friedmann, *Tolerance and Coercion in Islam: Interfaith Relations in the Muslim Tradition* (Cambridge: Cambridge University Press, 2003) 149; Lutz Wiederhold, 'Blasphemy against the Prophet Muhammad and His Companions (Sabb al-Rasul, Sabb al-

Sahabah): The introduction of the topic into Shafi'i legal literature and its relevance for legal practice under Mamluk rule' *Journal of Semitic Studies* XLII/1 Spring 1997 39–70.

16. Imam Fazl-e-Haq Khairabadi, *Matbae Hidaya* (Delhi: no publisher identified, 1852).

17. Altaf Husain Hali, *Yaadgar-e-Ghalib* (Kanpur: Nami Press, 1897) 79.

18. Ibid.

19. A concise biography of Mirza Ghalib (1797–1869) can be found in Frances W. Pritchett and Owen T.A. Cornwall (ed.), *Ghalib: Selected Poems and Letters* (New York: Columbia University Press, 2017) ch 1.

20. Altaf Husain Hali, *Yaadgar-e-Ghalib* (Kanpur: Nami Press, 1897) 79.

21. On the strategies Indian Muslims adopted after the Mutiny, see Wilfred Cantwell Smith, *Modern Islam in India* (Lahore: Minerva Books, 1943).

22. For the opposite view that the Khairabdi-Shah Isamail debate was key in the formation of a South Asian Muslim 'political theology', see Sherali Tareen, *Defending Muhammad in Modernity* (Notre Dame, IN: University of Notre Dame Press, 2020).

23. Pankaj Mishra, *Age of Anger: A History of the Present* (New York: Macmillan, 2017).

24. Asad Ahmed, 'Adjudicating Muslims: Law, Religion and the State in Colonial India and Post-Colonial Pakistan.' PhD diss., University of Chicago, 2006; Many studies have strengthened Ahmed's argument and used the Foucauldian power/knowledge paradigm to find ever more ways in which the colonial state's legal practices produced emotional and affective responses from colonial subjects; see: Neeti Nair, 'Beyond the "communal" 1920s: The problem of intention, legislative pragmatism, and the making of section 295A of the Indian Penal Code.' *Indian Economic and Social History Review* vol. 50 no. 3 (2013) 317–40; Julia Stephens, *Governing Islam: Law, Empire, and Secularism in Modern South Asia* (Cambridge: Cambridge University Press, 2018).

25. Venkat Dhulipala, *Creating a New Medina: State Power, Islam, and the Quest for Pakistan in Late Colonial North India* (Cambridge: Cambridge University Press, 2016).

26. Ayesha Jalal, *The Struggle for Pakistan: A Muslim Homeland and Global Politics* (Cambridge, MA: Harvard University Press, 2014).

27. Martin Lau, *The Role of Islam in the Legal System of Pakistan* (Leiden: Brill, 2006).

28. Election Commission of Pakistan Form-14, 'Statement Containing Particulars of Eligible Voters', see https://www.ccp.gov.pk/

documents/laws2017/1-3-2020/The%20Election%20Rules,%20
2017%20as%20on%2024th%20February%202020.pdf on p. 2,
accessed December 15, 2020.

29. Partly this bias comes from Friedmann's early work on late medieval
Islamic history, which he connects to his work on the late nineteenth
century: Yohanan Friedmann, *Prophecy Continuous: Aspects of Ahmadi
Religious Thought and Its Medieval Background* (New Delhi, Oxford
University Press, 2003); Adil Hussain Khan, *From Sufism to Ahmadiyya:
A Muslim Minority Movement in South Asia* (Bloomington: Indiana
University Press, 2015); Spencer Lavan, *The Ahmadiyah Movement: A
History and Perspective* (New Delhi: Manohar Books, 1974).

30. Notable exceptions are: Bruce Desmond Graham, *Hindu Nationalism
and Indian Politics: The Origins and Development of the Bharatiya Jana Sangh*
(Cambridge: Cambridge University Press, 1990) and Christophe
Jaffrelot, *The Hindu Nationalist Movement in India* (New York: Columbia
University Press, 1998).

31. The only study that attempts to examine Hindu, Muslim, and Sikh
revivalism in nineteenth-century India in parallel is Bob van der
Linden, though he sees them as reactions to the colonial state and is
not primarily interested in exploring their conversations with each
other. Bob van der Linden, *Moral Languages from Colonial Punjab: The
Singh Sabha, Arya Samaj, and Ahmadiyah* (New Delhi: Manohar, 2008).

32. Faisal Devji, *Muslim Zion: Pakistan as a Political Idea* (London: Hurst,
2013); Ali Usman Qasmi and Megan Eaton Robb (eds), *Muslims
against the Muslim League: Critiques of the Idea of Pakistan* (Cambridge:
Cambridge University Press, 2018); Ayesha Jalal, *The Struggle for
Pakistan: A Muslim Homeland and Global Politics* (Cambridge, MA:
Harvard University Press, 2017); Francis Robinson, *The Muslim
World in Modern South Asia: Power, Authority, Knowledge* (New York: State
University of New York Press, 2020); David Gilmartin, Pamela Price
and Arild Engelsen Ruud (eds) *South Asian Sovereignty: The Conundrum
of Worldly Power* (London: Routledge, 2020).

33. Pratab Bahanu Mehta, *The Burden of Democracy* (New Delhi: Penguin,
2017); Gyan Prakash, *Emergency Chronicles: Indira Gandhi and
Democracy's Turning Point* (Princeton: Princeton University Press,
2019); Tripurdaman Singh, *Sixteen Stormy Days* (New Delhi: Penguin,
2020); Ishtiaq Ahmed, *Jinnah: His Successes, Failures and Role in History*
(New Delhi: Penguin, 2020).

34. Madhav Khosla, *India's Founding Moment: The Constitution of a Most
Surprising Democracy* (Cambridge, MA: Harvard University Press,
2020).

35. Rohit De, *A People's Constitution: The Everyday Life of Law in the Indian Republic* (Princeton: Princeton University Press, 2018).

36. For an overview see: David Gilmartin, 'Partition, Pakistan, and South Asian History: In Search of a Narrative.' *Journal of Asian Studies* Vol. 57, no. 4 (1998) 1068–95.

37. For a notable exception to this trend, see: Shruti Kapila, *Violent Fraternity: Indian Political Thought in the Global Age* (Princeton, NJ: Princeton University Press, 2021).

38. The exception here is Kenneth Jones, *Arya Dharm: Hindu Consciousness in 19th-Century Punjab* (Berkeley: University of California Press, 1976) 139–45.

39. The precise timing of when the idea a Muslim nation state on Indian soil was first conceived, and how it eventually came into being, is fiercely contested between so-called primordial approaches, which root the presence of a separate nation well into the past and modernist positions, which tie a state's emergence closer to its nationalist movement. Both positions agree, however, that glimpses of Muslim separatism became visible in the late colonial period, particularly in northern India. See: Adeel Hussain, *Law and Muslim Political Thought in Late Colonial North India* (Oxford: Oxford University Press, 2022) ch. 1.

40. All South Asian religions underwent fundamental transformations and took their distinct shape that we recognise today under colonialism in the late nineteenth century. See: Qasim Zaman, *Islam in Pakistan* (Princeton: Princeton University Press, 2018) 14–27.

41. For a comprehensive overview of this position, see David Gilmartin, *Empire and Islam: Punjab and the Making of Pakistan* (Berkeley: University of California Press, 1988).

42. Vali Nasr, 'Sectarianism and Shia Politics in Pakistan, 1979-present' in *Cahiers d'Études sur la Méditerranée Orientale et le monde Turco-Iranien* Vol. 28 (1999) 311–23; Tahir Kamran, 'Contextualizing Sectarian Militancy in Pakistan: A Case Study of Jhang' in *Journal of Islamic Studies* Vol 20 no. 1 (2009) 55–85.

43. General Zia-ul-Haq implemented a strict version of the Hanafi *fiqh*, which differs from the Jafarite school that most Shia ascribe to. For an overview of Sunni Shia violence see: Khaled Ahmed, *Sectarian War: Pakistan's Sunni-Shia Violence and its links to the Middle East* (Karachi: Oxford University Press, 2013).

44. Eamon Murphy, *Islam and Sectarian Violence in Pakistan: The Terror Within* (New York: Routledge, 2019) ch. 8.

45. Ashok K. Behuria 'Sects Within Sect: The Case of Deobandi-Barelvi Encounter in Pakistan' in *Strategic Analysis* Vol. 32, no. 1 (2008) 57–80.

46. On the events that led up to the constitutional exclusion of Ahmadis in 1974, see: Ali Usman Qasmi, *The Ahmadis and the Politics of Religious Exclusion in Pakistan* (London: Anthem Press, 2015) 167–85.

47. For an elaboration of this argument, see: Kenneth W. Jones, *Arya Dharm: Hindu Consciousness in 19th-century Punjab* (Berkeley, University of California Press).

48. According to the Pakistan Census of 1961, out of 10 million Hindus that lived in Pakistan, 9.4 million resided in East Pakistan, where they made up 18.4 per cent of the population. In West Pakistan, 97.2 per cent of the population was Muslim. M. Sanaullah, 'Second and Third Release from the Second Population Census of Pakistan, 1961' in *The Pakistan Development Review*, Vol. 2 no. 1 (1962) 110f.

49. This insight is taken from Hannah Arendt's reading of how national majorities react to minority groups who, despite their small numbers and lapsed utility for the state and society at large, occupy a prominent role in public life. Hannah Arendt, *The Origins of Totalitarianism* (New York: Schocken Books, 1951).

CHAPTER 1. REBIRTH

1. All translations are the author's own unless otherwise noted. For biographical details see Yohanan Friedman, *Prophecy Continuous: Aspects of Ahmadi Religious Thought and Its Medieval Background* (Oxford: Oxford University Press, 2010); Adil Hussain Khan, *From Sufism to Ahmadiyya* (Bloomington: Indiana University Press, 2015); Spencer Levan, *The Ahmadiyah Movement* (New Delhi: Manohar, 1974); Basharat Ahmad, *Mujaddid-e-Azam* (Lahore: Ahmadiyya Anjuman Isha'at-i-Islam Lahore, 1949); Dost Mohammad Shahid, *Taareekh-e-Ahmadiyyat* (Amritsar: Nazarat Nashro Ishaat Qadian, 2007) vols 1–2.

2. Since Grisworld's classic essay of 1902, scholars have linked the etymology of 'Ahmadiyya' to its founder Mirza Ghulam Ahmad; however, Mirza repeatedly raises the point that the movement derives its name from the Prophet Muhammad; see: H.D. Griswold, *Mirza Gulam Ahmad: The Mehdi Messiah of Qadian* (Ludhiana, The American Tract Society, 1902) 1; Murtaza Khan, *The Name Ahmadiyya and its Necessity* (Lahore: The Ahmadiyya Anjuman Isha'at-i-Islam, 1945); for Mirza's claims see: Mirza Ghulam Ahmad, *Tohfa-e-Ghuznaviyyah* (Qadian: Zia-ul-Islam, 1902).

3. Arya Samaj was a religious reformist movement in late nineteenth-century India that sought to rid Hinduism of corruption, see: Lajpat Rai, *The Arya Samaj* (London: Longmans, Green and Co., 1915).

4. Mirza largely shared his prophecies with his followers after the *maghrib* prayer. The Arabic revelation translates to 'A lifeless calf devoid of spirituality'. Mirza interpreted this to mean 'Lekh Ram is Samiri's calf and will be cut into pieces like Samiri's calf'. In another verse, he also suggested that a sign from God would manifest on the day of (or close to) Eid, 'just like Samiri's calf was burnt on Eid.' For the original prophecy, see: Mirza Ghulam Ahmad, *Aaina-e-Kamalat-e-Islam* (Amritsar: Riaz Hind Press,1893); Mirza Ghulam Ahmad, *Barakaat-ud-Dua* Mutaba (Amritsar: Riaz Hind Press, 1893). For Mirza's interpretation, see Mirza Ghulam Ahmad, *Haqiqatul-Wahi:The Philosophy of Divine Revelation* (Farnham, Surrey: Islam International Publications, 2018 [1907]) 360f. For Lekh Ram's biographical details, see Kenneth W. Jones, 'Communalism in the Punjab: The Arya Samaj Contribution', *Journal of Asian Studies* 28, no. 1 (1968); David Emmanuel Singh, '"The Malicious Arya"? Pundit Lekhram ji's Portrayal of Christianity in the 19th Century South Asia', *International Journal of Asian Christianity* 1 (2018) 198–224.

5. Ibid., 2f.

6. Mirza Ghulam Ahmad, *Siraj-e-Muneer* (Qadian: Zia-ul-Islam, 1897) 12f.

7. Ibid, 14.

8. Mirza claimed that the Arabic revelation concerning Lekh Ram was 'his work will be completed in six', which he first understood to mean that Lekh Ram will die within six years. On further inspection upon Lekh Ram's death, Mirza wrote that the prophecy had also hinted at the date and the time of the attack: Lekh Ram was stabbed on 6 March at six o'clock. There is no written proof that this revelation occurred before Lekh Ram's murder, which Mirza openly conceded: Mirza Ghulam Ahamad 'Istafata' in *Ruhani Khazain Vol. 12* (Tilford, Surrey: Islam International Publications, 2009) 125.

9. 'The Late Pundit Lekh Ram', *Tribune*, March 17, 1897.

10. 'The Late Pundit Lekh Ram', *Tribune*, March 24, 1897.

11. 'Assassination of Pandit Lekh Ram', *Tribune*, March 10, 1897; on *shuddhi* see only G.R. Thursby, *Hindu–Muslim Relations in British India* (Leiden: Brill, 1975) 136–58.

12. 'The Late Pundit Lekh Ram', *Tribune*, March 24, 1897.

13. For an extensive description of house structures in Lahore's Old City, see: William Glover, *Making Lahore Modern: Constructing and Imagining a Colonial City* (Minneapolis: University of Minnesota Press, 2008) 102–5.

14. Lekh Ram used the word 'kambacht', which has been translated as 'wretch' but corresponds more closely to 'someone who brings bad luck', see 'The Late Pundit Lekh Ram', *Tribune*, March 17, 1897.

15. 'Assassination of Pandit Lekh Ram', *Tribune*, March 10, 1897.

16. For an overview see: Tahir Kamran and Ian Talbot, *Lahore: In the Time of the Raj* (Gurgaon: Penguin Random House, 2016) 24–36.

17. The conflict seemed to have erupted on how to devise a curriculum for the DAV school, especially on the place meat consumption should have in it. Sunder Das and an unknown man died after a heated exchange of lathi blows; see Feroz Chand, *Lajpat Rai: Life and Work* (New Delhi: Ministry of Information and Broadcasting, Government of India, 1978) 76.

18. Lekh Ram's dying words were 'Pameshwar [God] can save me'. According to the attending intern he uttered them multiple times over. A British gynaecologist, Colonel Edmond Ludlow Perry, later operated on Lekh Ram but could not save him, Mirza Yaqub Beg 'Pandit Lekh Ram ka waqiyah', *Paigham-e-Sulh*, May 26, 1923; *Indian Medical Gazette* 1927 Sep; 62(9): 541.

19. 'Assassination of Pandit Lekh Ram', *Tribune*, March 10, 1897.

20. 'Assassination of Pandit Lekh Ram', *Tribune*, March 10, 1897.

21. Mirza Ghulam Ahmad, *Siraj-e-Muneer* (Qadian, Zia-ul-Islam, 1897) 39.

22. The Prophet used to eat and drink with his right hand. Mirza Ghulam Ahmad, *Siraj-e-Muneer* (Qadian, Zia-ul-Islam, 1897) 21f.

23. Ibid., 25.

24. Murders triggered by sexual jealousy were not unusual and this seems to be a plausible narrative. Mirza Ghulam Ahmad, *Siraj-e-Muneer* (Qadian, Zia-ul-Islam, 1897) 32.

25. Mirza Ghulam Ahmad, *Siraj-e-Muneer* (Qadian, Zia-ul-Islam, 1897) 45 in footnote.

26. Tripurdaman Singh, *Imperial Sovereignty and Local Politics: The Bhadauria Rajputs and the Transition from Mughal to British India*, 1600-1900 (Cambridge: Cambridge University Press, 2019).

27. Carl von Hügel, *Kaschmir und das Reich der Siek Band 2* (Stuttgart: Hallberger'sche Verlagshandlung, 1840) 149ff.

28. Sir Lepel H. Griffin, *The Panjab Chiefs Vol. II* (Lahore: Civil and Military Gazette Press, 1890) 49f.

29. Ibid.

30. Carl von Hügel, *Kaschmir und das Reich der Siek Band 2* (Stuttgart: Hallberger'sche Verlagshandlung, 1840) 149ff.

31. Sir Lepel H. Griffin, The Panjab Chiefs Vol. II (Lahore: Civil and Military Gazette Press, 1890) 49f.

32. Ibid.; There is considerable controversy regarding Mirza's day of birth. He writes himself that he was born in the year.
33. William Francklin, *Military Memoirs of Mr. George Thomas* (London: John Stockdale, 1805) 343
34. J.M Wilson to Mirza Ghulam Murtaza Khan, 11.6.1849 reprinted in Mirza Ghulam Ahmad, *Kitab-al-Bariyyah* (Qadian: Zia-ul-Islam, 1898) 5f.
35. His foremost biographers provide 1835 as Mirza's birthyear, but according to his own writings he was born 'in 1839 or 1840'. This is further substantiated by the fact that Mirza also recalls the Mutiny. He even remembers his age and writes that he was 'sixteen or seventeen'. I have therefore assumed that he was born in 1840; see Mirza Ghulam Ahmad, *Kitab-al-Bariyyah* (Qadian: Zia-ul-Islam, 1898) 177.
36. Colonel Malleson and John Kaye, *Kaye's and Malleson's History of the Indian Mutiny Vol. II* (London: 1897) 301f; Reginal G. Wilberforce, *An Unrecorded Chapter of the Indian Mutiny* (London: John Murray, 1894) 39f and 87f;
37. Robert Cast to Mirza Ghulam Murtaza Khan, n.d ca. 1858, as reprinted in Mirza Ghulam Ahmad, *Kitab-al-Bariyyah* (Qadian: Zia-ul-Islam, 1898) 6. Upon the demise of Mirza Ghulam Murtaza this *khilat* was transferred to Mirza's brother Ghulam Qadir in 1876; see ibid., 8. These recommendations letters have aged poorly. What were genuine recommendations in the nineteenth century, when India was under British colonial rule, have started looking like proofs of colonial excess and misplaced loyalty in the twentieth century. Amongst other things, this reveals the structural shift towards democratic forms of governance that the twentieth century has brought in.
38. Basharat Ahmad, *The Great Reformer Vol. I* (Dublin, Ohio: Ahmadiyya Anjuman Ishaat Islam, 2007) 52. According to biographer A.R. Dard, Mirza estimated that barring the time and energy that went into the court cases his father fought, 'close upon Rs. 70,000'. This number seems excessively high. It is more likely that the costs ran into several thousand rupees. A.R. Dard, *Life of Ahmad: Founder of the Ahmadiyya Movement* (Tilford, Surrey: Islam International Publications, 2008) 39.
39. Basharat Ahmad, *The Great Reformer Vol. I* (Dublin, Ohio: Ahmadiyya Anjuman Ishaat Islam, 2007) 38.
40. Ibid., 73.
41. Mirza Bashir Ahmad, *Sirat-ul-Mahdi I* (Qadian: Ahmadiyya Kitabghar, 1935) 43.
42. Basharat Ahmad, *The Great Reformer Vol. I* (Dublin, Ohio: Ahmadiyya Anjuman Ishaat Islam, 2007) 58.

43. Ibid., 73.
44. John F.W. Youngson, *Forty Years of the Panjab Mission of the Church of Scotland 1855-1895* (Edinburgh: R.&.R. Clark, 1896) 137.
45. Ibid., 138.
46. Basharat Ahmad, *The Great Reformer Vol. I* (Dublin, Ohio: Ahmadiyya Anjuman Ishaat Islam, 2007) 58.
47. C.A. Bayly, *The Birth of the Modern World, 1780-1914* (Oxford: Wiley-Blackwell, 2003).
48. This incident probably occurred in 1865, when Government College Lahore was recruiting. The professorship went to Maulvi Alumdar Hussain. Mir Hassan gives a salary estimate of 100 rupees per month, which would be at the upper end of the Government's pay-scale. Mirza was earning around 10 rupees a month as a law clerk. H.L.O Garrett, *A History of Government College, Lahore 1864-1914* (Lahore: Civil and Military Gazette, 1914) 2 and 40.
49. Basharat Ahmad, *The Great Reformer Vol. I* (Dublin, Ohio: Ahmadiyya Anjuman Ishaat Islam, 2007) 58.
50. Basharat Ahmad, *The Great Reformer Vol. I* (Dublin, Ohio: Ahmadiyya Anjuman Ishaat Islam, 2007) 58.
51. Ibid; Mirza Bashir Ahmad, *Sirat-ul-Mahdi I* (Qadian: *Ahmadiyya Kitabghar*, 1935) 43.
52. Mirza Ghulam Ahmad, *Barahin-e-Ahmadiyya I+II* (Tilford, Surrey: Islam International Publications, 2012) 74.
53. Ibid., 9.
54. Ibid., 8f.
55. Ibid., 49.
56. There was a procedural web attached to getting that money, which may be another reason that there wasn't more of a buzz in accepting that challenge. Mirza had promised 'awards' before but then dismissed the claims of those who stepped forward. He did this either on procedural grounds (composition of the jury and so on) or by arguing outright that an award was only binding if it was based on 'reasoned judgement'. Mirza would judge what constituted 'reasoned judgement', which left plenty of leeway to wiggle out of an unfavourable decision, see Basharat Ahmad, *The Great Reformer Vol. I* (Dublin, Ohio: Ahmadiyya Anjuman Ishaat Islam, 2007) 112.
57. Ibid., 50.
58. Mirza sent this letter to Bishop Matthew from the Archdiocese of Lahore. The word in the original German is 'schwärmerisch': Joh. Hesse (ed.), *Evangelisches Missions-Magazin* (Basel: Verlag der Missionsbuchhandlung, 1885) 298.

59. Mirza Ghulam Ahmad, *Barahin-e-Ahmadiyya IV* (Tilford, Surrey: Islam International Publications, 2016) 264.

60. For a short autobiographical note, see: Swami Dayanand Saraswati, *Satyarth Prakash* (Lahore: Virjanand Press, 1908) 1–49.

61. Max Müller, *Biographical Essays* (London: Longmans, Green, and CO., 1884) 92.

62. There is an acknowledged link between Dayanand's criticism of colonial rule and the staunch nationalism of fervent Arya Samaj supporters in the early twentieth century. For instance, one of the most prominent Arya Samajis, Lala Lajpat Rai, writes in 1928 that 'from a national point of view, no curse is greater than that of political subjection to another people.' Lala Lajpat Rai, *Unhappy India* (Calcutta: Banna Publishing, 1928) XIV.

63. Mirza called the Arya Samaj a 'new sect'. He justified this in the following way: 'all the principles it [Arya Samaj] adheres to and all the doctrines it imputes to the Vedas are generally not found in any ancient Hindu sect, or in the Ved Bhash and other reference works. It is rather an amalgamation of miscellaneous ideas—some the product of the Pundit's own imagination and others taken haphazardly from various religious texts.' Mirza Ghulam Ahmad, *Barahin-e-Ahmadiyya I + II* (Tilford, Surrey: Islam International Publications, 2012) 86 in footnote.

64. H.L.O Garrett, *Government College Lahore, 1864-1914* (Lahore: Military Gazette Press, 1914) 35.

65. Mirza Ghulam Ahmad, *Barahin-e-Ahmadiyya I + II* (Tilford, Surrey: Islam International Publications, 2012) 123.

66. Mirza wrote his first letter to Syed Ahmed Khan already in the 1860s, when Syed Mir Hassan told him about Sir Syed's views on divine revelation in the modern age. Syed Ahmed denied such experiences, whereas Mirza sought them still possible. After that Mirza wrote another letter to criticise Syed Ahmed's commentary on the Quran, though he was mighty impressed with his insistence that Jesus had not died on the cross, as was conventional Christian belief, and dedicated several books to him. Mirza also liked Sir Syed's negation of jihad under British rule. However, he received no response from Sir Syed.

67. Basharat Ahmad, *The Great Reformer Vol. I* (Dublin, Ohio: Ahmadiyya Anjuman Ishaat Islam, 2007) 108–12.

68. A.R. Dard, *Life of Ahmad: Founder of the Ahmadiyya Movement* (Tilford, Surrey: Islam International Publications, 2008) 39.

69. Contrary to this, John Morrison, in his study on Indian religious movements, asserted that Dayananda was 'out of caste altogether,

being the son of a brahman father and a low-caste mother', see John Morrison, *New Ideas in India During the Nineteenth Century: A Study of Social, Political, and Religious Developments* (Edinburgh: George A. Morton, 1906) 30.

70. Lala Lajpat Rai, *The Arya Samaj* (London: Longmans, Green and Co., 1915) 8.
71. Max Müller, *Biographical Essays* (London: Longmans, Green and Co., 1884) 167f.
72. Ibid.
73. Dayanand preacher his condemnation of idol worship in at least three Indian languages, see: 'Occasional Notes', *Madras Mail*, March 29, 1876.
74. 'The Great Swami Dayanand', *Madras Mail,* January 8, 1875.
75. *Pioneer*, March 11, 1876.
76. Swami Dayanand Saraswati, *Satyarth Prakash* (Lahore: Virjanand Press, 1908) 22.
77. 'The Late Swami Dayananda Saraswati', *Tribune*, November 3, 1883.
78. Just like Mirza, Dayanand was keen on maintaining conversation with high-profile religious leaders. When a low-ranking missionary challenged Dayanand in 1880, he declined the request and answered that he would only discuss theological matters with a "well-educated bishop"'. 'Pundit Dayanand Saraswati', *Weekly Ceylon Observer*, March 8, 1880.
79. Swami Dayanand Saraswati, *Satyarth Prakash* (Lahore: Virjanand Press, 1908) 41.
80. The Ajmer episode is something of the foundational myth in Lekh Ram hagiographies and usually dated to 1880. Since Dayanand did not spend any significant time in Ajmer in 1880, it is more likely that Lekh Ram came to see him in 1878. Swami Dayanand Saraswati, *Satyarth Prakash* (Lahore: Virjanand Press, 1908) 41–4.
81. Pandit Lekh Ram, *Kulyaat-e-Ariya-Musafir* (Lahore: Mufeed-e-Aam Press, 1903) Introduction 4.
82. Ibid.; Kenneth W. Jones, *Arya Dharm: Hindu Consciousness in 19th-century Punjab* (London: University of California Press, 1976) 147–50.
83. On *samadhi* see: Stuart Ray Sarbacker, *Samadhi: The Numinous and Cessative in Indio-Tibetan Yoga* (Albany, NY: SUNY Press, 2006).
84. Pandit Lekh Ram, *Kulyaat-e-Ariya-Musafir* (Lahore: Mufeed-e-Aam Press, 1903) Introduction 4.
85. Kenneth W. Jones, *Arya Dharm: Hindu Consciousness in 19th-century Punjab* (London: University of California Press, 1976) 147–50; Jones relies solely on material printed by the Arya Samaj, which is highly

hagiographical, and makes it difficult to reconstruct his life before he adopted a public role from the 1880s onwards.

86. Pandit Lekh Ram, *Kulyaat-e-Ariya-Musafir* (Lahore: Mufeed-e-Aam Press, 1903) Introduction 4.
87. Basharat Ahmad, *The Great Reformer Vol. I* (Dublin, Ohio: Ahmadiyya Anjuman Ishaat Islam, 2007) 140.
88. Ibid., 151.
89. Mirza Ghulam Ahmad, *Barahin-e-Ahmadiyya* (Tilford, Surrey: Islam International Publications, 2018) 200.
90. Pandit Lekh Ram, *Kulyaat-e-Ariya-Musafir* (Lahore: Mufeed-e-Aam Press, 1903) Introduction 4.
91. Ibid., 502–692.
92. Ibid.
93. Mirza Ghulam Ahmad, Chashma-e-Ariya (Amritsar, Riaz Hind Press, 1886).
94. Mirza acknowledges him as a source of inspiration in his last book: Mirza Ghulam Ahmad, *A Message of Peace* (Tilford, Surrey: Islam International Publications, 2007) 34.
95. Pandit Lekh Ram, *Kulyaat-e-Ariya-Musafir* (Lahore: Mufeed-e-Aam Press, 1903) 599–619.
96. Farina Mir, *The Social Space of Language: Vernacular Culture in British Colonial Punjab* (Berkeley: University of California Press, 2010); Bob van der Linden, *Moral Languages from Colonial Punjab: The Singh Sabha, Arya Samaj, and Ahmadiyah* (New Delhi: Manohar, 2008); the importance of masculinity is visible from the advertisements in many of Mirza Ghulam Ahmad's first editions. Here one can find ads for several stimulants to overcome 'nervous and sexual debility', see only: *Review of Religion*, January 1902, 42.
97. Even though Dayanand Saraswati mentioned in passing that *niyoga* was part of the Arya *dharm*, there was a lot of pushback on this in the Arya Samaj. Ruchi Ram Sahni warned in 1897 that, if practised, *niyoga* could 'lead to a considerable dislocation in the social life of the Hindus'. Since many of the discussions around *niyoga* remain theoretical and there is no evidence that Punjabi Hindus practicsed it on any measurable scale, *Niyoga* had little practical relevance. Ruchi Ram Sahni, *The Niyoga Doctrine of Arya Samaj* (Lahore: Punjab Economical Press, 1897) 1f.
98. Adeel Hussain, *Muslim Political Thought in Modern India* (Oxford: Oxford University Press, 2022) 12–21.
99. Mirza Ghulam Ahmad, *Paigham-e-Sulha* (Lahore: Nawlakshwar Press, 1907) 8.

100. Ibid., 11–13.
101. Ibid., 26.
102. Ibid., 31.
103. Ibid., 30.
104. 'Mirza Gholam Ahmed's Last Message: A Message of Peace', *Tribune*, March 23, 1908.

CHAPTER 2. BETRAYAL

1. Anish Vanaik, *Possessing the City: Property and Politics in Delhi, 1911-1947* (Oxford: Oxford University Press, 2019) 139.
2. Abdul Rashid v. Emperor, 1927 A.I.R. Lahore 567.
3. For a historical appreciation of the Indian Army in the First World War: Kaushik Roy, *Indian Army and the First World War, 1914-18* (Oxford: Oxford University Press, 2018); for the frequent use of pistols in the Delhi crime scene: 'Review of the Police Administration in the Delhi Province for 1926', Home/Public, File No. 75/17/1927, 6, National Archives of India, New Delhi.
4. Abdul Rashid v. Emperor, 1927 A.I.R. Lahore 567.
5. Swami Shraddhanand, *Aryapathik Lekh Ram* (Calcutta: Vaidik Pustakalaya, 1914).
6. Gandhi narrated this incident in his speech at the A.I.C.C. Meeting in Gauhati on December 24, 1924. It is likely that he took this information from Shraddhanand's son, Indra Vidyavachaspati: *The Collected Works of Mahatma Gandhi Vol. 32* (New Delhi: Ministry of Information and Broadcasting, Government of India, 1969) 452f.
7. *The Collected Works of Mahatma Gandhi Vol. 32* (New Delhi: Ministry of Information and Broadcasting, Government of India, 1969) 452f.
8. Abdul Rashid v. Emperor, 1927 A.I.R. Lahore 567.
9. Ibid.
10. Ibid.
11. Muhammad Zafarullah Khan, *Tehdees-e-Ne'mat* [autobiography] (no place identified: no publisher given, 1941).
12. 'Mianji, idhar ao,' were the words that Rashid claimed to have heard someone whisper from inside Shraddhanand's haveli, see Abdul Rashid v. Emperor, 1927 A.I.R. Lahore 568.
13. Abdul Rashid v. Emperor, 1927 A.I.R. Lahore 569.
14. Ibid., 568.
15. Ibid., 569.
16. For biographical details of Munshi Ram's early years, see: J.T.F.

Jordens, *Swami Shraddhananda: His Life and Causes* (New York: Oxford University Press, 1981) ch. 1.

17. M.R. Jambunathan (ed.), *Swami Shraddhanand* [autobiography] (New Delhi: Vedic Prakasnan, 2016) 27.

18. Ibid., 28.

19. Ibid.

20. Ibid., 29–36.

21. Ibid., 38f.

22. Ibid., 59.

23. Ibid., 65.

24. Ibid.

25. Ibid.

26. Ibid., 75.

27. Rudyard Kipling, *Something of Myself and Other Autobiographical Writings*, ed. Thomas Pinney (Cambridge: Cambridge University Press, 1990) 282.

28. Munshi Ram and his peers studied *Elements of Jurisprudence*, which was first published in 1880 and quickly become the standard textbook on the subject. M.R. Jambunathan (ed.), *Swami Shraddhanand* [autobiography] (New Delhi: Vedic Prakasnan, 2016) 79.

29. Ibid.

30. Larpantan increased the fees in the coming years to 1500 rupees and ultimately to the royal sum of 2000 rupees: 'The Great Punjab Bribery Case', *Tribune* (Lahore), February 4, 1888.

31. 'The Great Punjab Bribery Case', *Tribune* (Lahore), February 4, 1888.

32. M.R. Jambunathan (ed.), *Swami Shraddhanand* [autobiography] (New Delhi: Vedic Prakasnan, 2016) 96.

33. Ibid., 98.

34. Ibid., 120.

35. Swami Shraddhanand, *Inside Congress* [collection of articles published in the Liberator in 1926] (Bombay: Phoenix Publications, 1946) 21.

36. Munshi Ram, 'The Great Congress Meeting at Jullundhur', *Tribune* (Lahore), May 30, 1888.

37. Munshi Ram, 'The Great Congress Meeting at Jullundhur', *Tribune* (Lahore), May 30, 1888.

38. Syed Ahmed Khan, *Sir Syed Ahmed on the Present State of Indian Politics, Consisting of Speeches and Letters Reprinted from the 'Pioneer'* (Allahabad: The Pioneer Press, 1888) 31.

39. Munshi Ram, 'The Great Congress Meeting at Jullundhur', *Tribune* (Lahore), May 30, 1888.

40. M.R. Jambunathan (ed.), *Swami Shraddhanand* [autobiography] (New Delhi: Vedic Prakasnan, 2016) 137.

41. Swami Shraddhanand, *Inside Congress* (Bombay: Phoenix Publications, 1946) 24.

42. Ibid., 25.

43. Swami Shraddhanand, *Inside Congress* (Bombay: Phoenix Publications, 1946) 24.

44. M.R. Jambunathan (ed.), *Swami Shraddhanand* [autobiography] (New Delhi: Vedic Prakasnan, 2016) 141.

45. Ibid., 139.

46. Ibid., 190.

47. Ibid., 188.

48. Ibid., 189.

49. Ibid., 193.

50. Swami Shraddhanand, *Inside Congress* (Bombay: Phoenix Publications, 1946) 31.

51. Ibid.

52. Ibid.

53. 'The Gurukula Anniversary', *Leader* (Allahabad), April 23, 1920.

54. Swami Shraddhanand, *Inside Congress* (Bombay: Phoenix Publications, 1946) 40.

55. For the debate in the Legislative Council, where the Bill was moved against the opposition of all Indian members, see: Home/Political/B, File No. 82/1919, 5–30, National Archives of India, New Delhi.

56. Swami Shraddhanand, *Inside Congress* (Bombay: Phoenix Publications, 1946) 64.

57. Home/Political/B, File No. 82/1919, 5-30, National Archives of India, New Delhi.

58. 'Rowlatt Act', *Amrita Bazar Patrika* (Calcutta), 22 July 1919.

59. Shraddhanand Sanyasi, 'Message to Satyagrahies', *Tribune* (Lahore), March 15, 1919.

60. Swami Shraddhanand, *Inside Congress* (Bombay: Phoenix Publications, 1946) 60.

61. Letter from the Chief Commissioner, Delhi to H.D. Craig, the Deputy Secretary to the Government of India, April 23, 1919 in Home/Political/Deposit, File No. 20/1919, 5, National Archives of India, New Delhi.

62. 'The Delhi Tragedy: Swami Shraddhanand's Statement', *Mahratta* (Poona), April 6, 1919 as reprinted in Home/Political/Deposit, File No. 619-640/1919, 17, National Archives of India, New Delhi.

63. Ibid.

64. Ibid.
65. 'The Delhi Tragedy', *Bombay Chronicle* (Bombay), April 1, 1919.
66. Letter from C.A. Barron, Chief Commissioner, Delhi to Sir J.H. DuBoulay, Secretary to the Government of India, March 31, 1919, in Home/Political/B, File No. 141-147/1919, 2f, National Archives of India, New Delhi.
67. 'The Delhi Tragedy', *Bombay Chronicle* (Bombay), April 1, 1919.
68. Letter from C.A. Barron, Chief Commissioner, Delhi to Sir J.H. DuBoulay, Secretary to the Government of India, March 31, 1919, in Home/Political/B, File No. 141-147/1919, 2f, National Archives of India, New Delhi.
69. 'The Delhi Tragedy', *Bombay Chronicle* (Bombay), April 1, 1919.
70. Letter from C.A. Barron, Chief Commissioner, Delhi to Sir J.H. DuBoulay, Secretary to the Government of India, March 31, 1919, in Home/Political/B, File No. 141-147/1919, 3, National Archives of India, New Delhi.
71. Report from P.L. Orde, Superintended of Police on April 8, 1919 in Home/Political/B, File No. 268-273/1919, 5, National Archives of India, New Delhi.
72. Letter from M.K. Gandhi to J.L Maffey, Private Secretary to His Excellency the Viceroy, March 12, 1919 as reprinted in Home/Political/A, File No. 250/1919, 7, National Archives of India, New Delhi.
73. Letter from C.A. Barron, Chief Commissioner of Delhi to Sir J. DuBoulay, Secretary to the Government of India, April 7, 1919, in Home/Political/B, File No. 141-147/1919, 11, National Archives of India, New Delhi.
74. Telegram from His Excellency the Viceroy to The Secretary to the Government of India, Home Department, April 8, 1919 in Home/Political/A, File No. 455-472/1919, 3f, National Archives of India, New Delhi.
75. There is also reason to believe that his movement was decreasing in popularity. This was partly due to the counter-propaganda of the colonial state, which printed over a hundred thousand leaflets on the Rowlatt Act for free distribution in the Punjab. See: Report from Sheikh Asghar Ali, Additional Secretary to Government, Punjab to the Secretary to the Government of Punjab, Home Department, July 26, 1919 in Home/Political/B, File No. 447-448/1919, 5f, National Archives of India, New Delhi.
76. Letter from M.K. Gandhi to J.L. Maffey, Private Secretary to His

Excellency the Viceroy, April 15, 1919, in Home/Political/A, File No. 455-472/1919, 11, National Archives of India, New Delhi.

77. Ibid.
78. Ibid.
79. Swami Shraddhanand, *Inside Congress* (Bombay: Phoenix Publications, 1946) 95f.
80. Letter from Shraddhanand Sanyasi to Gandhi, May 2, 1919 as reprinted in 'Swami Shraddhanand Resigns from Satyagraha Sabha', *Leader* (Allahabad), May 29, 1919.
81. Letter from Swami Shraddhanand to Mahatma Gandhi, September 9, 1921 in Swami Shraddhanand, *Inside Congress* (Bombay: Phoenix Publications, 1946) 137.
82. Swami Shraddhanand, *Inside Congress* (Bombay: Phoenix Publications, 1946) 137.
83. Ibid., 139.
84. Shraddhanand Sanyasi, 'Urgently Wanted for Famine-Stricken in Garhwal', *Leader* (Allahabad), July 1, 1918.
85. Swami Shraddhanand's Chairman Address as reprinted in *Report of the Thirty Fourth Session of the Indian National Congress held in Amritsar On The 27th, 29th, 30th, 31st, December 1919 and 1st January 1920* (Amritsar: Reception Committee 34th Indian National Congress, 1922) 3.
86. Swami Shraddhanand's Chairman Address as reprinted in *Report of the Thirty Fourth Session of the Indian National Congress held in Amritsar On The 27th, 29th, 30th, 31st, December 1919 and 1st January 1920* (Amritsar: Reception Committee 34th Indian National Congress, 1922) 3.
87. Ibid., 4.
88. Ibid., 7.
89. M.R. Jambunathan (ed.), *Swami Shraddhanand* [autobiography] (New Delhi: Vedic Prakasnan, 2016) 206f.
90. Munshi Ram Jyasu, *The Arya Samaj and Its Detractors:Vindication*, 1910 in Home/Political/B, File No. 55-58/1911, 339, National Archives of India, New Delhi.
91. Ibid.
92. Swami Shraddhanand, *Inside Congress* (Bombay: Phoenix Publications, 1946) 140.
93. *Report of the 36th Indian National Congress:Ahmedabad 1921* (Ahmedabad: Reception Committee Office, 1922) 39.
94. Swami Shraddhanand, *Inside Congress* (Bombay: Phoenix Publications, 1946) 131f.
95. Ibid., 154.

96. *Report of the 36th Indian National Congress: Ahmedabad 1921* (Ahmedabad: Reception Committee Office, 1922) 34.

97. Swami Shraddhanand, *Inside Congress* (Bombay: Phoenix Publications, 1946) 1a.

98. 'All-India Congress Committee: Mahatma Gandhi's Triumph', *Amrita Bazar Patrika* (Calcutta), February 28, 1922.

99. Swami Shraddhanand, *Inside Congress* (Bombay: Phoenix Publications, 1946) 169.

100. 'Swami Shraddhanand Arrested', *Tribune* (Lahore), September 12, 1922.

101. Letter from Shraddhanand Sanyasi to L.B. Amroil, District Magistrate Bijnore, July 1, 1921 as reprinted in *Leader* (Allahabad) July 7, 1921.

102. M.K. Gandhi, 'Malegaon Misbehaviour', *Leader* (Allahabad), May 16, 1921.

103. For an overview of the political, social and religious demands of the Mahasabha see: 'Swami Shraddhanand and a District Magistrate, *Leader* (Allahabad), July 7, 1921.

104. Br. R. Sheikh Muhammad, 'Hindu–Muslim Problem: Who is Responsible for the Present Condition', The *Muslim Outlook* (Lahore), February 16, 1924.

105. Moulvi Rafuddin Ahmed, 'Hindu-Moslem Relations: The Benares Edict – Why Not a Rival Organisation to the Maha Sabha', *Times of India* (Bombay), August 24, 1923.

106. 'Hindu Mahasabha ka Salana Jalsa', *Oudh Akhbar* (Lucknow), January 6, 1923.

107. Gail Minault, *The Khilafat Movement: Religious Symbolism and Political Mobilization in India* (New York: Columbia University Press, 1982) ch. 1.

108. Faisal Devji, *The Impossible Indian: Gandhi and the Temptation of Violence* (Cambridge, MA: Harvard University Press, 2013) 29–33.

109. 'Communal Frictions in United Provinces' Confidential Report, Home/Political, File No. 140/1925, 22, National Archives of India.

110. Though numerically negatable, the discourse around the conversion of Malkana Rajputs put the *shuddhi* campaign at the centre of Muslim political discourse, see: 'U.P. Social Conference', *Leader* (Allahabad), 27. August 1923.

111. David Gilmartin, 'Partition, Pakistan and South Asian History: In Search of a Narrative' *Journal of Asian Studies*, Vol. 57, No. 4 (1988) 1068–1095.

112. E.A. Gait, *Census of India, 1911 Volume 1: Part I. Report* (Calcutta: Superintendent Government Printing India, 1913) 117.

113. Ibid., 118.
114. Ibid.
115. Ibid.
116. Ibid.
117. Shraddhanand Sanyasi, *Hindu Sangathan: Saviour of the Dying Race* (Place of publication not identified: Publisher not identified,1924) 15.
118. Ibid., 18.
119. Ibid., 20–33.
120. Ibid., 17.
121. Ibid.
122. Ibid.
123. These are the two ways in which the *shuddhi* episode of the 1920s is conventionally framed, see: Yoginder Sikand and Manjari Katji, 'Mass Conversions to Hinduism among the Indian Muslims', *Economic and PoliticalWeekly* Vol. 29, No. 34 (1994) 2214–2219.
124. 'Report on the political situation in India during the month of March 1923', Home Department/Political, File No. 25/1923, 66, National Archives of India, New Delhi.
125. 'Communal Frictions in United Provinces' Confidential Report, Home/Political, File No. 140/1925, 26, National Archives of India, New Delhi.
126. 'Communal Frictions in United Provinces' Confidential Report, Home/Political, File No. 140/1925, 29, National Archives of India, New Delhi.
127. 'Communal Frictions in United Provinces' Confidential Report, Home/Political, File No. 140/1925, 29, National Archives of India, New Delhi.
128. 'Communal Frictions in United Provinces' Confidential Report, Home/Political, File No. 140/1925, 30, National Archives of India, New Delhi.
129. 'Communal Frictions in United Provinces' Confidential Report, Home/Political, File No. 140/1925, 22, National Archives of India, New Delhi.
130. 'Private informal meeting of leaders of all shades of opinions', Home/Political, File No. 277/1923, 79, National Archives of India, New Delhi.
131. 'Private informal meeting of leaders of all shades of opinions', Home/Political, File No. 277/1923, 83f, National Archives of India, New Delhi.
132. 'Private informal meeting of leaders of all shades of opinions',

Home/Political, File No. 277/1923, 83, National Archives of India, New Delhi.

133. 'Private informal meeting of leaders of all shades of opinions', Home/Political, File No. 277/1923, 84, National Archives of India, New Delhi.

134. 'Private informal meeting of leaders of all shades of opinions', Home/ Political, File No. 277/1923, 102, National Archives of India, New Delhi.

135. Shabbir Ahmed Usmani, their spokesman, went even further and exclaimed he would never 'leave the congress and form [an] independent organisation', as he was bound 'by the fatwa [from] Sheikhul Hind', Hussain Ahmed Madani, only to abandon the Congress and turning into one of the biggest supporters of the Pakistan movement two decades later. 'Private informal meeting of leaders of all shades of opinions', Home/Political, File No. 277/1923, 81, National Archives of India, New Delhi.

136. 'Communal Frictions in United Provinces' Confidential Report, Home/Political, File No. 140/1925, 31, National Archives of India, New Delhi.

137. Though Chamupati never admitted to having written *Rangila Rasul*, it seems very much in line with his writing style. After his death the Arya Samaj began to ascribe the book to him more openly, 'Communal Frictions in United Provinces' Confidential Report, Home/Political, File No. 140/1925, 31, National Archives of India, New Delhi.

138. Letter Police Commissioner (J.J. Johnson) to Chief Commissioner of Delhi (A.M. Stow), 11 August 1927, in Home/Political, F11/x/1927, 42, National Archives of India, New Delhi.

139. Letter Police Commissioner (J.J. Johnson) to Chief Commissioner of Delhi (A.M. Stow), 11 August 1927, in Home/Political, F11/x/1927, 42, National Archives of India, New Delhi.

140. Letter Police Commissioner (J.J. Johnson) to Chief Commissioner of Delhi (A.M. Stow), 11 August 1927, in Home/Political, F11/x/1927, 43, National Archives of India, New Delhi.

141. *The Collected Works of Mahatma Gandhi Vol. 32* (New Delhi: Ministry of Information and Broadcasting, Government of India, 1969) 459.

142. Nripendra Nath Mitra (ed.), *The Indian Quarterly Register, Volume 2, July-December 1926* (Calcutta: The Annual Register Office, 1927) 355.

143. Ibid., 354.

144. Nripendra Nath Mitra (ed.), *The Indian Quarterly Register, Volume 2, July-December 1926* (Calcutta: The Annual Register Office, 1927) 356.

145. Ibid.

146. 'Communal Frictions in United Provinces' Confidential Report, Home/Political, File No. 140/1925, 23, National Archives of India.

147. Bob van der Linden, *Tradition, Rationality and Social Consciousness: The Singh Sabha, Arya Samaj and Ahmadiyah: Moral Languages From Colonial Punjab* (Universiteit van Amsterdam, PhD unpublished, 2004) 118–20.

148. Veer Savarkar 'Introduction' Indra Prakash (ed.), *A Review of the History & Work of the Hindu Mahasabha and the Hindu Sanghatan Movement* (New Delhi: The Akhil Bhartiya Hindu Mahasabha, 1938) XVII; 'Of all the institutions which are referred to above as being allied with the Hindu Mahasabha in the common cause of the Hindu Sanghatan Movement, the Arya Samaj must rank as being not only the first but the foremost advocate of the Hindu Cause. The Maha Sabha itself is in fact but an enlarged and more comprehensive edition of the Arya Samaj.' Bhai Parmanand 'Foreword', in Indra Prakash (ed.), *A Review of the History & Work of the Hindu Mahasabha and the Hindu Sanghatan Movement* (New Delhi: The Akhil Bhartiya Hindu Mahasabha, 1938) XVII.

149. 'The All-India Hindu Mahasabha', *Indian Social Reformer*, August 28, 1923.

150. 'Pandit Malviya and Muslims', *New India* (Madras), August 25, 1923.

151. 'The Hindu Mahasabha', *Justice* (Madras), August 28, 1923.

152. 'A Moving Appeal', *Daily Express* (Madras), August 22, 1923.

153. Nripendra Nath Mitra (ed.), *The Indian Quarterly Register, Volume 2, July-December 1926* (Calcutta: The Annual Register Office, 1927) 369.

154. Ibid., 371.

155. Ibid.

156. Ibid., 372.

157. Resolution and Speech at Congress Session Gauhati, December 26, 1926, as reprinted in *The Collected Works of Mahatma Gandhi Vol. 32* (New Delhi: Ministry of Information and Broadcasting, Government of India, 1969) 459.

158. Ibid., 445.

159. Ibid.

160. Ibid., 459.

161. Home/Political, File no. 132/1927, 45, National Archives of India, New Delhi.

162. Home/Political, File No. 132/1927, 46, National Archives of India, New Delhi.

163. Home/Political, File No. 132/1927, 47, National Archives of India, New Delhi.

164. Home/Political, File No. 132/1927, 48, National Archives of India, New Delhi.

165. Home/Political, File No. 132/1927, 48, National Archives of India, New Delhi.

166. Home/Political, File No. 132/1927, 49, National Archives of India, New Delhi.

167. *Al-Fazl* (Qadian), Janaury 11, 1927 as translated and quoted in *Tadhkira: English rendering of the divine revelations, dreams and visions vouchsafed to Mirza Ghulam Ahmad of Qadian* (Qadian: Nazarat Nashro Isha'at, 2019) 304.

168. Speech at Meeting of Women, Banaras, January 9, 1927 in *The Collected Works of Mahatma Gandhi Vol. 32* (New Delhi: Ministry of Information and Broadcasting, Government of India, 1969) 538.

169. Ibid., 540.

170. 'Report on the Disturbances at Delhi on 14.11.1927' in Home/Political, File No. 3/VII/1928, 42, National Archives of India, New Delhi.

171. 'Report on the Disturbances at Delhi on 14.11.1927' in Home/Political, File No. 3/VII/1928, 43, National Archives of India, New Delhi.

CHAPTER 3. SIN

1. 'Trial of Ghazi Ilam Din Shaheed', Abstract Translation of Zimni Report No 1(a), 43, Punjab Archives, Lahore.

2. Telegram R. No. A-75, August 6, 1927, Home/Political, File No, 132/III/1927, 67, National Archives of India, New Delhi.

3. Gene R. Thursby, *Hindu–Muslim Relations in British India: A Study of Controversy, Conflict, and Communal Movements in Northern India 1923-1928* (Leiden: Brill, 1975) 43.

4. Letter from C.M.G. Ogilvie, Deputy Commissioner Lahore to H.D. Craik, Chief Secretary to the Government Punjab, June 4, 1927 in Home/Political, File No. 11/x/1927, 24, National Archives of India, New Delhi. Apart from posters, Mufti Muhammad Sadiq, the secretary of Mirza Mahmud, also forwarded a reprint of *Rangila Rasul*, apparently from Banaras, to the authorities, see: Letter from H.G. Haig, Secretary to the Government of India to P.C. Bamford, September 15, 1927 in Home/Political, File No. 132/II/1927, 4, National Archives of India, New Delhi.

5. Telegram from the Chief Commissioner and Agent to the Govel non-

General in the North-West Frontier Province to the Secretary to the Government of India and the Chief of the General Staff and Army, May 10, 1919 in Home/Political/B, File No. 32 Proceedings June 1919, 79, National Archives of India, New Delhi.

6. 'Position of Hindus in the Frontier', *Tribune* (Lahore), August 20, 1927.

7. The *mohalla* has been renamed 'Sarfaroshan' in Ilm Din's memory; 'Trial of Ghazi Ilam Din Shaheed', Abstract Translation of Zimni Report No 1(a), 43, Punjab Archives, Lahore.

8. 'Trial of Ghazi Ilam Din Shaheed', Abstract Translation of Zimni Report No 1(a), 43, Punjab Archives, Lahore.

9. Ibid.

10. Ibid.

11. Ibid.

12. Ibid.

13. 'Trial of Ghazi Ilam Din Shaheed', Abstract Translation of Zimni Report No 1(a), 45, Punjab Archives, Lahore.

14. Ibid.

15. Ibid.

16. Ibid.

17. *Ilam ud Din v. Emperor*, A.I.R. 1930 Lahore, 158.

18. Ajit Singh, Bhagat Singh's uncle, was a close confidant of Lala Lajpat Rai and active in the Arya Samaj infused radical freedom struggle of the Ghadar movement. Both men were deported in 1908, but only Lajpat Rai was allowed to return. 'Weekly Report of the Director of Criminal Intelligence, dated the 4th January 1908' Home/Political/B, File No. 111-118/January 1908, 9, National Archives of India, New Delhi; On Bhagat Singh's case, see: Home/Political, File No. 4/20/1931, 53, National Archives of India, New Delhi.

19. Apart from the Zimni Report, which was recorded immediately after arresting Ilm Din, most subsequent legal proceedings are accurately reprinted from the original in Zafar Iqbal Nagina, Ghazi Ilmuddin Shaheed (Lahore: Jang Publishers, 1988) 118.

20. *Ilam ud Din v. Emperor*, A.I.R. 1930 Lahore, 158.

21. Ibid.

22. Mohammad Isaak Bhatti, Mian Abdul Aziz Malwada (Lahore: Nashriat, 2006) 210.

23. 'Inside Story of Mumtaz Begum', *The New Statesman* (London), August 1, 1925.

24. Letter from the Commissioner of Police Bombay to the Secretary to the Government of Bombay, Home Department, January 13, 1925

in Home/Political, File No. 114/I/1925, 24, National Archives of India, New Delhi.

25. Letter from the Commissioner of Police Bombay to the Secretary to the Government of Bombay, Home Department, January 13, 1925 in Home/Political, File No. 114/I/1925, 25, National Archives of India, New Delhi.

26. Jinnah organised the defence together with Mr Gupte and wove his defence strategy along similar lines as in the Ilm Din case (perhaps his signature move in criminal cases), see: Home/Political, File No. KW to 114/II/1925, 58–120, National Archives of India, New Delhi.

27. 'The Tilak Case', *Amrita Bazar Patrika* (Calcutta), July 1, 1908.

28. 'Mr. Tilak's Case', *Amrita Bazar Patrika* (Calcutta), August 9, 1916.

29. 'Alleged Contempt of Court: Bombay Chronicle Charged', *Leader* (Allahabad), November 27, 1922.

30. *Ilam ud Din v. Emperor*, A.I.R. 1930 Lahore, 158.

31. Ibid.

32. *The Legislative Assembly Debates (Official Report) Volume IV, Fifth Session of the Third Legislative Assembly 1929* (Simla: Government of India Press, 1930) 755.

33. Ibid.

34. Home/Political/B, File No. 810/1922, 11, National Archives of India, New Delhi.

35. Letter from Chief Secretary of Government Punjab to C.W. Gwynne, Deputy Secretary to the Government of India, June 9, 1922 in Home/Political/B, File No. 810/1922, 18, National Archives of India, New Delhi.

36. *The Collected Works of Mahatma Gandhi: XXIV May-August 1924* (New Delhi: The Director, Publications Division Ministry of Information and Broadcasting, Government of India, 1967) 145.

37. Ibid., 261.

38. *The Collected Works of Mahatma Gandhi: XXIV May-August 1924* (New Delhi: The Director, Publications Division Ministry of Information and Broadcasting, Government of India, 1967) 153.

39. Ibid., 261.

40. *Raj Paul vs. Crown*, P&J 1576 1927, IOR/L/PJ/1941, British Library, London.

41. The prosecution appealed that historical facts should be marshalled in the court room as this would infinitely extend the case without ever coming to a conclusion. Judge Martineau of Lahore High Court rejected their appeal and, agreeing with Phailbus, held that history

matters, even when it would take time to establish the facts. See *King Emperor v. Raj Paul* A.I.R. 1926 Lahore 195.

42. *Raj Paul vs. Crown*, P&J 1576 1927, IOR/L/PJ/1941, British Library, London.
43. Ibid.
44. Letter from Chief Secretary to the Government of the Punjab, September 29, 1927 in Home/Political, File No. 102/1928, 8, National Archives of India, New Delhi.
45. Letter from Chief Secretary to the Government of the Punjab, September 29, 1927 in Home/Political, File No. 102/1928, 7, National Archives of India, New Delhi.
46. Letter from Chief Secretary to the Government of the Punjab, September 29, 1927 in Home/Political, File No. 102/1928, 8, National Archives of India, New Delhi.
47. *Crown v. Raj Paul*, in P&J 1567 1927, IOR/L/PF/6/1941, British Library, London; also republished in File No. 132/1927, 31–6, National Archives of India, New Delhi.
48. Ram Lal Tara, 'Sir Gokul Chand Narang', in *Punjab's Eminent Hindus*, ed. N.B. Sen (Lahore: New Books Society, 1943) 36.
49. *Rajpal v. Crown*, in Home/Political, File No. 132/1927, 36–9, National Archives of India, New Delhi.
50. Dalip Singh's great-grandfather had given Mirza Ghulam Ahmad's father refuge after the Sikh rulers ousted them from Qadian in the early nineteenth century.
51. *Crown v. Raj Paul*, in P&J 1567 1927, IOR/L/PF/6/1941, British Library, London.
52. Ibid.
53. Most scholarly evaluation have not given enough weight to this point that it was blasphemous insults and killings that produced rage not legal rulings.
54. Sir Zafarullah Khan claims to have heard this through his brother from one of the sitting members of the bench, Justice Harrison, in Zafarullah Khan, *My Mother* (London: The London Mosque, 1981) 55.
55. 'Report on Communal Disturbances at Lahore – May 1927' in Home/Political, File No. 11/x/1927, 112f, National Archives of India, New Delhi.
56. 'Report on Communal Disturbances at Lahore – May 1927' in Home/Political, File No. 11/x/1927, 114, National Archives of India, New Delhi.
57. In cases of emergency, the Deputy Superintendent can also take

such decisions. He took thirteen of his men to the Sikh gurdwara but found 'all quiet': 'Report on Communal Disturbances at Lahore – May 1927' in Home/Political, File No. 11/x/1927, 114, National Archives of India, New Delhi.

58. Teja Singh was later charged with murder and lost his job: 'Report on Communal Disturbances at Lahore – May 1927' in Home/Political, File No. 11/x/1927, 114, National Archives of India, New Delhi.

59. 'Report on Communal Disturbances at Lahore – May 1927' in Home/Political, File No. 11/x/1927, 114, National Archives of India, New Delhi.

60. 'Report on Communal Disturbances at Lahore – May 1927' in Home/Political, File No. 11/x/1927, 122, National Archives of India, New Delhi.

61. 'Rangila Rasul Case: M. Rajpal's Statement', *Tribune* (Lahore), June 9, 1926.

62. Ibid.

63. Ibid.

64. 'Report on Communal Disturbances at Lahore – May 1927' in Home/Political, File No. 11/x/1927, 125, National Archives of India, New Delhi.

65. Letter from C.M.G. Ogilvie, Deputy Commissioner Lahore to H.D. Craig, Chief Secretary to Government, Punjab, June 30, 1927 in Home/Political, File. No. 132/III/1927, 8, National Archives of India, New Delhi.

66. 'Resign!' *Muslim Outlook* (Lahore), June 14, 1927.

67. Ibid.

68. Ibid.

69. *In the Matter of Muslim Outlook*, A.I.R. 1927 Lahore 610.

70. Ibid., 612.

71. Ibid., 613.

72. Ibid.

73. *Guru Ghantal* (Lahore), July 11, 1927 as cited in Mirza Tahir Ahmad, *Ahmadiyya Muslim Jama'at and the Muslims of India* (Tilford, Surrey: Islam International Publications, 2007) 11.

74. 'Rangila Rasul Case', *Sind Observer* (Karachi), June 23, 1927.

75. This figure is debated: Muslim Outlooks reported fifty thousand attendees but the colonial authorities spoke of a mere fifteen thousand. The truth probably lies somewhere in between. 'Ultimatum of Lahore Musalmans', *Muslim Outlook*, June 24, 1927.

76. 'Agitation for the "Muslim Outlook": Muslim Hartal and Meetings', *Hindu Herald* (Lahore), June 24, 1927.

77. 'Lahore Muslim's Indignation: "Muslim Outlook" Conviction Sequel', *Hindustan Times* (New Delhi), June 24, 1927.
78. '"Muslim Outlook" Contempt Case', *Tribune* (Lahore), June 24, 1927.
79. Ibid.
80. The correspondent of The Tribune claims that Mr. Phailbus attended the meeting 'throughout', 'Rangila Rasul Judgement: Lahore Musalman's Protest', *Tribune* (Lahore), June 24, 1927.
81. Telephone Message from Deputy Commissioner, Lahore to H.D. Craik, Chief Secretary, July 3, 1927 in Home/Political, File No. 132/1927, 5, National Archives of India, New Delhi.
82. Habib's words were: 'suar', 'surni ka bachcha', 'kanjar' in Telephone Message from Deputy Commissioner, Lahore to H.D. Craik, Chief Secretary, July 3, 1927 in Home/Political, File No. 132/1927, 5, National Archives of India, New Delhi.
83. 'Rowdy Scenes at Lahore Meeting', *Bombay Chronicle* (Bombay), July 4, 1927.
84. Telephone Message from Deputy Commissioner, Lahore to H.D. Craik, Chief Secretary, July 3, 1927 in Home/Political, File No. 132/1927, 8, National Archives of India, New Delhi.
85. Letter from Justice Dalip Singh, Lahore High Court to Malcolm Hailey, Governor of the Punjab, August 14, 1927 in Home/Political, File No. 132/III/1927, 31, National Archives of India, New Delhi.
86. Letter from Sir Malcolm Hailey, Governor of the Punjab to India Office, June 16, 1927 in Home/Political, File No. 132, 3, National Archives of India, New Delhi.
87. Ibid.
88. Letter from Justice Dalip Singh, Lahore High Court to Malcolm Hailey, Governor of the Punjab, August 14, 1927 in Home/Political, File No. 132/III/1927, 33, National Archives of India, New Delhi.
89. *Devi Sharan Sharma and others v. Emperor*, A.I.R. 1927 Lahore 594; 'The "Vartman" Judgement: Dr. Gokal Chand's Statement', *Tribune* (Lahore), August 11, 1927.
90. Justice Broadway ordered the transfer of *Risala Vartman* from the Amritsar district magistrate's court to the High Court on 5 July 1927. At the time he was planning to conduct the hearing alone. To increase the legal standing of the ruling, Justice Skemp joined the bench later. Home/Political, File No. 132/1927, 66, National Archives of India, New Delhi.
91. Telegram from the Government of the Punjab to the Government of Bombay, July 6, 1927 in Home/Political, File No. 132/1927, 10, National Archives of India, New Delhi.

92. Ibid.

93. *Devi Sharan Sharma and others v. Emperor*, A.I.R. 1927 Lahore 601.

94. Uma Shanker interview of Jang Bahadur Singh, July 27, 1975 as reprinted in Audio, Interview Number 208, 83f, Archive Centre of South Asian Studies, Cambridge.

95. Uma Shanker interview of Jang Bahadur Singh, July 27, 1975 as reprinted in Audio, Interview Number 208, 84, Archive Centre of South Asian Studies, Cambridge.

96. Insults on Prophets and Saints: Maulana Mohamed Ali's View, *The Leader* (Allahabad), July 23, 1927.

97. 'Muslim Outlook Case: Governor's Reply to Ahmadiyas' *Civil and Military Gazette* (Lahore), July 10, 1927.

98. Letter from Mufti Muhammad Sadiq, 'Foreign Secretary to His Holiness the Khalifatul Mesih' to His Excellency the Right Honourable Edward Frederick Lindley Wood, Baron Irwin of Kirby, Viceroy and Governor-General of India, August 27, 1927 in Home/Political, File No. 132/III/1927, 71, National Archives of India, New Delhi.

99. Ibid.

100. *Ata-Ullah Shah Bokhari v. Crown,* in Home/Political, File No. 36/5/35, 26, National Archives of India, New Delhi.

101. Letter from M.B. Mahmud Ahmad, Head of the Ahmadiya Community to Baron Irwin of Kirby, Viceroy and Governor General of India, October, 1926 in Letter from Mufti Muhammad Sadiq, 'Foreign Secretary to His Holiness the Khalifatul Mesih' to His Excellency the Right Honourable Edward Frederick Lindley Wood, Baron Irwin of Kirby, Viceroy and Governor-General of India, August 27, 1927 in Home/Political, File No. 132/III/1927, 80, National Archives of India, New Delhi.

102. Letter from Mufti Muhammad Sadiq, 'Foreign Secretary to His Holiness the Khalifatul Mesih' to His Excellency the Right Honourable Edward Frederick Lindley Wood, Baron Irwin of Kirby, Viceroy and Governor-General of India, August 27, 1927 in Home/Political, File No. 132/III/1927, 72, National Archives of India, New Delhi.

103. Ibid.

104. Letter from M.B. Mahmud Ahmad to Baron Irwin, Viceroy of India, 31 August 1927, in in Home/Political, File No. 132/III/1927, 80, National Archives of India, New Delhi.

105. For instance, the newspapers *Badr*, *Nur*, and *Al-Fazl*. See: Fortnightly report on the internal political situation in India during the month of February 1927, Home/Political, File No. F-36/1927, 9, National Archives of India, New Delhi; Fortnightly report on the internal

political situation in India during the month of June 1927, Home/ Political, File No. 32/1927, 37, National Archives of India; Fortnightly Report on the Internal Political Situation in India for the Month of November 1927, Home/Political, File No. 32/1927, 14, National Archives of India, New Delhi.

106. 'Rasul-i-Karim ki muhabbat ka dawa karne wale kiya ab bhi bedar na hone', in Fortnightly report on the internal political situation in India during the month of June 1927, Home/Political, File No. 32/1927, 37, National Archives of India.

107. Letter from W.T.M. Wright, Secretary of the Legislative Assembly to Abdul Latif Farookhi, August 20, 1927 in Home/Political, File No. 44/VII/1927, 29, National Archives of India, New Delhi.

108. Letter from G.H. Spence, Secretary of the Council of State, to Saiyad Muhammad Padshah Sahib Bahadur, July 21, 1927 in Home/Political, File No. 44/VII/1927, 29, National Archives of India, New Delhi.

109. 'Report of the Select Committee on the Bill further to amend the Indian Penal Code and the Code of Criminal Procedure, 188, for certain purpose, with the Bill as amended' in File No. 132/1927, 66, National Archives of India, New Delhi.

110. 'Select Committee: Minutes of Dissent', Home/Political, File No. 132/1927, 68, National Archives of India, New Delhi.

111. Home/Political, File No. 132/1927, 108, National Archives of India, New Delhi.

CHAPTER 4. TRANSGRESSION

1.   On Pakistan's creation and the early debates on the notions of community, nationhood, and power, see: Farzana Sheikh, *Making Sense of Pakistan* (London: Hurst & Company, 2018) 1–40.

2.   *The Reminiscences of Sir Muhammad Zafrulla Khan* (Maple, Ontario: Oriental Publishers, 2004) 36.

3.   Stephen Legg, 'Imperial Internationalism: The Round Table Conference and the Making of India in London, 1930–1932.' *Humanity: An International Journal of Human Rights, Humanitarianism, and Development* 11, no. 1 (2020) 32-53.

4.   *The Reminiscences of Sir Muhammad Zafrulla Khan* (Maple, Ontario: Oriental Publishers, 2004) 31.

5.   Ibid., 40.

6.   Appointment to the Viceroy's Executive Council and Appointment to the Federal Court in 1941: Public, File No. 20(1) GGB/1941, National Archives of India, New Delhi.

7. *The Reminiscences of Sir Muhammad Zafrulla Khan* (Maple, Ontario: Oriental Publishers, 2004) 114.

8. There has been a lot of controversy about the line drawn to divide West Punjab (Pakistan) from East Punjab (India). To this day Pakistanis hold that Mountbatten, the Viceroy, altered the Award because of the marked delay in conveying Radcliffe's decision to the public. The thorn of contention centres around the Ferozepur and Gurdaspur districts, which were Muslim-majority areas but were awarded to India. Radcliffe did this on the basis of 'other factors', like water works, railways, and communication. But even Radcliffe remained 'conscious that there are legitimate criticisms to be made' of his Award. Report from Sir Cyril Radcliffe to His Excellency the Governor General, August 12, 1947, in Foreign Office Files for India, Pakistan and Afghanistan, 1947–1964 [FOF], DO 133/59, 217–18, UK National Archives, Kew.

9. Zafarullah Khan lobbied extensively for the passing of the United Nations Security Council Resolution S/RES/47(1948). It is still widely believed in Indian diplomatic circles, that Zafarullah's personal connections with the delegates were a major factor. For Zafarullah's efforts see: Letter from Sir Zafrulla Khan to the President of the Security Council, April 30, 1948, FOF, FO 371/69716, 86–9, UK National Archives, Kew.

10. F.K. Khan Durrani, *The Meaning of Pakistan* (Lahore: Sh. Muhammad Ashraf, 1944).

11. Ibid., 112–13.

12. Durrani features more than fifty times in Prasad's book, see: Rajendra Prasad, *India Divided* (New Delhi: Penguin Book, 2010 [1946]).

13. Zafarullah Khan, 'Pakistan's Place in Asia', *International Journal* Vol. 6, No. 4 (1951) 266.

14. Ibid., 269.

15. Ibid., 271.

16. Waheed Ahmad (ed.) *Diary and Notes of Mian Fazl-i-Husain* (Lahore: Research Society of Pakistan, University of Punjab, 1977) 141.

17. Home/Political, File No. 36/5/1935, 33, National Archives of India, New Delhi.

18. Home/Political, File No. 36/5/1935, 31, National Archives of India, New Delhi.

19. Home/Political, File No. 36/5/1935, 21, National Archives of India, New Delhi.

20. Home/Political, File No. 36/5/1935, 23, National Archives of India, New Delhi.

21   Mirza Mahmud had been exaggerating his influence on the colonial government. Calling Ahmadis pro-British was not necessarily an insult: 'So far as the Qadianis are concerned, the Governor in Council believes that part of the influence, which they have been able to exercise in the past, is due to the impression which they take every means of propagating that they have influence in high quarters and are able to affect the course of affairs.' Letter from the Government of the Punjab to the Political Secretary to the Government of India in the Foreign and Political Department, July 1934 in Home/Political, File No. 108/1934, 4, National Archives of India, New Delhi.

22.   Jawaharlal Nehru, 'The Solidarity of Islam', *The Modern Review* 58 (1935), 504f.

23.   Latif Ahmed Sherwani (ed.) *Speeches, Writings and Statements of Iqbal* (Lahore: Iqbal Academy Pakistan, 1977) 174.

24.   Ibid., 176.

25.   A scholarly attempt to credit the ulema with impacting the Muslim League in the immediate years before partition can be found in Venkat Dhulipala, *Creating a New Medina: State Power, Islam, and the Quest for Pakistan in Late Colonial North India* (Cambridge: Cambridge University Press, 2014).

26.   For the broader historical context, see Farzana Shaikh, *Making Sense of Pakistan* (London: Hurst & Company, 2018) ch. 3.

27.   The Indian Independence Act of 1947 was passed by the British Parliament and received Royal Assent on July 18, 1947.

28.   M.A. Jinnah, Constituent Assembly of Pakistan [CAP], August 11, 1947.

29.   Ibid.

30.   One of Jinnah's greatest fears was that, in the name of secularism, Hindus would treat Muslims in a united India like untouchables.

31.   Liaquat Ali Khan, CAP, August 11, 1947.

32.   Ibid.

33.   Dhirendra Nath Datta, CAP, May 18, 1947.

34.   H.S. Suhrawardy, CAP, May 18, 1947.

35.   For the ensuing language movement and the collapse of the Muslim League in East Pakistan, see Ian Talbot, *A History of Modern South Asia: Politics, States, Diasporas* (New Haven: Yale University Press, 2016) 198-206.

36.   Bhupendra Kumar Datta, CAP, February 25, 1948.

37.   Bhupendra Kumar Datta, CAP, February 25, 1948.

38.   Ghazanfar Ali Khan, CAP, February 25, 1948.

39.   Ibid.

40. Liaquat Ali Khan, CAP, February 25, 1948.

41. For a micro-historical account of violence in a Punjabi city, see Ian Talbot, 'The August 1947 Violence in Sheikhupura City' in Ian Talbot (ed.), *The Independence of India and Pakistan: New Approaches and Reflections* (Karachi: Oxford University Press, 2013) 90–119.

42. The full text of the resolution reads: 'That this Assembly resolves that Mr. Mohammad Ali Jinnah, President of the Constituent Assembly of Pakistan and Governor-General designate of Pakistan be addressed as 'Quaid-i-Azam Mohammad Ali Jinnah, Governor-General of Pakistan' in all official Acts, documents, letters and correspondence from Augist 15, 1947.' Liaquat Ali Khan, CAP, August 12, 1947.

43. M. Munir and M.R. Kayanai, *Report of the Court of Inquiry Constituted under Punjab Act II of 1954 to Enquire into the Punjab Disturbances of 1953* (Lahore: Superintendent, Government Printing Punjab, 1954) 302f.

44. Ibid., 304.

45. Ibid., 309.

46. Ibid., 289f.

47. Ibid., 75.

48. Ibid., 100f.

49. Ibid., 338.

50. Ibid., 155.

51. Ibid., 155–60.

52. Ibid., 291.

53. Ibid., 296.

54. Ibid., 291.

55. On Nazimuddin's reluctance see: *The Reminiscences of Sir Muhammad Zafrulla Khan* (Maple, Ontario: Oriental Publishers, 2004) 243.

56. This narrative has been proposed by, amongst others, Samad Yunus. A more recent account by Aqil Shah suggests that the army under Ayub Khan was eagerly waiting for an occasion to expand the role of the military in the nascent state, which portrays Ayub Khan unfairly as a power-hungry general. Aqil Shah, *The Army and Democracy: Military Politics in Pakistan* (Cambridge, MA: Harvard University Press, 2014) 67–9.

57. For an insider's account of the events leading up to Partition see: Abul Kalam Azad, *India Wins Freedom: An Autobiographical Narrative* (New Delhi: Orient Longman Limited, 1959).

58. 'Pakistan National Assembly Election 1970–71', *Dawn* (Karachi), December 11, 1970.

59. Zulfikar Ali Bhutto, *The Great Tragedy* (Karachi: Pakistan Peoples Party, 1971) 16.

60. Zulfikar Ali Bhutto's speech from 28 February 1971 at Iqbal Park, Lahore, Audio Tape, Author's Archive.
61. Zulfikar Ali Bhutto, *The Great Tragedy* (Karachi: Pakistan Peoples Party, 1971) 8f.
62. Zulfikar Ali Bhutto, *The Great Tragedy* (Karachi: Pakistan Peoples Party, 1971) 16.
63. Memorandum of Conversation, Washington, September 18, 1973 in Ford Library, National Security Adviser, Kissinger-Scowcroft West Wing Office File, Box 19, India/Pakistan. https://static.history.state.gov/frus/frus1969-76ve08/pdf/d147.pdf.
64. Zulfikar Ali Bhutto speech at Nishtar Park, Karachi. March 1, 1972, https://bhutto.org/wp-content/uploads/2020/04/101-Speech-at-the-public-meeting-in-nishtar-park-karachi-03-01-19972.mp3.
65. Legislative, File No. 588-590/1920, National Archives of India, New Delhi.
66. Legislative, File No. 591-593/1920, National Archives of India, New Delhi.
67. Legislative/Council/B, File No. 3/1921, National Archives of India, New Delhi.
68. Ibid.
69. 'Against Non-Cooperation: Non-official Members' Manifesto', *Leader* (Allahabad), August 29, 1920.
70. 'Khan Bahadur', *Amrita Bazar Patrika* (Calcutta), June 4, 1921.
71. Letter from H.K. Kirpalani, Chief Secretary Government Sind to M. Maxwell, Secretary to the Government of India, February 19, 1937 in Home/Political, File No. 18/2/1937, 45, National Archives of India, New Delhi.
72. In his letter to Nehru, Shah Nawaz wrote 'in view of the complete breakdown of administration resulting in chaotic condition in the State, you should take over the administration forthwith and ensure peace and order at the earliest possible moment.' Letter from Shah Nawaz Bhutto, Dewan of Junagadh to Pandit Nehru, Prime Minister of India, November 8, 1947 in FOF, DO133/76, 124, UK National Archives, Kew.
73. She converted to Islam and changed her name to Khurshid Begum; see Owen Bennett-Jones, *The Bhutto Dynasty* (New Haven: Yale University Press, 2020) 33f.
74. Only a year later, Bhutto would refuse to acknowledge his associations with Iskander Mirza and say similar things to General Ayub Khan, who was then in charge: *Iskander Mirza Speaks: Speeches, Statements and Private Papers* (Lahore: Gora Publishers, 1997) 246.

75. Salman Taseer, *Bhutto: A Political Biography* (London: Ithaca Press, 1979) ch. 1.

76. Bhutto pleaded at the Supreme Court of India on November 3, 1958 that he was 'now settled in Karachi and does not propose to prosecute appeal No. 489 of 1957 pending in this honourable court any further.' See Rajya Sabha Debates, Vol. LIV, No. 12, November 19, 1965.

77. Rajya Sabha Debates, Vol. LIV, No. 12, November 19, 1965.

78. Ibid.

79. Shri Mahavir Tyagi, India's Minister of Rehabilitation stated the following in parliament: 'While on the one hand he [Zulfikar Ali Bhutto] was contesting the decision that he was an evacuee and disowned any connection with Pakistan, its nationality or domicile, on the other hand he had filed an application in Pakistan as an evacuee claiming payment of a court deposit lying with the High Court Bombay.' Rajya Sabha Debates, Vol. LIV, No. 12, November 19, 1965.

80. Rajya Sabha Debates, Vol. LIV, No. 12, November 19, 1965.

81. Diary note March 3, 1967 in Craig Baxter (ed.), *Diaries of Field Marshal Mohammad Ayub Khan, 1966-1972* (Karachi: Oxford University Press, 2008) 69.

82. The speech at the UN Security Council in 1965, in which Bhutto claimed Indian-occupied Kashmir to be a part of Pakistan 'in flesh' and that he was willing to 'wage a war of a thousand years' is usually singled out as a prime example of his oratorical skills. Though the BBC's positive coverage of the speech ('most impressive and effective speech of its kind in the Council's history') was soon challenged by India as biased. External Affairs/AMS, File No. WII 307(5)/1969, 44, National Archives of India, New Delhi.

83. UN Security Council. S/7221, March 25, 1966.

84. Ibid.

85. Diary entry September 2, 1966 in Crag Baxter (ed.) *Diaries of Field Marshal Mohammad Ayub Khan, 1966-1972* (Karachi: Oxford University Press, 2008) 3.

86. Tariq Ali, *Uprising in Pakistan: How to Bring Down a Dictatorship* (London: Verso, 2018) 27–30.

87. Shahid Javed Burki, *Pakistan under Bhutto, 1971-1977* (London: The Macmillan Press, 1980) 70.

88. Even Zulfikar Ali Bhutto's land reforms largely targeted those landlords politically opposed to the PPP. Those on PPP tickets retained their landholdings. Banks which had been nationalised were forced to issue cheap loans to PPP landlords, who felt no need to pay them back.

See Craig Baxter, 'The People's Party Vs. the Punjab "Feudalists"' in *Journal of Asian and African Studies*, Vol. 8, Issue 3-4 (1973).

89. Seyyed Vali Reza Nasr, *The Vanguard of the Islamic Revolution: The Jama'at-i Islami of Pakistan* (Berkeley, CA: University of California Press, 1994) 76.

90. Ibid.

91. Bhutto dismissed the Governors of NWFP and Baluchistan with the reasoning that arms had been hidden in the Iraqi Embassy that were going to be used for the Baluchistan freedom movement: External Affairs/Historical, File No. HI/1012(57)/1973, 30, National Archives of India, New Delhi; for a vivid account of the events that led up to the military intervention, see: Tariq Ali, *Can Pakistan Survive: The Death of a State* (New York: Penguin Books, 1983) 99-133.

92. Interviews with a former *Jamaat-i-Taliba* student, who had participated in the brawl. Conducted by the author, 10 August 2019.

93. Ibid.

94. Letter from Shagufta to The Prime Minister of the UK, July 19, 1947, in FOF, FCO 37/1500, 300, UK National Archives, Kew.

95. 'Shops set on fire in Pakistan', *Guardian* (Manchester), March 31, 1974; 'Tension in Punjab Mounts', *Times* (London), June 13, 1974; 'All in the Name of Allah', *Economist* (London), June 15, 1974; 'Shops Set on Fire in Pakistan', *Daily Telegraph* (London) May 31, 1974; Ali Usman Qasmi, *The Ahmadis and the Politics of Religious Exclusion in Pakistan* (London: Anthem Press, 2014) 175ff.

96. Ali Usman Qasmi, *The Ahmadis and the Politics of Religious Exclusion in Pakistan* (London: Anthem Press, 2014) 176.

97. Z.A. Bhutto, *National Assembly of Pakistan Debates* [NAD], June 3, 1974.

98. Ibid.

99. Bhutto's brief moment of resistance in this matter can hardly justify the laudatory account that he receives in Owen Bennett-Jones' otherwise measured account. Owen Bennett-Jones, *The Bhutto Dynasty* (New Haven, Yale University Press, 2020).

100. *Jang* (Karachi), July 10, 1974.

101. Z.A. Bhutto, NAD, June 3, 1974.

102. Sahibzada Ahmad Raza Khan Qasuri, NAD, June 3, 1974.

103. Ibid.

104. Sahibzada Ahmad Raza Khan Qasuri, NAD, June 2, 1974.

105. YouTube. AmeerAbbasOfficial84 'Special interview of Complainant against Zulfiqar Ali Bhutto | Real Facts Exposed | Ahmed Raza Kasuri', uploaded on April 4, 2020 https://www.youtube.com/watch?v=_RTY0WSHarM [16:25] Accessed December 15, 2020.

106. YouTube. AmeerAbbasOfficial84 'Special interview of Complainant against Zulfiqar Ali Bhutto | Real Facts Exposed |Ahmed Raza Kasuri', uploaded on April 4, 2020 https://www.youtube.com/watch?v=_RTY0WSHarM [17:41] Accessed December 15, 2020.

107. Adeel Hussain, 'Muhammad Iqbal's Constitutionalism', *Indian Law Review* (2018) Vol. 2.

108. *The National Assembly of Pakistan: Proceedings of the Special Committee of the Whole House held in Camera to Consider the Qadiani Issue August 5-September 7, 1974* [SCQ] 90f.

109. Yahya Bakhtiar, SCQ, 28.

110. *Zulfikar Ali Bhutto v. The State*, PLD 1979, 68.

111. Abdul Hafeez Pirzada, SCQ, 3075.

112. Ibid.

113. H.L.A. Hart, 'Oxford and Mrs. Thatcher', *The New York Review of Books*, March 28, 1985.

114. Tariq Ali, *Can Pakistan Survive: Death of a State* (New York: Penguin Books, 1983) 213.

115. Stanley Wolpert, *Zulfi Bhutto of Pakistan: His Life and Times* (Oxford, Oxford University, 1993) 330.

116. Diary-note September 19, 1972 in Craig Baxter (ed.), *Diaries of Field Marshal Mohammad Ayub Khan, 1966-1972* (Karachi: Oxford University Press, 2008) 529.

117. *Zulfikar Ali Bhutto v. The State*, PLD 1979, 53.

CHAPTER 5. PUNISHMENT

1.   'A Funeral Mass for Sister Susan', *St Louis Post-Dispatch* (St. Louis), August 15, 1988.

2.   Barbara Crossette, 'Who Killed Zia?', *World Policy Journal* Vol. 22, No. 3 (Fall, 2005), 94.

3.   Pakistan-trained counterrevolutionaries were especially outraged by the freedoms granted to women, mandatory schooling for girls, and outlawing of child marriages. Sam Deaderick, 'The Russians, Yanks, Persians and Afghanis are coming!!' *Freedom Socialist*, Spring 1980, Vol. 6. Issue 2, 14f.

4.   'Zia Dies in Plane Crash', *Dawn* (Karachi), August 18, 1988.

5.   General Khalid Mahmud Arif, 'Zia the Soldier' in Salem Azzam (ed.), *Shaheed-ul-Islam Muhammad Zia-ul-Haq* (London: Indus Thames, 1990) 35.

6.   Ibid., 36.

7.   For an overview of the activities of Al-Zulfikar, see: Raja Anwar, *The*

Terrorist Prince: The Life and Death of Murtaza Bhutto (Lahore: Vanguard Books, 1998); their plots ranged from a bomb hoax (bizarrely from their own telephone line in their 'student flat' on 42 Lowndes Square, SW1 London) to the hijacking of a PIA plane and murder. Bhutto's son, denied all charges against them and claimed that he 'had been framed by the Dirty Tricks Department of the Pakistani Government'. When the police said that they had done a scientific test to determine that the telephone was not hacked, he simply said 'Well, let me tell you that I did it.' See Metropolitan Police Report, Police Station B Divn. October 11, 1978 in FOF, FCO 37/2108, 86-106, UK National Archives, Kew.

8. 'Who Killed Pakistan's Zia: The Fear and the Theories', *Washington Post* (Washington) August 28, 1988; 'Missile Killed Zia, Pakistan Indicates', *Washington Times* (Washington), August 29, 1988.

9. PTV transmission of the funeral, VHS tape, Author's Archive.

10. In an interview with Gavin Young from the Observer, Zia stated that 'If the Supreme Court says "acquit him [Bhutto], I'll acquit him". If it says, "hang the blighter", I'll hang him'. Even the Pakistani press was surprised by such statements as it was clear that Zia could not afford to let Bhutto out of prison without risking a fresh power struggle. Letter from C.P. Burdess, British Embassy Islamabad to J.M. Candlish, Foreign and Commonwealth Office October 6, 1978 in FOF, FCO 37/2108, 183, UK National Archives, Kew.

11. A short-cut to this conclusion can be reached by looking at the accusations levelled against both men.

12. Letter from O.G. Forster, British Embassy Islamabad to W.K.K. White, South Asia Department, Foreign and Commonwealth Office, July 23, 1979 in FOF, FCO 37/2188, 23, UK National Archives, Kew.

13. 'Leading Personality Report: Muhammad Zia-ul-Haq', FOF, FCO 37/2032, 15, UK National Archives, Kew.

14. 'Bhutto's Trial was Fair: Govt. Will not Influence Courts: CMLA', *Pakistan Times*, Rawalpindi, March 25, 1978; A surprisingly broad alliance of states petitioned Zia for clemency and to convert the death sentence into life imprisonment. A fraction of those are collected in FOF, FCO 37/2014, UK National Archives, Kew; for an early draft of Carter's urgent message to Zia to 'spare Mr. Bhutto's life' as this 'would be seen in the United States as an act of clemency, courage and statesmanship, consistent with the humane values our religion teaches us. It would be welcomed and applauded by Pakistan's many friends in the United States and around the world.' Though Bhutto always saw

the charges against him as an American ploy to eradicate a socialist leader, there seems to have been a genuine push to save his life from Jimmy Carter. See, Draft Letter from Jimmy Carter, President of the United States to His Excellency, General Zia-ul-Haq in FOF, FCO 37/2108, 79, UK National Archives, Kew.

15. For an exhaustive economic analysis on which this argument is based, see: Shahid Javed Burki, "Pakistan's Economy under Zia" in Shahid Javed Burki and Craig Baxter (eds), *Pakistan Under the Military: Eleven Years of Zia ul-Haq* (Boulder: Westview Press) 93.

16. Ibid., 94–5.

17. This was made up of the Jamaat-e-Islami, the Jamiat Ulema-e-Islam, the Jamiat Ulema-e-Pakistan, National Democratic Party, Baluchistan National Party, Muslim League Qayyum, Muslim League Functional, Democratic Party, Tehreek-e-Istaqlal.

18. Mary Anne Weaver 'Pakistan's General Zia: From Soldier to Politician', *Christian Science Monitor* (Boston), May 16, 1984.

19. Ibid.

20. Jack O'Connell, *King's Counsel: A Memoir of War, Espionage, and Diplomacy in the Middle East* (New York: W.W. Norton & Company, 2011) 103.

21. Valedictory Report by the Defence Attaché Brigadier G.N. Powell in FOF, FCO 32/2049, 48, UK National Archives, Kew.

22. Valedictory Report by the Defence Attaché Brigadier G.N. Powell in FOF, FCO 32/2049, 49, UK National Archives, Kew.

23. Valedictory Report by the Defence Attaché Brigadier G.N. Powell in FOF, FCO 32/2049, 50, UK National Archives, Kew.

24. Youtube. 'General Zia- imposing Martial Law (5-07-1977)).wmv' https://www.youtube.com/watch?v=pJIFbJX-cY8 Uploaded July 4, 2011 [7:47] Accessed December 15, 2020.

25. Youtube. 'General Zia ul Haq Inteview in 1977 regarding PM Bhutto' https://www.youtube.com/watch?v=QldlpYv_dEE Uploaded March 30, 2019 [1:22] Accessed December 22, 2020 (account since deleted).

26. Speech at the Majlis-e-Shura c. 1984, VHS Tape, Author's Archive. A snippet is also available at: https://www.youtube.com/watch?v=UuybwsOphdw.

27. Letter from S.J. Hiscock, British Embassy Islamabad to R.D. Lavers, Foreign and Commonwealth Office, November 23, 1978 in FOF, FCO 37/2108, 57f, UK National Archives, Kew.

28. Letter from A.R. Murray, British Embassy Islamabad to FCO Karachi,

Kabul, Delhi, Tehran September 19, 1978 in FOF, FCO 37/2107, 17, UK National Archives, Kew.

29. Letter from C.P. Burdess, British Embassy Islamabad to J.M. Candlish, Foreign and Commonwealth Office, October 2, 1978 in FOF, FCO 37/2108, 190, UK National Archives, Kew.

30. Only from this angle is Martin Lau's argument that the judiciary was a driving factor in the Islamisation of laws tenable. See, Martin Lau, *The Role of Islam in the Legal System of Pakistan* (Martinus Nijhoff: Leiden, 2006).

31. Corporal punishments and veiling efforts of women that Zia undertook were widely reported abroad, even in fringe newspapers: 'Man Whipped for Attack on Girl', *Gaysweek* (New York) March 30, 1978; 'Students ordered to Cover up', *Multiple Vision* (Kansas City) December 1, 1980.

32. Letter from A.R. Murray, British Embassy Islamabad to FCO Karachi, Kabul, Delhi, Tehran September 19, 1978 in FOF, FCO 37/2107, 17, UK National Archives, Kew.

33. 'Four Nationalities Theory Advocated: No Basis for Muslim Nationhood', *Pakistan News* (Rawalpindi) August 28, 1978.

34. Pakistan's newspaper blamed terrorist activities occurring in the border region on refugees, which led to growing tensions between locals and Afghan refugees. See, 'CIA Report, Pakistan: Coping with Afghan Refugees – An Intelligence Assessment' https://www.cia.gov/library/readingroom/docs/CIA-RDP88T00096R000600770001-2.pdf.

35. 'Zia Ul Haq', *Bangkok Post* (Bangkok), September 26, 1982.

36. Shias were the wealthier community so proportionately they would be subsidising the Sunnis with their *zakat* payments, which were distributed according to the size of the population. Restricted Report SAD Karachi, May 21, 1979 in FOF FCO 37/2188, 149, UK National Archives, Kew.

37. 'President amends relevant laws for separate electorate', Pakistan Times (Rawalpindi), September 25, 1978.

38. PLD 1978, Lahore, 139.

39. Zia-ul-Haq speech at the Majlis-e-Shura, May 1984, VHS tape, Author's Archive.

40. Most of the roughly three thousand men charged were released on bail shortly afterwards 'Report: Ordinance XX', *Nawaiwaqt* (Karachi), September 11, 1988.

41. For a comparison, in India's general election a year later that number was

well above sixty and in Bangladesh, where an army putsch had led to a similar period of disenchantment and where a number of major parties were boycotting the poll, the vote was still higher than fifty per cent.

42. Even her coalition partner, the *Mohajir Qaumi Movement*, a broadly secular party of Urdu-speaking migrants settled in Karachi, doubted her intentions when they realised that most of their people remained in jail. See: Anthony Hyman, 'No Great Change in Human Rights', *Index on Censorship* 10/89, 24.

43. Benazir Bhutto, Commencement Address Harvard University 1989, https://www.c-span.org/video/?7979-1/commencement-address.

44. John F. Burns, 'House of Graft: Tracing the Bhutto Millions; A Special Report; Bhutto Clan Leaves Trail of Corruption', *New York Times* (New York), January 9, 1998.

45. Anthony Hyman, 'No Great Change in Human Rights', *Index on Censorship* 10/89, 26.

46. 'Emergency Declared', *Dawn* (Karachi) August 7, 1990.

47. Ibid.

48. PPP claimed that the polls had been rigged. More than a decade later, a Supreme Court decision reprimanded the military for having funded IJI candidates.

49. PLD 91 FSC 10.

50. Ibid.

51. See only: Tripurdaman Singh and Adeel Hussain, *Nehru: The Debates That Defined India* (London: William Collins, 2021) ch. 1.

52. PLD 91 FSC 10.

53. *Zaheeruddin v. State* 26 SCMR 1993, 1753f.

54. Ibid., 1777.

55. Ibid.

56. Ibid., 1775.

57. The cases on which Chaudhary dwells at length are: *Cox v. New Hampshire*, *Cantwell v. Connecticut*, *Reynolds v. United States*, and *Hamilton v. Regents of the University of California*.

58. *Zaheeruddin v. State* 26 SCMR 1993, 1775.

59. Amnesty International, Use and Abuse of the Blasphemy Laws, 1 July 1994, ASA/33/08/94, available at: https://www.refworld.org/docid/3ae6a9aa4.html [accessed 27 October 2020].

60. https://www.pakembassyankara.com/userfiles/files/Form_A_Passport_Form.pdf.

61. For Muhammad Iqbal's legitimising narrative for this aspect see only Adeel Hussain, 'Muhammad Iqbal's Constitutionalism', *Indian Law Review* Vol 2 (2) 2018, 135-158.

62. See Christophe Jaffrelot, *The Pakistan Paradox: Instability and Resilience* (New York: Oxford University Press, 2015) 239–59.
63. For the view that primarily holds the army responsible, see Aqil Shah, *The Army and Democracy: Military Politics in Pakistan* (Cambridge, MA: Harvard University Press, 2014) ch. 5.
64. See Ayesha Jalal, *The Struggle for Pakistan: A Muslim Homeland and Global Politics* (Cambridge, MA: Harvard University Press, 2014) 311.
65. Ibid., 322–8.
66. United Nations General Assembly Fifty-Eighth Session, 9th Plenary Meeting, Wednesday, 24 September 2003, p. 18 http://undocs.org/en/A/58/PV.9.
67. Ibid.
68. See Martin Lau, 'Twenty-Five Years of Hudood Ordinances – A Review' *Washington and Lee Law Review* Vol. 64, Issue 4, 1300.
69. Muhammad Khalif Masud, 'Modernizing Islamic Law in Pakistan: Reform or Reconstruction?' *Journal of South Asian and Middle Eastern Studies*, Vol. 42, No. 2 (Winter 2019) 80.
70. 'Sufism to be promoted, says Shujaat' *Dawn*, October 13, 2006. https://www.dawn.com/news/214641/sufism-to-be-promoted-says-shujaat.

CHAPTER 6. REDEMPTION

1. 'Pakistaner Verbrennen Deutsche Flaggen' *Berliner Zeitung*, May 8, 2006.
2. 'Alptraum Einzeltäter', *Der Spiegel*, May 11, 2006.
3. Ibid.
4. For German penal law, the critical point is the moment the attack commences from the perspective of the attacker. As Cheema was still inquiring into the whereabouts of Köppel, he had not done everything to begin the attack. See, §22 Strafgesetzbuch.
5. 'Pakistan schickt Ermittler' *Die Tageszeitung*, May 10, 2006.
6. 'Zweifel an Suizid von Pakistaner' *Die Tageszeitung*, May 27, 2006.
7. For an elaboration on the theme of 'lone wolf attacks' and some further background on attacks along the same pattern, see Guido W. Steinberg, *German Jihad: On the Internationalization of Islamist Terrorism* (New York, Columbia University Press, 2013) ch. 2.
8. 'Alptraum Einzeltäter', *Der Spiegel*, May 11, 2006.
9. Ibid.
10. 'Taliban rüsten in Pakistan auf' *Rheinische Post*, May 15, 2006.
11. At least this is what Rizvi claimed in a video recorded more than a decade later, after Cheema had become a driving force for his *Tahreek-*

e-LabaikYa RasoolAllah [I am here to serve you, Oh Prophet] movement: YouTube. AllamaKhadimHussainRizvi9263 'Allama khadim Hussain Rizvi/Urs Ghazi Aamir Cheema Shaheed Alehrehmah' https:// www.youtube.com/watch?v=axCwC-pywJk uploaded November 23, 2016 [37:45] Accessed December 3, 2020.

12. 'Anti-deutsche Proteste' *Berliner Zeitung*, May 8, 2006.

13. The National Assembly of Pakistan. Debates. Official Report, Friday, the 5ᵗʰ May, 2006 (35ᵗʰ Session), Volume XXXV Contains No. 1-6, 457.

14. 'Suicide Leads to Aamir Cheema Death: German Ambassador', *Frontier Star*, May 12, 2006.

15. Opposition came only from the *Muttahida Qaumi Movement* [United National Movement], a secular party that draws its membership largely from the migrants who settled in Karachi after Partition. See 'MQM has reservations about Aamir Cheema's martyrdom: Farooq Sattar', *Baluchistan Times*, May 16, 2006.

16. 'PTI To Adopt Joint Strategy With Opposition About Aamir Cheema Issue: Imran', *Baluchistan Times*, May 17, 2006.

17. Ishfaqullah Shawl, 'Government to be pressurised to make probe report public: Imran visits Cheema's house', *Business Recorder*, May 18, 2006.

18. 'Government Plans to Bury Aamir Cheema Secretly', *Baluchistan Times*, May 12, 2006.

19. The right-wing Islamist party *Muttahida Majlis-e-Amal* [United Council for Action] would have preferred a public holiday for the entire country. See 'MMA berates Government Attitude on Aamir Cheema's Martyrdom', *Baluchistan Times*, May 14, 2006.

20. 'Government Plans to Bury Aamir Cheema Secretly', Baluchistan Times, May 12, 2006.

21. 'Aamir Cheema Buried in Saroki Amidst Thousands of Mourners' *Frontier Star* (Peshawar), May 13, 2006.

22. 'MMA berates Government Attitude on Aamir Cheema's Martyrdom', *Baluchistan Times*, May 14, 2006.

23. Early newspaper headlines fuelled these theories, see 'Germans Cold-Shouldered FIA', *Nation*, May 25, 2006; Over time these torture accusations have grown in magnitude:YouTube. FTM105FarooqTayyab 'The Story Of Amir Cheema Shaheed And Full Interview Father Of Amir Cheema Haji Nazeer Ahmad|FTM105|', https://www. youtube.com/watch?v=ZzX-bGUKMxE uploaded May 17, 2019 [5:45]. Accessed December 15, 2020.

24. This would be like levelling a vindicatory genealogy of Enlightenment reason against the vindicatory genealogy of theological thought.

25. For a diverging view, which sees ethical acts as relating more immediately to a new form of global politics, see Faisal Devji, *The Terrorist in Search of Humanity: Militant Islam and Global Politics* (London: Hurst & Company, 2008) 171–73.

26. This explains why Deobandis and Barelvis fail to enter a fruitful conversation. Barelvis push for the recognition of their constructed narratives as ethical acts, worthy of high praise. For rationalist Deobandis they simply look like invented fairy tales, which in turn leads Barelvis to accuse them of *gustakhi-e-Rasool* (insult to the Prophet) and *kuffar* (disbelief). For a diverging view that regards the respect given to the founders of their traditions as the nub of the Deobandi-Barelvi problem see, Mohammad Waqas Sajjad, *For the Love of the Prophet: Deobandi-Barelvi Polemics and the Ulama in Pakistan* (The Faculty of the Graduate Theological Union, PhD unpublished, 2018) 121–203.

27. YouTube. MuhammadShoaibTahir 'Jab Allama khadim Hussain Rizvi k Samnay Allama Tahir ul Qadri k Fav Naat Khawa Syed Fasih ud din Ae', https://www.youtube.com/watch?v=0kcuXKqwlkI uploaded December 5, 2020 [4:01] Accessed December 7, 2020.

28. On the interplay of sovereignty and blasphemy in Pakistan, see Faisal Devji, *Muslim Zion: Pakistan as a Political Idea* (London: Hurst & Company, 2013) 239f; Mashal Saif, *The 'Ulama in Contemporary Pakistan: Contesting and Cultivating an Islamic Republic* (Cambridge: Cambridge University Press, 2021) ch. 2.

29. Amongst the blasphemy cases that often get overlooked was the burning alive of eight Christians after allegations of insulting the Prophet Muhammad in Toba Tek Singh, see 'Shameful Behaviour', *The Nation*, August 1, 2009.

30. 'A Blot on Pakistan', *India Currents*, November 29, 2010.

31. Sessions Case No. 402/2019, *The State v. Mst. Asia Bibi*, p. 44, para 15, http://www.documentcloud.org/documents/2104049-trial-court-judgement.html Accessed December 15, 2020.

32. Ibid., p. 48, para. 26.

33. Ibid., para 15.

34. 'Salman Taseer backs Christian's blasphemy death appeal', *Daily Messenger*, November 17, 2010; 'Punjab Governor calls on President Zardari', *Baluchistan Times*, November 19, 2010.

35. 'Condemned Christian woman seeks mercy', *The Nation*, November 20, 2010.

36. Salman Taseer, *Bhutto: A Political Biography* (New Delhi: Vikas Publication, 1980) 151f.

37. YouTube. TheGovernorPunjab 'Governor Punjab- Aasia Bibi Press

Conference'   https://www.youtube.com/watch?v=HxvlLpSy4BI
uploaded November 22, 2020 [0:21] Accessed December 7, 2020.
38. YouTube. Shooter1pk 'Salman Taseer's Last Interview part4.flv'
https://www.youtube.com/watch?v=sTYA2s57Iwo uploaded
January 4, 2011 [1:32] Accessed December 7, 2020.
39. 'Blasphemy case: Zardari warned not to grant pardon', *Express Tribune*,
November 23, 2010.
40. 'ATAS protests Governor's support for Asia Bibi', *The Nation*,
November 23, 2010.
41. Ibid.
42. 'Lawyers observe strike, boycott courts', *The Nation*, November 23,
2010.
43. For instance, Sahibzada Fazal Karim of the Sunni Ittehad Council
feared the erosion of Sharia Law under Western pressure, see
'Handle Blasphemy Law with Care', *Pakistan Observer*, November,
28, 2020.
44. Loosely grouped together as the *Tehreek-e-Hurmat-e-Rasool* [Respect
the Prophet Movement] and far from being ideologically streamlined,
this faction threatened a countrywide movement if Asif Ali Zardari
was to go ahead with the pardon. 'THR holds rallies against "support"
to Asia today', *The Nation*, November 25, 2010; 'City witnesses
protests', *The Nation*, November 26, 2010.
45. A constant theme during the demonstration was that politicians
should not disrupt the judicial process. 'Jamiat-e-Ulema-e-Pakistan
(JUP) threatens Sherry Rahman', *The Baluchistan Times*, December 1,
2010.
46. 'Govt warned against repealing Blasphemy Laws', *The Nation*,
November 29, 2010.
47. YouTube. BlasphemyLaw 'Analyzing Salman Taseer's statement | | Kia
wo Kafir / Gustakh tha? aur Kia Mumtaz Qadri Ghazi hay?' https://
www.youtube.com/watch?v=fr9VW_T2egM uploaded October 28,
2011 [2:21] Accessed December 15, 2020.
48. Ibid.
49. 'No idea why Governor met Asia, says Badar', *The Nation*, November
27, 2010.
50. Ibid.
51. 'Rehman Malik sees accord on blasphemy laws', *Dawn*, March 12,
2011 https://www.dawn.com/news/612552/rehman-malik-sees-
accord-on-blasphemy-laws. Accessed December 15, 2020.
52. 'New death threats against "blasphemous" Christian', *Guardian*,
December 7, 2010.

53. 'No proposal under consideration to amend anti-blasphemy law: Sumsam', *Baluchistan Times*, December 30, 2010.

54. 'Taseer insists on review of blasphemy laws', *The Nation*, December 23, 2010.

55. Saba Hakeem and Zahid Bag, 'Complete shutter-down strike observed in Lahore', *Business Recorder*, January 1, 2011; 'Blasphemy Protests', *The Nation*, January 1, 2011; M. Wali Afridi, 'Proposed amendment in Blasphemy Law Government warned of dire consequences', *Frontier Post*, January 1, 2011.

56. Tanvir Siddiqi and Nasir Mehmood 'Strike brings country to standstill', *Pakistan Observer*, January 1, 2011; 'Pakistan Rally in Support of Blasphemy Law Seen as Harmful to Christians', Salman Masood, *New York Times*, January 1, 2011; Anita Joshua, 'Walking the tightrope on Pakistan's blasphemy laws', *The Hindu*, January 1, 2011.

57. 'Effigy of Taseer burnt in Ahmedpur East', *Frontier Post*, January 1, 2011.

58. 'Taseer presents prizes to winners', *Business Recorder*, January 3, 2011.

59. Mushtaq Mughal, 'Taseer gunned down', *The Nation*, January 4, 2011.

60. 'Govt. to probe murder thoroughly: Malik', *Baluchistan Times*, January 4, 2011.

61. 'Governor Punjab assassinated', *Baluchistan Express*, January 4, 2011.

62. 'Elite Force gunman assassinates Salman Taseer', *Daily Frontier Star*, January 4, 2011.

63. The statement has been reprinted in the original without correction as the constant usage of [sic] would make it hard to read. *Muhammad Malik Mumtaz Qadri v. State*, 6 PLD 2016 SC 17, 6.

64. *Muhammad Malik Mumtaz Qadri v. State*, 6 PLD 2016 SC 17, 5.

65. For the book that allegedly drove Mumtaz Qadri, see Aatish Taseer, *Stranger to History: A Son's journey through Islamic Lands* (Edinburgh: Canongate Books, 2009).

66. Qadri later claimed to have acted spontaneously but his later version seemed to correspond more to legal strategy. In his confessional statement at the Anti Terrorism Court in Islamabad, Qadri submitted that Hanif Qureshi's sermons 'not only moved me to act against the man who spoke against the sanctity of the Holy Prophet Muhammad (PBUH) but compelled me to stand up against those who were demanding changes in the blasphemy laws', see 'Why did Qadri kill Governor Taseer', *Express Tribune*, January 12, 2011.

67. After a personal meeting with Qureshi in May 2012, Mashal Said won the impression that Qureshi is 'an exceptional and provocative public speaker'. She also called him 'a compelling author'. Mashal Saif, *The*

'Ulama in Contemporary Pakistan: Contesting and Cultivating an Islamic Republic (Cambridge: Cambridge University Press, 2021) 107.

68. Omar Waraich, 'Why Did a Trusted Bodyguard Turn Fanatical Assassin', *The Independent*, January 28, 2011.

69. Israr Ahmed, 'Court defers Qadri's indictment', *The Nation*, February 1, 2011.

70. DVD in Author's Archive.

71. Ibid.

72. Ibid.

73. YouTube. Almujtaba100 'Hanif Qureshi's sermon which made Mumtaz Qadri to Kill Salman Taseer Gustakh e Rasool khanqah dogran', https://www.youtube.com/watch?v=8QEtLWYY6Tk uploaded August 27, 2011 [0:27] Accessed December 15, 2020.

74. A thoughtful analysis on this point can be found in: Juergen Schaflechner, "Blasphemy and the appropriation of vigilante justice in 'hagiohistoric' writing in Pakistan" in Paul Rollier, Kathinka Froystad, and Arild Engelsen Ruud (eds), *Outrage: The Rise of Religious Offence in Contemporary South Asia* (London: UCL Press, 2019) 208–235.

75. YouTube. 'Mufti Hanif Qureshi's hate speech with English Subs which made Mumtaz Qadri to kill Salman Taseer', https://www.youtube. com/watch?v=rlEPYtVo014 uploaded March 1, 2016 [2:40] Accessed December 15, 2020.

76. YouTube. TheIslamdefender180 'Mufti Hanif Qureshi -Shan-e-Ikhtiyarat-e-Mustafa', https://www.youtube.com/watch?v=KI4LM_13k-o uploaded October 8, 2011 [1:35:40] Accessed December 15, 2020; YouTube. TheIslamdefender180 'Mufti Hanif Qureshi 2012' uploaded May 22, 2012 [1:16:01] Accessed December 15, 2020.

77. YouTube. BrailveeOnline 'mufti HANIF QURESHI angry on SALMAN TASEER before his DEATH' https://www.youtube.com/watch?v=VwUnuGDbh6U uploaded May 25. 2020 [0:35] Accessed December 15, 2020.

78. YouTube. BrailveeOnline 'mufti HANIF QURESHI angry on SALMAN TASEER before his DEATH' https://www.youtube.com/watch?v=VwUnuGDbh6U uploaded May 25. 2020 [2:04] Accessed December 15, 2020.

79. 'A Game of Dare', *Economist*, March 3, 2016.

80. *Muhammad Malik Mumtaz Qadri v. State*, 6 PLD 2016 SC 17, 4.

81. For the colonial legacy of the term 'terrorism' see Joseph McQuade, *A Genealogy of Terrorism: Colonial Law and the Origins of an Idea* (Cambridge: Cambridge University Press, 2020).

82. Anti-Terrorism Act, 1997 (20 August 1997), PLD 1997 Central

Statutes (unreported) 535 as cited in Charles H. Kennedy, 'The Creation and Development of Pakistan's Anti-terrorism Regime, 1997-2002' in Satu P. Limaye, Mohan Malik and Robert G Wirsing (eds.), *Religious Radicalism and Security in South Asia* (Honolulu: Asia-Pacific Center for Security Studies, 2004), 390.

83. 'Death Haunts Pakistan', *India Today*, March 14, 2011.

84. *Mst. Asia Bibi v. The State*, PLJ 2019 Cr.C. (Note) 1 (DB) para. 2.

85. Ibid., para. 3.

86. Ibid., para. 19.

87. Ibid.

88. M.A. Niazi, 'Blasphemy case shakes the nation', *The Nation*, December 2, 2010; Saba Imtiza, 'Pakistan court upholds death penalty in Christian woman's blasphemy case', *Christian Science Monitor*, October 17, 2014 https://www.csmonitor.com/World/Asia-South-Central/2014/1017/Pakistan-court-upholds-death-penalty-in-Christian-woman-s-blasphemy-case Accessed 15 December 2020.

89. I take this point from Laurent Gayer's study on the attraction of the MQM for what he calls 'disgruntled youths in search of rapid upward social mobility', see Laurent Gayer, *Karachi: Ordered Disorder and the Struggle for the City* (London: Hurst & Company, 2014) 112.

90. On the motive of urban fun and violence, see Oskar Verkaaik, *Migrants and Militants: Fun and Urban Violence in Pakistan* (Princeton, NJ: Princeton University Press, 2004).

91. YouTube. 'justice nazir ahmed ghazi says about mumtaz qadri 2018 | mumtaz qadri namaz e janaza | mumtaz qadri naat' https://www.youtube.com/watch?v=qhbRdMP8-Ik uploaded June 7, 2018 [5:10] Accessed December 15, 2020.

92. Ibid. [0:45].

93. Ibid. [7:01].

94. YouTube. TayyibaProduction 'Justice nazir ahmed ghazi speech imam norani convention 2016' uploaded June 23, 2016 [9:45] Accessed December 15, 2020.

95. In its ruling on March 9, 2015, the Islamabad High Court dismissed the appeal against his death sentence but followed Nazir Ahmed's point that the case was not a matter that fell under the Anti Terrorism Act.

96. See, Sherali Tareen, *Defending Muhammad in Modernity* (Notre Dame, Indiana: University of Notre Dame Press, 2020); YouTube. TayyibaProduction 'Khadim Hussain Rizvi aiwan e iqbal Lahore', https://www.youtube.com/watch?v=2ZS2RM04BO8 uploaded June 15, 2016 [4:50] Accessed December 15, 2020.

97. YouTube. TayyibaProduction 'Khadim Hussain Rizvi aiwan e iqbal Lahore', https://www.youtube.com/watch?v=2ZS2RM04BO8 uploaded June 15, 2016 [21:58] Accessed December 15, 2020.

98. YouTube. Asaderaza 'Ya Rasool Allah Tere Chahne walo ki Khair By Malik Mumtaz Hussain Qadri', https://www.youtube.com/watch?v=vr_v0kcIZ2Q uploaded January 6, 2011 [0:21] Accessed December 15, 2020.

99. YouTube. Mani007aag 'Mumtaz Qadri reciting naat under police custody', https://www.youtube.com/watch?v=p95jH90vpjw uploaded January 6, 2011 [0:40] Accessed December 15, 2020.

100. *Muhammad Malik Mumtaz Qadri v. State*, 6 PLD 2016 SC 17, 37.

101. Ibid., 38.

102. YouTube. MuhammadUsmanNathanie'MumtazQadri | Sadr e Pakistan se appeal', https://www.youtube.com/watch?v=LG1j7Picj6c uploaded March 13, 2016 [0:28] Accessed December 15, 2020.

103. Inamullah Khattak, 'Mumtaz Qadri begs president for mercy', *The Nation*, January 20, 2016 https://nation.com.pk/20-Jan-2016/mumtaz-qadri-begs-president-for-mercy Accessed December 15, 2020.

104. YouTube. MuhammadNaqeebAhmad, 'Allama Khadim Hussain Rizvi | Mumtaz Qadri | Death', https://www.youtube.com/watch?v=UZh-cPJzFxc uploaded November 24, 2017 [0:48] Accessed December 15, 2020.

105. YouTube. Kudkhan 'Ghamidi - Mumtaz Qadri Ka Asal Jurm' https://www.youtube.com/watch?v=Vbc0zWBiC2M uploaded February 8, 2011 [5:20] Accessed December 15, 2020.

106. YouTube, RizviMedia92 'Allama Khadim Hussain Rizvi | Agr Haland Ne Gustakhi Ki To 'Atom Bomb' Chla Do Agr Nhi Chla sakte to', August 4, 2018 [at 0:21] Accessed December 15, 2020.

107. 'Declarations by the Candidate 1. I, _____(nominated candidate), hereby declare that, […] (iii) I believe in the absolute and unqualified finality of the Prophet-hood of Muhammad (Peace Be Upon Him), the last of the Prophets and that I am not the follower of anyone who claims to be a prophet in any sense of the word or of any description whatsoever after Prophet Muhammad (Peace be Upon Him), and that I do not recognize such a claimant to the prophet or a religious reformer, nor do I belong to the Qadiani group or the Lahori group or call myself Ahmadi.' *The Gazette of Pakistan*, Islamabad, Thursday, October 2, 2017, 1553 https://www.ecp.gov.pk/Documents/laws2017/25-6-2018/TEA-2017%20First%20Amendment.pdf Accessed December 15, 2020.

108. *The Gazette of Pakistan*, October 19, 2017 https://www.ecp.gov.
pk/Documents/laws2017/25-6-2018/TEA-2017%20First%20
Amendment.pdf Accessed December 15, 2020.

109. Zahid Hamid even continued to dispute the accusation that he was
Ahmadi in the resignation letter to the President dated 27 November
2017.

110. YouTube, RizviMedia92 '8 November 2017' https://www.youtube.
com/watch?v=0HJF-YodF70 uploaded November 8, 2017 [0:44]
Accessed December 15, 2020.

111. Suo Moto Action Regarding Islamabad-Rawalpindi Sit-in/Dharna,
PLJ 2019 SC (Cr.C) 190 para. 4.

112. Ibid., 190 para. 15.

113. Ibid., 190 para. 16.

114. YouTube, MediaTalkPakistan, 'Khadim Hussain Rizvi Last Speech
at Faizabad Sit-In.' https://www.youtube.com/watch?v=73r9Zi
MlrKg uploaded November 17, 2017 [0:59] Accessed December 15,
2020.

115. *Mst. Asia Bibi v. The State* PLD 2019 SC 64.

116. Ibid.

117. YouTube. RabwahTimes 'Imran Khan finds out his finance minister
to be Atif Mian is Ahmadi Muslim, rants against Ahmadiyya' https://
www.youtube.com/watch?v=x9HEMDJnmfI uploaded on October
5, 2014 [2:11].

118. 'Liberal Apostasy', *Economist*, September 13, 2018.

119. 'Imran Khan criticised for axing Ahmadi adviser', *Financial Times*,
September 10, 2018.

120. YouTube, UCGp31xq0H_kAH10u5H129Zg 'Peer afzal qadri TLP
order to murder judges who give verdict in favor of Asia Bibi' https://
www.youtube.com/watch?v=jKweByd7Y9E uploaded November 1,
2018 [1:27].

121. Twitter. @fawadchaudhry, https://twitter.com/fawadchaudhry/
status/1066053257171210240 November 23, 2018 at 8:37pm.

122. YouTube. Dawnnewspakistan '– Pir Afzal Qadri resigns, apologises
on statements against army, courts', https://www.youtube.com/
watch?v=E874O02pU5E uploaded on May 1, 2019 [1:37] Accessed
December 15, 2020.

123. Amongst those arrested and sentenced to fifty-five years in prison
were Rizvi's brother and his nephew. 'Harsh Sentences', *Dawn*,
January 20, 2020.

124. YouTube. AllamaKhadimHussainRizvi9263 'Allama Khadim Hussain

Rizvi | Ghazi ilm Deen Shaheed | Complete Bayan | Friday 8 November 2019' https://www.youtube.com/watch?v=x_5q8iX7A4Q uploaded November 16, 2019 [18:01]; there are certain stories Rizvi likes and freely attributes to other Ghazis as well, which underlines the point that historical accuracy is not the prerogative of the TLP.

125. YouTube. 'Allama Khadim Hussain Rizvi Paying Tribute to Ghazi Faisal' https://www.youtube.com/watch?v=JsHpjYnLWbU uploaded August 7, 2020 [2:51] Accessed December 15, 2020.

126. On the mystical dimension of these individualised sacrificial practices, see: Olivier Roy, *Globalized Islam: The Search for a New Ummah* (London, Hurst & Company, 2004) 246.

127. I.A. Rehman, 'High Drama in Islamabad' *Dawn*, November 19, 2020; 'Khadim Rizvi dies', *Frontier Post*, November 19, 2020.

128. YouTube. AllamaKhadimHussainRizvi9263 'Allama Khadim Hussain Rizvi | Imran Khan France Ke Khilaf Jahad Ka Elan Karo | Latest Bayan' https://www.youtube.com/watch?v=tdILu5lNxCk uploaded October 24, 2020 [7:00] Accessed December 15, 2020; According to French prosecutors, the suspect of a double-stabbing in Paris outside Charlie Hebdo's former newspaper offices in September 2020 looked 'abundantly at Khadim Hussain Rizvi's videos'. 'Paris Stabbings: Suspect Claims Prophet Caricatures Prompted Attack', *The Hindu*, September 30, 2020.

129. YouTube. AllamaKhadimHussainRizvi9263 'Allama Khadim Hussain Rizvi | Imran Khan France Ke Khilaf Jahad Ka Elan Karo | Latest Bayan' https://www.youtube.com/watch?v=tdILu5lNxCk uploaded October 24, 2020 [7:00] Accessed December 15, 2020.

130. Twitter. @ImranKhanPTI https://twitter.com/ImranKhanPTI/status/1329485070344839168 November 19, 2020 at 7:01pm; Twitter. @OfficialDGISPR https://twitter.com/OfficialDGISPR/status/1329507306254573575 November 19, 2020 at 8:30pm. Accessed December 15, 2020.

131. Sabir Shah, 'Khadim Rizvi funeral one of the biggest in Lahore's history', *News International*, November 22, 2020.

CONCLUSION

1. Compare Christophe Jaffrelot 'Introduction: The Invention of an Ethnic Nationalism' in Christophe Jaffrelot (ed.), *Hindu Nationalism: A Reader* (Princeton, New Jersey: Princeton University Press, 2007) 3–27.

2. Imran Khan, U.N. GA, 74th Session, 9th plenary meeting, U.N. Doc. A/74/PV.9 (27 September 2019) available at https://digitallibrary. un.org/record/3835055 [accessed 15 December 2021].

3. 'The Mahatma Gandhi Murder Case', in Home/Political, File No 59/8/49, 33, National Archives of India, New Delhi.

4. 'The Mahatma Gandhi Murder Case', in Home/Political, File No 59/8/49, 101f, National Archives of India, New Delhi.

5. 'The Mahatma Gandhi Murder Case', in Home/Political, File No 59/8/49, 32, National Archives of India, New Delhi.

6. 'The Mahatma Gandhi Murder Case', in Home/Political, File No 59/8/49, 104f, National Archives of India, New Delhi.

7. Yasmin Khan writes that the Congress party 'was able to use the funeral, mortuary rituals and distribution of Gandhi's ashes to assert the power of the state and to stake the Congress Party's right to sovereignty.' Yasmin Khan, 'Performing Peace: Gandhi's assassination as a critical moment in the consolidation of the Nehruvian state.' *Modern Asian Studies* 45, no.1 (2011): 57–80, at 57.

8. See, Faisal Devji, *The Impossible Indian: Gandhi and the Temptation of Violence* (London: Hurst & Company, 2012) 41-43.

9. 'Mahatma Gandhi Murder Case: Volume 4. Statement of Accused', in Private/Gandhi Trial Papers, File No. 41, 43, National Archives of India, New Delhi.

10. 'Mahatma Gandhi Murder Case: Volume 4. Statement of Accused', in Private/Gandhi Trial Papers, File No. 41, 44, National Archives of India, New Delhi.

11. Ibid.

12. 'Mahatma Gandhi Murder Case: Volume 4. Statement of Accused', in Private/Gandhi Trial Papers, File No. 41, 45, National Archives of India, New Delhi.

13. 'Mahatma Gandhi Murder Case: Volume 4. Statement of Accused', in Private/Gandhi Trial Papers, File No. 41, 53, National Archives of India, New Delhi.

14. Ibid.

15. Ibid.

16. To spread the blame evenly amongst communal organisation, the Union Government extended the ban to the Hindu Rashtra Dal, the Khaksars and the Muslim League National Guards, see: 'Memorandum', States/Political, File No. 74-P/48, 49, National Archives of India, New Delhi.

17. Letter from Sant Indar Singh Chakarwarti, General Secretary of Patiala State Prajamandal to The Prime Minister, His Highness Govt.,

Patiala, February 2, 1948 in State/Political, File No. 74-P/48, 18, National Archives of India, New Delhi.

18. For the opinion that Hinduism was already 'symbolically represented in the activities and rhetoric of political operators across a spectrum of classes and political affiliations within the Congress', see William Gould, *Hindu Nationalism and the Language of Politics in Late Colonial India* (Cambridge: Cambridge University Press, 2004) 33.

19. For a brief overview of the conflict between the orthodox followers of a Sanatan (eternal) Dharma and the Arya Samaj within the Mahasabha, see Christophe Jaffrelot 'Introduction: The Invention of an Ethnic Nationalism' in Christophe Jaffrelot (ed.), *Hindu Nationalism: A Reader* (Princeton, New Jersey: Princeton University Press, 2007) 12.

20. 'Secret Report: Rashtriya Swayam Sewak Sangh' Home/Political(Internal), File No. 28/8/42, 10f, National Archives of India, New Delhi.

21. As the RSS had no political wing at this time, many of their members continued to work under the Mahasabha. From the Mahasabha platform they passed a resolution that endorsed 'Hindus in general and youths in particular to join it [the RSS] in large numbers', see: 'Mahasabha Working Committee Meets' Home/Political, File No. 104/34, 10, National Archives of India, New Delhi; For the impact of the Arya Samaj on Hedgewar, see also Christophe Jaffrelot, *The Hindu Nationalist Movement in India* (New York: Columbia University Press) 66–9.

22. 'Secret Report: Rashtriya Swayam Sewak Sangh' Home/Political(Internal), File No. 28/8/42, 11, National Archives of India, New Delhi.

23. 'Secret Report: Rashtriya Swayam Sewak Sangh' Home/Political(Internal), File No. 28/8/42, 15, National Archives of India, New Delhi.

24. 'Secret Report: Rashtriya Swayam Sewak Sangh' Home/Political(Internal), File No. 28/8/42, 17, National Archives of India, New Delhi.

25. 'Secret Report: Rashtriya Swayam Sewak Sangh' Home/Political(Internal), File No. 28/8/42, 17, National Archives of India, New Delhi.

26. 'Secret Report: Rashtriya Swayam Sewak Sangh' Home/Political (Internal), File No. 28/8/42, 20, National Archives of India, New Delhi.

27. In his defence statement, Veer Savarkar claimed that after Partition, Godse had become a member of the more orthodox Sangathan

faction of the Mahasabha. This camp thought that 'a recognition of the Indian Union amounted to a recognition of Pakistan.' This turn may well be true, but it did not erase Godse's close alliance to Arya Samaj thought and ideology. 'Judgement in the Mahatma Gandhi Murder' Home/Political, File No. 54/8/49, 263f, National Archives of India, New Delhi.

28. 'Judgement in the Mahatma Gandhi Murder' Home/Political, File No. 54/8/49, 16, National Archives of India, New Delhi.

29. A Marathi [Savarkar], Hindutva (Nagpur: V. V. Kelkar, 1923) 3–6.

30. Vinayak Damodar Savarkar, The Indian War of Independence 1857 (London: Publisher not given).

31. 'Judgement of Special Tribunal in the High Court of Judicature at Bombay' in Home/Political-A, File No. 21-67/1911, 98, National Archives of India, New Delhi.

32. 'Judgement of Special Tribunal in the High Court of Judicature at Bombay' in Home/Political-A, File No. 21-67/1911, 100, National Archives of India, New Delhi.

33. 'Judgement of Special Tribunal in the High Court of Judicature at Bombay' in Home/Political-A, File No. 21-67/1911, 98, National Archives of India, New Delhi.

34. Ibid.

35. 'Declaration Mr Charles John Power' in Home/Political-A, File No. 21-67/1911, 172, National Archives of India, New Delhi.

36. 'The Submission', in Home/Political-A, File No. 21-67/1911, 152, National Archives of India, New Delhi.

37. Letter from E. Daeschner, Ambassador of France in London to Sir Edward Grey, Secretary of State, August 2, 190 in in Home/Political-A, File No. 21-67/1911, 176, National Archives of India, New Delhi.

38. 'Comité Consultatif Du Recueil Général: L'Affaire Savarkar' in Home/Political-A, File No. 21-67/1911, 229, National Archives of India, New Delhi.

39. France v. Great Britain, Permanent Court of Arbitration February 254, 1911 https://pcacases.com/web/sendAttach/515 Accessed December 15, 2020.

40. V.D. Savarkar to The Chief Commissioner, October 3, 1914 in Home/Political-B, File No. 245/1914, 4, National Archives of India, New Delhi.

41. See, Pir Syed Muhammad Akhtar Hussain Shah, Sirat Amer-e-Millat Pir Syed Jamaat Ali Shah (Narowal: Faridi Press, 1971).

42. Note Regarding the Double Murder in Mirozai Village on 10th September 1924 by a Recently Converted Muhammadan', in Home/

Political, File No. 249/VIII/1924, 15, National Archives of India, New Delhi.

43. Note Regarding the Double Murder in Mirozai Village on 10th September 1924 by a Recently Converted Muhammadan', in Home/ Political, File No. 249/VIII/1924, 15, National Archives of India, New Delhi.

44. Letter from V.D. Savarkar to J.A. Shillidy, April 6, 1925 in Home/ Political, File No. 91/I/1925, 8, National Archives of India, New Delhi.

45. Ibid.

46. Bhai Parmanand, *The Story of My Life* (New Delhi: Ocean Books, 2003) 45.

47. Sardar Patel, *The Working of His Mind* (New Delhi: Rajhans Publications, 1948) 87.

48. Ibid., 92.

49. Ibid.

50. Bruce Desmond Graham, *Hindu Nationalism and Indian Politics: The Origins and Development of the Bharatiya Jana Sangh* (Cambridge: Cambridge University Press, 1990) 18f.

51. After Gandhi's murder RSS membership fell from 500,000 members to about 100,000 but already in the first quarter of 1951 it rose to 'a little above 600,000' Bruce Desmond Graham, *Hindu Nationalism and Indian Politics: The Origins and Development of the Bharatiya Jana Sangh* (Cambridge: Cambridge University Press, 1990) 17.

52. Letter from Syama Prasad Mookerjee to Pandit Nehru, April 6, 1950 in Durga Das (ed.), *Sardar Patel's Correspondence 1945-50 Vol. 10* (Ahmedabad: Navajivan Press, 1974) 130.

53. For the internal ideological fissures that occur within the BJP and the political development Hindu nationalist thought took over the twentieth century see only Christophe Jaffrelot, *The Hindu Nationalist Movement in India* (New York: Columbia University Press, 1998).

54. YouTube. BJP 'Shri Narendra Modi's speech at Maharshi Dayanand Saraswati's Birth Anniversary Celebrations', https://www.youtube.com/watch?v=UXKVDlUVV34 [21:20] Accessed December 20, 2020.

INDEX

Tanzania, 118
Taranai Shuddhi (The Slogan of
Shuddhi), 62
Taseer, Salman, 144–6
appointed as Governor by
Musharraf, 147
Tashkent Declaration, 103
Tashkent, 103
tawhid, 131
Taylor, John, 20, 22
Tazkiyah al Shuhood, 153
Tehreek-e-Hurmat-e- Rasool, 146,
219n44
*Tehreek-e-Tahafuze-e-Namoos-e-
Risalat Pakistan*, 147–8
The Hague, 105, 170
Third Anglo-Sikh War (1919), 70
Tiananmen Square, 130
TLP [*Tahreek-e-Labaik Pakistan*], 137
See Tahreek-e-Labaik Pakistan (TLP)
Tribune (newspaper), 16, 43
Truman (President), 94, 112
Twitter, 3
298-A Pakistan Penal Code, 10

U.S. Supreme Court, 132
U6 subway, 139
Uganda, 118
UN Security Council, 88, 209n82
Unisveen Saddi Ka Maharishi, 62, 82
United Kingdom (UK), 102
United Nations General Assembly,
136, 164
United Provinces, 47, 57
United States (US), 94, 102, 116,
160
Afghanistan, military campaign
against, 135
Taliban, war efforts against,
135–6

United States Commission, 4
University of Applied Science, 140
University of Sindh, 101
Urdu, 19, 93
Usmani, Shabbir Ahmad, 94

vakil, 41, 42
Vedas, 27, 33
Vietnam, 115
Virjanand, Swami, 27
Vishnu, 13

Wachowali *galli*, 14
'Wahabi', 4, 6
wajib-ul-qatl, 3, 5, 94, 160
Wazir Khan mosque, 96
West Pakistan, 99, 103, 180n48
Wilders, Geert, 158
Wojciechowski, Susan, 115
Women Protection Act (2006),
136
World War I, 35, 48, 169, 188n3
World War II, 90, 120

YouTube, 2, 3

Zafar, Bahadur Shah, 6
Zaheeruddin decisions, 133
zakat (tax), 125
Zamindar (newspaper), 81, 94
Zardari, Asif Ali, 137, 152
Zia. *See* Zia-ul-Haq
Zia-ul-Haq, 113, 115, 117, 212n10
Bhutto arrested by, 118
death of, 116
Islam usage for political
legitimacy, 122–3
Islamisation, move towards,
119–21
Ordinance XX issued by, 126–8